Railroaded

in

Cooperstown

A TRUE STORY

BY

David K. Butler, Sr.

Edited by Nancy Lee Varnum

Publishing and printing authorized by
Railroaded In Cooperstown, LLC
140 Main Street
Richfield Springs, New York 13439

First published in 2006

Copyright © Railroaded in Cooperstown, LLC, 2005
All rights reserved

ISBN-10
0-615-13279-0

ISBN-13
978-0-615-13279-2

Printed in the United States of America

To Mary,
who suffered immeasurably through all that happened,
because of no fault of her own;
and yet steadfastly remained the sunshine, inspiration, and strength
that allowed me to endure...

Prologue

*"The horror of that moment, the King went on, I shall never forget. You will,
though, the Queen said, if you don't make a memorandum of it."*

— Lewis Carroll

I'm sitting alone in my living room basking in the warmth radiating from
the fireplace that I just stoked. Another long, bitter cold winter has settled in over
the Village of Cooperstown, New York. Mary is working the night shift again at
the Clara Welch Thanksgiving Home, Cooperstown's historic assisted living facility.
Mary is a wonderful nurse. In fact, that's how we met. When my oldest son,
David, Jr., was small, his arm was severely broken during little league practice and
he was hospitalized for a few days. Mary, a hospital nurse at the time, was more
than a caregiver. She was an inspiration. She still is. Her effervescent personality
and cheerful smile are charged with that infectious kind of positive energy that
encourages your spirit and nurtures your soul. We've been married twenty-six
years. Her love and support is constant. Thank God for her.

Nursing is Mary's career, but it has also been her temporary escape each
day from the nightmare that we have lived for more than twenty years now. I was
then Chief of Police for the subsidiary railroads owned by Cooperstown's Delaware
Otsego Corporation. In the aftermath of my investigations of a double fatality
accident at a railroad crossing and a sexual harassment complaint by a young male
railroad employee, I lost my job and suffered incomprehensible consequences when
I chose integrity over loyalty to Walter Rich, the corrupt railroad president (and
subject of the sexual harassment complaint). It should have never unfolded the
way it did. That is, not if truth, honor, and integrity matter at all in American
corporate, political, and judicial systems.

Slowly, I speak each of those words aloud: "truth...honor...integrity."
Simple words, really. It occurs to me that it's in the context of deliberate daily
decisions to choose honesty over fraud, respect over contempt, and legitimacy
over vagary, even to one's peril, that those words ripen in significance.

"It sounds so philosophical," I think to myself. But, that's exactly what it
was all about. My life as the Chief of Police for Walter Rich's railroad became a
daily struggle to balance my ethical principles and moral values against Walter's

demands contrived, I believe, to feed his insatiable appetite of greed and self-gratification at the expense of others.

Walter Rich. His name nauseates me. To me, he represents everything that is the very antithesis of truth, honor, and integrity. Two innocent people die at the grade crossing accident because the damn train engineer, who was known by the railroad to deal in cocaine, failed to follow proper procedures and Walter orders me to forego a drug test on the engineer and falsify the police report to protect his railroad! Where is there any evidence of truth, honor, and integrity in that? A young, male employee requests Walter to buy back his vacation time so he can afford to buy heating oil to warm his home in the cold of winter, and Walter preys on him with humiliating sexual advances and threats of employment termination! Where is there any evidence of truth, honor, and integrity in that? I remember how often I thought Walter's sinister little smile boasted his contempt for the good and decent folks who worked for him as he systematically and with impunity challenged our integrity and used his position to strip us of our dignity and self-respect while feeding his greedy self-interests. Fraud, misrepresentation, bid rigging, abuse, bullying, manipulation, politics, character assassination, sexual harassment, smear campaigns – each was a powerful arrow in Walter's quiver and Walter is a clever archer. As his employees, we were vulnerable – good paying jobs are scarce in tiny little Cooperstown, New York, and we all had mortgages to pay, homes to heat, and families to feed. Blowing the whistle on Walter's misconduct was absolute suicide. Meanwhile, I saw Walter and his political cronies prosper; and they apparently continue to prosper.

Damn I hate sitting here mulling all of this over in my mind again.

An involuntary shiver ripples through my body as I gaze out the window at the blizzard relentlessly depositing more than a foot of new snow on the driveway that I just finished shoveling. "Severe winter conditions continuing through…," I hear a voice announce on the television to which I have been paying little attention. "It will be another early morning tomorrow," I think to myself, "shoveling snow from the driveway before I can venture out in sub-freezing temperatures to make progress on the project I started last week." Working outdoor construction in this weather is taking its toll on me. I think back to the heart attack I suffered in April. At sixty-one years old, I should be looking forward to retirement at the end of a successful law enforcement career. But, retirement has become nothing more than a dream. I wish Mary were home.

I glance at my journal lying on the table next to me, and I breathe a heavy sigh. The pages have yellowed over time, but the memory of the events I've chronicled over the years in factual detail on those yellowed pages stings as poignantly as did the experience of those events.

I'm not bitter; I'm angry. I'm angry at the political and judicial processes that effectively reward corruption and punish honor. I'm angry that here in America innocent people suffer, and some die, for the benefit of the politically corrupt. It's a righteous and indignant anger that now motivates me to publish my story.

I want people to know that official corruption is not confined to America's big metropolitan areas. It exists perhaps even more insidiously in quaint American towns and villages. It exists, for god sake, in Cooperstown, New York, the tiny one-stop-light picturesque Norman Rockwell village where baseball, the all-American past time, was born.

Most of all, I want my three sons to know and understand the truth. They are adults now. In the end, I want them to know that though the consequences were sometimes severe, I lived my life practicing the principles in which I believed: honesty, integrity, and ethical behavior.

Here's my story. It's a story of corporate and political corruption at the highest levels. Sex, fraud, abuse, corruption – it's all true. The towers of boxes stacked in my attic are filled with the evidence. I never had my day in court, but I was ready. Justice, I've learned, is within the province of the Universe, not the judicial system.

Was it all worth it? You decide.

David K. Butler, Sr.
December, 2005.

Chapter One

"There is a pleasure in the pathless woods,
There is a rapture on the lonely shore,
There is society where none intrudes,
By the deep sea, and music in its roar:
I love not man the less, but nature more,
From these our interviews, in which I steal,
From all I may be, or have been before,
To mingle with the universe, and feel
What I can never express, yet cannot all conceal."

— Childe Harold, as quoted in Chapter One of
James Fenimore Cooper's *The Deerslayer*.

I wasn't actually born in Cooperstown, New York, but I have lived here most of my life. I consider it "home." My family moved to the tiny village in the farmland of upstate New York from Greenwich, Connecticut, in 1947, when I was three years old. At the time, Cooperstown boasted a population of about 2,000 people. I think it still does. Not much changes in the quaint little village.

Cooperstown, the home of America's first major novelist, James Fenimore Cooper, sits at the base of shimmering Otsego Lake, the legendary "Glimmerglass," from which the mighty Susquehanna River begins its long winding journey south through the Appalachian Mountains to the Chesapeake Bay. Cooperstown is quintessential pastoral charm. Spring and summer are warm and balmy and Cooperstown becomes a picture postcard of green, rolling, wooded hills with tall white church steeples peaking through the trees and charming old houses and avenues adorned with baskets of crimson geraniums, pink and lavender impatiens, and fresh green vines. In the fall, the village is aglow in brilliant shades of gold, orange, and red as the air crispens and the maples and other hardwood trees surrounding the village display their radiant autumn colors. Blanketed with its winter snow, Cooperstown becomes a Norman Rockwell Christmas scene, complete with ice skaters gracefully gliding over the frozen waters of the Glimmerglass.

My parents purchased Cooperstown's historic Hickory Grove Inn located six miles north of the heart of the village on the west shore of Otsego Lake. Built around 1830, the Inn is a large, white clapboard Greek revival style farmhouse with a big front porch, wood beam ceilings, wide plank wood floors, and a large fieldstone fireplace. The majestic structure still sits in its original location on the shore of Otsego Lake.

The Inn was our home. My grandparents owned the adjoining property and a camp on the lake. My backyard was an expanse of lush green woods and the clear, deep, sparkling waters of Otsego Lake. The air was fresh and clean.

On warm summer days, I swam and fished and ran barefoot along the lake's sandy shore. With my Great Dane, Leaf, at my side, I roamed through the ferns and the woods around the lake, carrying my grandfather's civil war musket and pretending I was Deerslayer, the eighteenth century Indian hunter created by James Fenimore Cooper in his leatherstocking tale, *The Deerslayer*. The grand statue of Deerslayer, on which I climbed as a child still sits on the shore of Otsego Lake at the edge of the Village looking north over the lake.

In the fall, I would carve happy faces on great orange pumpkins fresh from the vine and gather wood with my father in anticipation of hot crackling fires in the hearth on frosty winter nights.

When winter was bitter cold and white, the frozen lake, decorated with little glowing ice-fishing huts, became my ice skating rink.

These are the kind of wonderful childhood memories that stay in your heart forever.

My parents sold Hickory Grove Inn and moved us all to Ft. Lauderdale, Florida when I was ten years old. It broke my heart to leave Cooperstown and I vowed that someday I would return. I could not have anticipated then where my journey would take me for the next twenty years and what I would find in Cooperstown when I returned.

Chapter Two

"Blue of the mighty deep; Gold of God's great sun
Let these colors be till all of time be done, done, done.
On seven seas we learn Navy's stern call:
Faith, courage, service true with honor over, honor over, all."

— Midshipman Royal Lovell (U.S. Naval Academy, Class of 1926);
concluding stanza of the official song of the U.S. Navy

Two words best describe how I was able to endure my adolescence in Florida: Port Everglades.

Port Everglades is a deep-water harbor at Fort Lauderdale, Florida. It is the world's largest cruise ship port. It is also the favorite east coast liberty port of call for United States Navy vessels.

I discovered Port Everglades one beautiful spring day in 1958. I was thirteen years old. My father took me to the port to see the Navy vessels docked there. It was Fleet Week at Port Everglades, an annual spring tradition sponsored by the local community to thank the Navy sailors for their dedicated service to our country and their ongoing patronage of the port. The port was crowded that day with locals and tourists. Children ran along the docks, giggling and urging on their strolling parents. Young girls cast coquettish glances at the handsome young uniformed sailors. Navy veterans, some wearing uniforms they had long ago outgrown, reminisced about the war and their own military service. It was a heady environment for a young boy from Cooperstown.

My father was a veteran. He had served as a U.S. Navy officer in World War II. For as long as I could remember, he would tell me stories and show me photographs of sailors in their blue dungarees aboard massive gray vessels misted with the ocean's salty spray. But nothing prepared me for my experience at Port Everglades.

There they were all lined up like giant trophies – a magnificent display of our nation's sea power: aircraft carriers, submarines, destroyers, tankers, frigates and cruisers.

"Would you like to take a tour of a Navy destroyer?" my father asked me.

I could hardly believe it! My heart was pounding with excitement as I boarded the massive floating edifice of gray steel and stood on the deck looking out into the wide-open sea. The salty air was laced with the scent of diesel fuel. The clanging noise of the ships' operational machinery reverberated inside of me.

I was thrilled. The camaraderie of the blue-dungareed sailors patiently answering my endless questions as they escorted me around the ship made me feel like a junior member of their crew. I closed my eyes and envisioned my future.

I had lived in Florida for about three years, desperately missing the hills and woods of my beloved Cooperstown and trying to fit in to this strange new environment. I hated the flat-roofed houses all lined up in convenient little neighborhoods. "How different," I often thought, "was my life at the Hickory Grove Inn on the shore of the peaceful waters of the Glimmerglass." I grew tired of being teased and taunted by my adolescent peers because I was the new kid in school. The only thing about Florida that I grew to like was the pounding surf and the sticky, salty ocean air.

I became a frequent visitor to Port Everglades, wanting to fill my senses with its smells and sounds. I loved talking to the sailors and watching the massive ships arrive and depart. When a ship pulled out to sea, I would stand on the dock and watch until it disappeared over the horizon. I longed to be on board. Visiting the port was a beguiling distraction from the melancholy mood in which I often found myself. At Port Everglades, every old photo from my father's scrapbook of Navy memories and every sea story he ever shared with me came alive.

I was so smitten with the life of the sailor that I attempted to feign maturity and join the Navy when I was sixteen. My effort was quickly dashed. "No way," proclaimed my parents. "You must first finish high school."

For the next year, I was relentless in campaigning for their consent. Finally, shortly after my seventeenth birthday, with my parents' consent on my word that I would finish high school while serving, I enlisted in the United States Navy. On December 29, 1961, I left Florida's winter sunshine for boot camp in the freezing clime of Great Lakes, Illinois. After nine bitter cold and exhausting weeks, I marched in the graduation review proudly donning the winter blue uniform of the United States Navy. My father beamed with pride.

My first assignment after boot camp was not at all what I expected.

"Shore duty!" I grumbled to myself as I read my orders, having dreamed of going to sea.

However, the year of amphibious boat school in Little Creek, Virginia, did allow me to fulfill an important commitment. Soon after my eighteenth birthday, true to my word, I presented my parents with the high school diploma I earned while learning the fine art of landing boats and troops on beaches and qualifying as an Assault Boat coxswain.

When my new orders came at the end of my year in Little Creek, I was delighted to learn that I would finally be serving on a Navy ship. The USS Arneb was stationed in Norfolk, Virginia. It was an amphibious attack cargo ship responsible for landing cargo on beaches during amphibious landings. I reported to Norfolk for duty aboard the USS Arneb in the spring of 1963, not expecting how dramatically my life would change.

I met Bobbie one day after I'd been in Norfolk for about year. By then I had been promoted to third class petty officer in the boatswains mate rating. Bobbie and I were both nineteen years old. She was a young pretty nurse in a Navy town, and I was a young lonely sailor. It was my first experience with romance. We were married within a year. Loneliness coupled with youthful romance, I was to learn, is a very inauspicious basis for a marriage.

Just days after our small civil wedding ceremony in April 1965, I left Norfolk for four and a half months of training in the Caribbean. A year later, I was deployed to Vietnam for amphibious search and destroy missions in the Mekong Delta. I wondered if I would return.

Chapter Three

Just before I was deployed to Vietnam, the Navy sent me to its Riverine Warfare School at Mare Island in Vallejo, California. Sailors from all over the country were there for training. It was 1966 and the Vietnam War was escalating quickly.

I was part of a nine-man crew and, as a boatswain's mate, was assigned as second-in-command. My primary job would be to maneuver a Navy Monitor gunboat through the maze of the Mekong Delta and, when necessary, act as a relief gunner. The Monitor was equipped with a mortar, a forty-millimeter cannon, several machine guns, and a multitude of small personal firearms, including shotguns and pistols. Our lives in Vietnam would depend upon our learning absolutely everything about every weapon aboard our boat.

In very realistic river operations in the swamps around Mare Island we were ambushed by instructors who shot at us with blank rounds of ammunition. In insufferable mock prison camp experiences, we were subjected to realistic and debilitating enemy torture techniques, pushing us almost beyond our physical and mental limitations to inculcate in us instinctive, involuntary survival, evasion, resistance, and escape reactions.

Training for the murky, enemy-infested swamps of Vietnam was absolute hell, but it paled in comparison to the actual combat experiences we would find there.

After successfully completing the Riverine Warfare School at Mare Island, I was immunized against every conceivable tropical disease I might encounter in Vietnam and issued jungle combat fatigues, weapons, and gear. I then had leave for five days before shipping out.

I flew home to Virginia where Bobbie and I said our good-byes. News coverage of the war in Vietnam daily reported the number of American casualties, a number that was escalating at an overwhelming pace. Sobered by the approaching reality, Bobbie and I found it difficult to talk.

As I boarded the flight to Vietnam, I looked around and wondered who of us on board would not return alive, and I shuddered.

In Vietnam, I was assigned to a heavily armed gunboat, the Monitor 112-1, to run gunfire support missions along the Mekong Delta. Between missions, our home was a large, olive drab barracks ship on the Mekong River. The ship had sleeping quarters, a mess, and boat repair shops, but it was cramped, noisy, and uncomfortable. Barges alongside the ship provided moorings for the dozens of gunboats that operated from the ship.

The Mekong Delta is located in the southern half of Vietnam. It is a vast delta formed by the multiple tentacles and tributaries of the mighty Mekong River, which has its origin in the Tibetan highland plateau 2,800 miles away. From its source, the Mekong River makes its way through China, Myanmar (Burma), Laos, Cambodia and South Vietnam before flowing out into the South China Sea. The Mekong Delta was a major combat zone in the Vietnam War, a war that raged between anti-communist South Vietnam and communist North Vietnam in the sixties and early seventies.

By 1963, South Vietnam had lost the fertile Mekong Delta to the Viet Cong. The abundant swampy rice fields and tall reeds that lined the river's banks provided ample cover for the Viet Cong guerrillas to ambush defenders of South Vietnam, the American gunboats that operated up and down the river. The Mekong Delta was a very dangerous place for an American sailor in the sixties.

The average age of a riverboat crewman in those days was eighteen years old. We arrived in Vietnam motivated by our training for war and with a naively youthful sense of invincibility. With a Polaroid camera I purchased at the Navy Exchange, I shot photos of my buddies, who posed in front of the cannons and machine guns, their newly tattooed muscles flexed.

Our boat escorted troops and supplies along the narrow, winding tendrils of the Mekong Delta. Our missions averaged about five days, after which we would return alongside the barracks ship to re-supply our gunboat and rest for a day or two. Our drinking water was heavily chlorinated, laced with Kool-Aid, and lukewarm.

Each time we completed another mission along the Mekong Delta, we returned more somber, wondering if we'd return from the next. Survival weighed heavily on our minds, and we vowed to take care of each other no matter what happened.

Looking back, the gallows humor that worked then to break the intensity of the moment seems now quite macabre.

"If you get killed today, can I have your boots?" one crew member would ask another, and then we'd all banter back and forth, laughing to relieve the immense anxiety we all felt.

Then one hot July day in 1967, the inevitable happened. On a mission down the Mekong River, our gunboat was ambushed and we encountered heavy enemy gun fire. I was positioned at the helm in the boat's pilothouse. The heavy, humid jungle air was thick with acrid gun smoke and I was having trouble seeing and breathing in the suffocating haze. When the gunfire subsided some, our boat captain, Chief Petty Officer Howard Bannister, shouted to me.

"If you want to get some water, I'll take the wheel," he offered.

"Yeah, thanks," I said with relief.

I stepped down and Bannister stepped up to the pilothouse, which was surrounded by inch-thick armored steel intended to provide some protection. As I moved forward toward the water tank in the mortar pit, new gunfire erupted from a tree line fifty feet away. I never made it to the water tank.

Instead, I grabbed the machine gun and started to return fire. An incoming rocket screamed over my right shoulder and made a direct hit on the pilothouse. The rocket pierced the thick armor shield and struck Bannister in the chest, killing him instantly. Two sailors behind him were wounded. Shrapnel from the exploded pilothouse tore into my arms, legs, and back. The force of the rocket's impact knocked my helmet off and blew me forward under the gun mount where hot, empty shell casings from returning fire dropped on my unprotected head.

Blood was spattered everywhere. Bannister's fallen body jammed the small helmsman's station in the demolished pilothouse. Another eighteen-year-old crew member, Thomas Stover, had to stand on Bannister's body to man the helm. One of the engines had been disabled, and I heard the remaining engine whine with strain as the hull beneath my head scraped the mud bottom of the shallow river.

With seven of the nine crew members wounded and one dead, Stover turned the boat back toward the ambush area to make his way upriver a half mile to where U.S. forces were staged. After reaching safety, he beached the boat. A helicopter landed nearby, its overhead blades battering the jungle air and whipping flat the swamp reeds.

I was still in the bottom of the boat, fighting to stay conscious, fearing I would die if I blacked out. Medics threw me onto a stretcher and into the helicopter next to an infantryman with a severe chest wound, his body going into shock. I tried to encourage him as he laid there writhing in pain.

The helicopter took off quickly and delivered us to the nearby medivac hospital. The pounding run in the canvas stretcher from the helicopter to the Quonset hut turned make shift hospital jarred the shards of shrapnel tearing at my flesh and I screamed in pain. Once inside the hut, aides rushed to the wounded, chaotically removing weapons, cutting off clothes, and performing triage. In a matter of minutes, I was pushed on a gurney through a plastic curtain and into the air-conditioned surgical section on the other side of the hut. Then, I was gone.

When I regained consciousness days later, I was wrapped in bandages, my leg in a cast, and tubes in my arms. I spent the next several weeks in various field hospitals lined with endless rows of cots holding the wounded, suffering young men who left their homes and their families to serve their country in war, no one now seemed to understand.

In September 1967, I was evacuated to the Naval Hospital in Portsmouth, Virginia. Bobbie and I were reunited, and after my wounds had sufficiently healed, I was released to light duty in the hospital's security office and went home. For about the next five months, I was in and out of the hospital undergoing a battery of tests to evaluate the extent of damage to my body.

On June 11, 1968, Bobbie gave birth to our first child, a son. We named him David Kirk Butler, Jr., and called him Davy. As I held him in my arms, gazing at his tiny form, I was conscious that this little being, who was a part of me, was utterly fragile and dependent. I wanted to protect him from all harm and ensure that he would have childhood memories of wholesome, simple pleasures like those I knew as a child growing up in Cooperstown. Filled with pride and joy, I was pleased to have a son to share my name. I was a parent – a father – and I couldn't image anything that could be more important.

The tests confirmed that the shrapnel had severed the nerves in my right leg. The hospital then submitted my medical information for review by the Navy Medical Board, who would determine my military fate. While waiting for the medical board to meet, I was designated a rehab patient and assigned light duty at the Naval Amphibious Base in Little Creek, Virginia.

In December 1968, after the Navy Medical Board determined that the damage to my leg was permanent, I was honorably discharged. I didn't know it at the time, but about a dozen or so pieces of shrapnel remained lodged in my right leg. I was approved for a disability pension.

Before I was discharged, I was presented with the Bronze Star, the Purple Heart, the Vietnam Cross of Gallantry, the Combat Action Award, and the Navy Unit Commendation. As I accepted the commendations, I felt guilt and regret thinking of the circumstances that resulted in the ultimate price Chief Petty Officer Howard Bannister paid to serve his country.

I had done nothing more than I had been trained to do.

Chapter Four

"His words are bonds, his oaths are oracles;
His love sincere, his thoughts immaculate;
His tears pure messengers sent from his heart;
His heart as far from fraud, as heaven from earth."

— William Shakespeare, as quoted in Chapter Eight of
James Fenimore Cooper's *The Deerslayer.*

As it turned out, my service in the U. S. Navy segued nicely into a new career in law enforcement.

While working at the hospital's security office during my recovery and evaluation, I became the liaison between the Navy and the local Portsmouth police in matters relating to accidents and crimes involving military personnel. I participated in police investigations and prepared reports for submission by the Navy to the police. When it came time for me to leave the hospital, the members of the Portsmouth Police Department encouraged me to apply to join their force.

Before being discharged from the Navy, I filed my application with the Portsmouth Police Department, took the written test, and was accepted. On the same day that I walked out of the base gate for the last time in December, 1968, I was sworn in as a Portsmouth Police Officer. While waiting for the next police academy class to begin, I was assigned to work with various patrols.

Portsmouth, with its large military community, was a rough town. Criminals and drug addicts infested the city's outlying housing projects, and race relations were tense. The opportunity to work patrols in the midst of all of that allowed me to acquire a wide variety of police experience in a very short period of time, and I was quickly accepted by my fellow police officers, who came to know me as a policeman they could count on in difficult situations.

I loved being a police officer. The job was everything I wanted it to be, and more. The precinct was alive with activity twenty-four hours a day, seven days a week, and charged with energy and excitement as officers and detectives regularly strode about with purpose, their radios crackling in constant communication. Most days, I was disappointed when my shift ended and it was time to go home; I spent my days off looking forward to going back to work. I knew I had found my calling in life.

It wasn't long before I was assigned to work alone in a busy patrol zone, signaling the department's confidence in me. Thereafter, I quickly rose through the ranks, becoming a member of the Accident Investigation Squad a year later and, shortly after that, being promoted to the Detective Bureau's burglary squad where I wore the coveted gold badge inscribed "Detective." I was proud of that badge; it meant more to me than anything I had ever owned.

Another year later, I was selected to join the Department's elite Homicide and Robbery Squad. I was thrilled. Although the job was dangerous, I seemed to thrive in its challenging and exciting environment.

Not too long after I joined the Homicide and Robbery squad, a string of armed robberies began to plague the city and victimize off-duty sailors. In discussing how the department should address the problem, I suggested that we set up our own decoys – police officers dressed in Navy uniforms walking down the street appearing intoxicated. Officer Don Hicks and I volunteered for the undercover operation, and I supplied the Navy uniforms. Armed with a .38 caliber handgun concealed by my Navy pea coat, and a small pistol in my back pocket, Hicks and I hit the dark streets of the seedy area where the menacing robberies had occurred. Within the first hour, we were aware of someone in the shadows stalking us.

"This is it, mother-fucker," a man screamed as he jumped out from behind a large tree and stood in front of us, a sawed-off shotgun under the denim coat draped over his arm. "Give me your money, now!" he shouted as he jammed the shotgun against my throat, pushing me back.

I reached for my pocket as if to retrieve my wallet, pulled out my .38 caliber pistol, and shot twice. Both shots hit the man who was holding me at gunpoint and he fell to the ground. The first bullet hit his shoulder; the second hit his chest after ricocheting off the stock of his shotgun, severing his finger. I shot at the second man, who took off running, Hicks in pursuit and calling for backup. Then the first man got up and ran into a nearby house. I followed him in and found him hunched over a chair, the residents of the house watching in disbelief. I arrested the wounded perpetrator, taking him out of the house in handcuffs. Hicks and the backup he had summoned caught and arrested the second offender.

Although Hicks and I did nothing more than what we were trained to do as police officers, we both received a commendation for the incident.

In December, 1969, as I was beginning my second year with the Portsmouth Police Department, Bobbie gave birth to our second child, another boy. We named him Donald Keith Butler so that his initials (D.K.B.) would be the same as mine and Davy's. I was a very proud father of two healthy, wonderful sons.

Maintaining our now family of four stretched our income to its limits. I earned just over $400.00 a month as a police officer. Although I worked many overtime hours and was regularly required to appear as a witness in court on my days off, I didn't get paid for either. Since my income was inadequate to support our family of four, Bobbie worked full time as a nurse, leaving the boys with a babysitter much of the time. To further supplement our income, I worked my off hours with a friend operating a tree service, which generated as much income for me in three days as I made in a week as a police officer. I regretted that working to make ends meet took so much time away from the boys, but it was necessary.

Four years later, in December, 1972, I left the Portsmouth Police Department and transferred to the city's fire department. Although I loved being a detective, the financial strain on my family was becoming overwhelming and because of the fire department work schedule, the transfer would allow me to substantially increase my income from the tree business while maintaining health benefits for my family through my city employment. Nonetheless, I knew I would miss police work.

During the last year that I worked the police department's homicide squad, I became aware that the Virginia State Police were investigating alleged corruption in the Portsmouth Police Department. I hadn't paid much attention to the investigation as I wasn't involved, I didn't engage in corrupt practices as a police officer, and I had an excellent record with the department. However, I was aware that corruption in the department did, to some extent, exist, and I was called to testify as a witness against an officer who was accused of stealing drugs. I testified truthfully that during a drug bust, the accused officer had confiscated 70 caps of heroin from a woman and instructed me to report only 30 caps. After testifying, I thought little more about the seemingly endless investigation. However, at one point, the state police questioned me seeking information about other detectives they suspected of wrongdoing. Truthfully, I told them that I wasn't aware of any wrongdoing by other detectives and had no information I could provide to them. They were disappointed with my answer, but it was the truth, and I had little interest in participating in what was beginning to look like a witch hunt. Amity between the state police and the Portsmouth policemen had significantly diminished by the time I transferred to the fire department.

After graduating from the fire academy, I was assigned to a busy engine company in the same area of the city I had worked as a policeman. While I missed police work, my personal financial situation had improved and I was learning to appreciate the kind of excitement that was associated with being a fireman. My friends in the department called me "Smokey the Pig" because they thought I acted more like a policeman than a fireman. But, I was settling into a routine and I liked what I was doing.

Then, that summer, my world started to crumble around me. I was playing volleyball one evening with the men of a ladder company and two engine companies when a state police car pulled into the parking lot. The volleyball game came to a halt. Two state police investigators got out of the car and asked to speak to me. I walked over to them.

"A special grand jury has returned an indictment against you; you're under arrest for larceny and bribery."

At first I thought it was a joke. But, as I looked at them, it was clear they were serious.

My heart pounded with fear, embarrassment, shock, and outrage.

"What are they talking about?" I wondered. "Larceny? Bribery? Me? No way; there wasn't that much money in the world."

I turned to my Captain and asked him to call Bobbie and to advise the fire chief. I didn't know what else to do or say. I didn't have a lawyer, and I didn't know what this was all about.

One of the investigators reached for his handcuffs.

"That's not necessary," I said as I got into their car with them.

As we pulled out of the parking lot, I heard one of the firemen shout, "Hang in there, D.K."

We rode in silence for the four or five blocks to police headquarters. There, I was led in like a common criminal, booked, fingerprinted, photographed, and put into the holding cell and told I could arrange for bail.

"Bail?" I thought. "For what? Where the hell do they think I'm going?"

Not knowing the details of the charges against me made things worse.

At the time the grand jury handed down the indictments, the magistrate set bail at $5,000.

It wasn't very long until I realized I wasn't alone. The Grand Jury returned indictments against a number of other Portsmouth Police officers and detectives, too, and they began to trickle in to police headquarters where they, too, were charged, fingerprinted, photographed, and put into a holding cell pending bail. Each was as stunned as I.

I didn't know who to call or what to do. My head was spinning. Suddenly, a friend of mine, a professional bondsman who frequented state police headquarters, walked over to the holding cell and looked at me.

"Don't worry about your bail," he said kindly. "I've posted bond for you."

I was out of there in less than two hours.

Bobbie was in tears when I arrived home. I didn't know what to say to her. Neither of us slept that night.

The next morning, the indictments were headlined in the newspaper and I was suspended from the fire department pending the outcome. I understood the suspension was standard procedure, but I felt humiliated. I couldn't look at my neighbors. I knew I had to fight back, but I didn't know where to begin. I took a deep breath and tried to think.

"Find a lawyer," was my first rational thought and I called around asking if anyone knew of a good criminal attorney in Portsmouth.

Stanley Sachs came highly recommended. I called him. He said he'd take the case, and I made an appointment to see him.

Sachs emanated success. He spoke well, he dressed well, and he lived well. There was a reason for his success – he was an outstanding criminal attorney, and that's exactly what I needed. Predictably, he didn't come cheap. I withdrew all of our savings and borrowed from my parents to pay his retainer. I had no choice.

Sachs filed a discovery motion and obtained the specifics of the indictments handed down against me. I read them in his office.

"Unbelievable," I thought.

The indictments included two counts of bribery and three counts of larceny. The two counts of bribery included one involving a purported ten dollar bribe and one involving a purported twenty dollar bribe.

"Who the hell is going to believe that a policeman could be bribed for twenty dollars?" I asked rhetorically. "That's ludicrous! These people clearly don't know me," I said to Sachs.

In Virginia, grand jury indictments result from witness statements taken at face value. There's no one in the grand jury room to challenge the veracity, reliability, or legitimacy of those statements.

The grand jury justified the ten dollar bribery indictment against me with a statement from a witness who said he had "seen another person put a ten dollar bill on the seat of an unmarked and unoccupied police car in a housing development." The witness statement was virtually the same for the twenty dollar bribery indictment. Nothing in either indictment alleged that the unmarked police car was assigned to me. So happens that it wasn't, but just like that, I was indicted for bribery because someone said they saw someone else put a ten dollar bill on the empty seat of an unmarked police car with no indication of what police officer was assigned the unmarked car.

I still can't believe it.

There were also three larceny indictments.

"These have just about as much merit as do the bribery charges," I told Sachs after reading the specifics supporting the three larceny indictments.

I was furious and I was ready to fight back.

"I'll do all of the leg work for investigating these charges," I told Sachs.

"There's a possibility that I can get some of the charges dismissed on technical grounds," he said.

"No way," I responded. "We've come this far, and I want each and every one of these charges before a jury in open court so I can clear my name."

Then I went to work gathering all of the evidence I could find, and we went to trial.

One of the larceny charges accused me of stealing a ham and a pistol from someone I had never heard of. When I researched the incident, I learned that the complainant was the subject of a search warrant that was executed back when I was a burglary and larceny detective. I was at the scene, but only as a backup car.

I had nothing to do with the search, nor did I have anything to do with what was seized. Apparently, the owner of the property said simply that these items turned up missing after the search, and the grand jury indicted every police officer that was there, whether the officer participated in the search and seizure or not.

"No prosecutor in his right mind would attempt to prosecute a case like that," I thought. "How does the grand jury get away with handing down an indictment like that?"

Of the other two larceny charges, one involved a drug suspect that I had arrested, again when I was still a burglary detective. He was a known heroin dealer and we grabbed him every legitimate chance we had. This guy hated me. I had arrested him several times hoping someday he'd be locked up for good. When I arrested him in this incident, he had $1,200 in cash in his pockets. Police department policy prohibited officers from putting a suspect in lockup with more than $5.00 in his possession. So, I took the $1,200, vouchered it as required, and filled out the required paperwork. At some point, the $1,200 was returned to him. But, during the corruption investigation, he claimed that he had $2,000 when I arrested him and that I had stolen $800. When I heard about his allegation, I joked to one of the police dispatcher's, "Of course I took it; that's how I was able to install air conditioning in my truck!" As it turned out, the dispatcher's brother was a state trooper with no sense of humor who relayed my smart aleck comment to one of the investigators working on the police corruption case. My comment didn't seem so funny when I heard it repeated in court.

The truth was that the suspect's attorney had picked up the suspect's money when he was released from jail. There was some question about whether his attorney gave any of the money to him. In any event, there was absolutely no evidence that I had taken any of his money.

The third larceny charge was the most ridiculous. I was actually accused of stealing my own camera.

In a drug and stolen property search, this time while I was in the homicide squad, we had searched an apartment in a housing project and arrested a woman and seized five stolen television sets. When we took her and the television sets to the detective bureau, my Polaroid camera was sitting on my desk. It was the same Polaroid camera I had purchased in 1967 at the Navy exchange when I was in Vietnam. I used it in the detective bureau because it produced instant pictures. When the woman we arrested saw the camera on my desk, she screamed, "That's my camera!" I told her to shut up and sit down. I thought that was the end of it until I read the third larceny indictment. During the corruption investigation, the woman I had arrested for possession of the five stolen television sets accused me of stealing "her" Polaroid camera. I couldn't believe it.

I rounded up a plethora of photos I had taken with the Polaroid camera in Vietnam. Each photo bore the specific marking created by the camera. The camera also had one major flaw – when using the flash to take a picture, the picture would come out black. I also requested and received a letter from the Polaroid Company that the particular model of my camera was not manufactured after 1967.

In court, the woman testified that she received the camera for Christmas in 1972 from her boyfriend and that he bought it new. Her boyfriend wasn't in court to testify and she claimed she didn't know where he was. Sachs handed my camera to her and told her to take a picture. She didn't know how to open the case, she could not explain how to operate the camera, and she couldn't answer any questions about what, if anything, was wrong with the camera. Sachs then presented the photos with the identifying marks that I took with the camera in Vietnam.

The judge had finally heard enough on the larceny charge involving the camera and said, "There's nothing here for a jury to decide. This charge is dismissed."

A record number of character witnesses came to court to testify on my behalf. Most of the Portsmouth police and fire departments were there. After several of them testified about my unimpeachable integrity, character, and reputation, the judge announced that he assumed each of the witnesses was going to testify likewise. He was right.

The prosecutor dropped all but two larceny charges. The jury deliberated twenty-two minutes on those two charges and returned a verdict of "not guilty" for each. I was elated, but not surprised. The charges were absurd and the experience left me bitter.

I had no recourse against the people who made the false allegations against me or the grand jury who believed them and I was out a considerable amount of money. But, I was innocent and it was time to get on with my life. However, there was another hurdle.

The jury had acquitted me of breaking any laws, but now I had to prove that I hadn't broken any rules. Before I could be reinstated as a firefighter with the Portsmouth Fire Department, a civil service investigation, which required that I take a polygraph examination, was required. I easily passed the polygraph examination. Within a couple of weeks, I received a letter from the Portsmouth City Manager advising me that all charges had been investigated and disposed of and I was reinstated to my position in the Portsmouth Fire Department.

Everyone at the fire department, from Chief Benton on down, welcomed me back to work. It felt good to be a fireman again. Then, after about six months, I was transferred to Truck (ladder) Company number 3, stationed at the west end of the city on Victory Boulevard.

Victory Boulevard was a busy fire station. In addition to its primary response territory, Victory Boulevard was the automatic second alarm for any fire anywhere in the city, so we responded to almost every major fire in Portsmouth.

Being part of a ladder company didn't thrill me. I had a fear of heights. Every day that we worked, we trained for two hours, frequently on the ladder. It terrified me.

Working an actual fire from the ladder terrified me even more. I hated the feeling of being whipped around by the 500 gallon per minute nozzle while strapped to the ladder fifty feet in the air. Dense smoke from the fire made it impossible to see and created in me an intense sense of claustrophobia. The air tanks and face masks contributed to the disconcerting sensation.

Our life in Portsmouth was taking its toll on our family. Bobbie and I worked different shifts and rarely saw each other any more. I was working most of the time, and the three-day shifts at the fire department were twenty-four hours a day. Our marriage was in trouble. Neither of us spent enough time with the boys, a circumstance I hated. Davy was in first grade and Donnie was in nursery school. When they weren't in school, they were with their babysitter. Race issues in the public schools were forcing busing, and soon Davy would likely be bused to an inner city school instead of the school in our neighborhood.

I thought about my boyhood and I wanted Davy and Donnie to experience the simple pleasures I had known as a child. I also wanted to be able to spend more time with them.

For many reasons, we desperately needed a vacation. So, after being at the Victory Boulevard station for about a year, I packed up Bobbie and the boys and hit the road.

I headed for Cooperstown.

Chapter Five

"We should have no regrets. We should never look back. The past is finished…Whatever it gave us in the experiences it brought us was something we had to know…They were years of preparation; a germinating time…Those things are deeply etched into your soul, and the soul will not forget. Just be assured when the time comes again, as it will come, and you reach a crisis where you must choose, the soul will know the path you should take."

— Rebecca Beard, *Everyman's Search* (1951)

In Cooperstown, we spent time together as a family, something we hadn't done for a long time. I swam with the boys in Otsego Lake, and they romped on its shore and played in the shadow of Deerslayer, gazing up in awe at the grand statue perched atop its massive bolder. As Davy and Donnie looked out across the blue reflective water, I explained to them that the lake was often called The Glimmerglass.

"What's a glimmerglass?" little Donnie asked, his face all scrunched up in childish bewilderment.

"A Glimmerglass," I said, "is like a mirror. People call Otsego Lake 'The Glimmerglass' because it is still, clear, and reflective – like a mirror." Then I pointed to the mirror image of the surrounding tree covered hills reflected at the water's edge.

It was the same clear, cool water that I remembered from my childhood.

I told Davy and Donnie stories about my childhood in this quaint little village called Cooperstown. I could see in their eyes that they were imagining my boyish escapades roaming through the ferns and the woods around the lake, carrying my grandfather's civil war musket and pretending I was Deerslayer. They giggled with delight.

The village was tranquil. Children played and people walked down sidewalks decorated with hanging flower baskets and planters spilling over with red geraniums and pink impatiens. It was safe, and it was peaceful. It was very different than Portsmouth.

After we put the boys to bed our first evening in Cooperstown, Bobbie and I sat outdoors, basking in the balmy night air and talking – something we rarely did anymore.

"I can't remember when we last had time to just sit and talk," I said. "We need this."

The next morning as we ate breakfast, I suggested that we spend the day walking around the village looking at its old quaint houses. As we walked, I talked about how nice it would be to raise the boys in a place like Cooperstown.

Finally, I said, "Let's talk to some people and find out what kind of job opportunities might exist here." Bobbie agreed, for no other reason I'm sure, than to patronize me. "We have nothing else in particular planned for the day anyway," she brooded.

Our morning walking tour of Cooperstown took us down Atwell Road past the large historic and impressive fieldstone building that is Bassett Hospital.

Mary Imogene Bassett Hospital is as important to Cooperstown as is the Baseball Hall of Fame, though in a less celebrated sense. As a child, I had no idea how Bassett Hospital came to be such a big part of Cooperstown; but for as long as I can remember, I knew that it was.

The hospital has a very interesting history that's worth reading. It was built by a member of Cooperstown's esteemed Clark family as a living memorial to Dr. Mary Imogene Bassett, the woman who, in the late 1800s, came to Cooperstown and, until her death in 1922, treated its sick and wounded.

For decades, the hospital has been among the best hospitals in America. That's no surprise to us that have lived in and around Cooperstown and benefited from the level of care the hospital provides and the quality of the hospital's medical staff. However, it's unusual to find a hospital of that magnitude in such a small village.

Bassett Hospital is also a major contributor to Cooperstown's economy, employing a very large team of doctors, nurses, and other health professionals. So Bobbie inquired about nursing positions that might be available. As luck would have it, a position in in-service training, for which Bobbie was well qualified, was available with an attractive salary.

That's all I needed to hear. It was as if I had moved in the right direction, and providence stepped in and started opening all of the right doors.

It seemed to me that with my police and firefighter training and experience, I, too, should have luck finding employment. After doing some checking, I discovered that in rural upstate New York, all of the fire departments are volunteer companies. So, I checked out the Cooperstown Police Department. Unlike Portsmouth where I was one of about 250 police officers, Cooperstown employed seven men and the department wasn't recruiting at the time.

So I visited the office of the County Sheriff. I spoke with the undersheriff, who told me he was impressed with my qualifications and that there was an excellent chance I would be hired if I moved to the area.

"Good," I thought, "I know that I am well qualified and will be able to get a job here in law enforcement." I was getting excited about the prospect of being able to move with my family back to Cooperstown.

We found a real estate office and talked to an agent about the housing market in and around Cooperstown. She asked if we had time to look at some houses.

"Sure!" I said, looking at Bobbie who looked a little chagrined by my enthusiasm, but agreed.

That very day, we found a house. It was an old, two-story farmhouse, circa 1900, with a nice front porch. It needed a little work, but nothing I couldn't fix. It was perfect. The owner was moving, but was in no hurry; and, the price was right, assuming we could sell our home in Virginia.

I couldn't stop thinking about the house and about how much I wanted to move home to Cooperstown.

At dinner that night, I looked at my family seated around the table and thought about what I wanted for our future.

"That's it," I said with a brashness that surprised even me. "I've made a decision. We're moving."

Sensing my excitement, the boys cheered with delight. Bobbie was somewhat less enthusiastic.

"Perhaps this is just what we need to get our marriage on track again," I suggested, my tone hopeful, and then I added, "Besides, it would be a wonderful place for the boys to go to school and grow up."

Bobbie looked at me, then turned and looked at the boys, all of us sitting there together as a family. She looked back at me and, reluctantly, said, "Okay," agreeing to support my decision.

The next day, I went back to the house we had found and spoke to the owner. I made an offer to purchase the house contingent on the sale of our house in Virginia, and, until then, to rent the house from him. The owner accepted the offer. I gave him a small deposit and he agreed to move out.

We returned to Portsmouth, put a "FOR SALE" sign in the yard, gave notice to our employers, and set a date for the move.

In August, 1975, I rented U-Haul's biggest truck and trailer and, after giving away everything we could get along without and packing the rest, we invited our friends to a "moving party" and loaded everything we owned into the truck and trailer.

The next day, I climbed into the cab of the truck and, without looking back, headed north. Bobbie and the boys followed me in our family car.

A day and a half later, we pulled up in front of the big old farmhouse in Cooperstown. Bobbie and I unloaded all of our possessions and carried them into the house. Eventually our house in Portsmouth sold, and we became owners rather than renters of the old farmhouse with the big front porch.

In September, the boys started school and Bobbie began her new job at Bassett Hospital.

I went to see the county sheriff about the job. This time I spoke with the sheriff, himself. After listening to me and reviewing my application, he told me that his deputies worked at his pleasure and he wasn't interested in hiring me because I was "overqualified" for the position. That took me quite by surprise. But, the position afforded no job security, I rationalized, and because the sheriff appeared to have more interest in getting himself elected than "making waves" by enforcing the law, I knew I would not be well suited for the position anyway.

From the sheriff's office, I walked to the east end of Main Street to the building that housed the village offices. It was a stately stone building with a row of white fluted columns across the front. The village library, with its elegant fireplace and leather chairs, occupied much of the first floor. The village Police Department operated out of the building's basement. I walked downstairs and asked to speak to the chief.

After I introduced myself and provided a brief overview of my law enforcement background, Chief Martin Healey reviewed my qualifications and said he was impressed with my credentials, but would have to wait for the results of a background investigation before he could offer employment.

During the background investigation, the subject of the Portsmouth grand jury indictments was raised. I spoke with Chief Healey about them and provided him with copies of all of the letters and documents I had related to the matter, including the jury's verdict finding me not guilty of the charges. He appeared to appreciate my honesty and understand the unwarranted nature of the charges against which I was required to defend myself. But, it was still embarrassing to me to have to answer to the matter in the context of a prospective employment opportunity and justify myself when I had done nothing wrong.

I was hired as a part-time police officer and went to work right away. After working as a police officer in Portsmouth, I felt a lot like Andy of Mayberry working as a policeman in Cooperstown. However, I liked the slower pace and I loved being back in my hometown.

After two years, it was clear to me that there was little, if any, opportunity for advancement in Cooperstown's small police department, and my salary was pretty much insufficient. So, as much as I enjoyed police work, I decided that, primarily for economic reasons, it was time to look for something else; I resigned.

At the same time, my marriage was failing and Bobbie and I separated. I rented a small efficiency apartment for myself and Bobbie kept the house and the boys so that their lives would be disrupted as little as possible.

I weighed my law enforcement options. I was too old for the state police, apparently over-qualified for the sheriff's department, and no longer interested in the local police department. So, for the next year, I worked odd jobs, mostly in construction, keeping an eye open for the right opportunity to get back to police work.

Just before Labor Day in 1978, Bobbie informed me that she was taking the boys and moving back to Virginia. My heart ached, but there was little I could do about it – I had no real job and lived in a one-bedroom apartment. She and the boys left Labor Day morning. It was a bitter cold day, and I never felt more alone. As the weeks passed, I missed the boys more and more. Depression overwhelmed me, and often I would sit in the apartment all day just staring out the window wondering how I could possibly live another day without them there with me.

Just a few months later, my father died and the unbearable sorrow I felt deepened my depression. Worried about my mental state, I called Bassett Hospital and made an appointment to see a psychiatrist. When the psychiatrist diagnosed my depression as "situational," I immediately identified the problem situation. I enrolled in the two-week treatment program recommended by the psychiatrist, but I knew that to be whole again, I had to find a way to change the situation that had me trapped in depression.

I called Davy and Donnie and asked how they were doing.

"Okay," they responded routinely, and then Davy told me that their mom was working nights and they stayed home alone while she was at work. I was deeply troubled that the boys were alone in the house all night without an adult who could protect them from harm. After I hung up, I was overcome with anxiety about their safety and wanted to rescue them, protect them, and bring them home. But, before I could formulate a plan, Bobbie called me.

"The boys want to live with you in your fantasy world," she announced abruptly and sarcastically. "I'm not going to object," she added, capitulating to their wishes.

I was on the road the next day, headed for Virginia to pick up my sons and bring them home. I was thrilled.

The three of us lived in my little one-bedroom apartment, Davy and Donnie sleeping in my bed in the bedroom and me on the sofa in the living room. The boys and I were happy to be reunited.

I filed for divorce and it was final in early 1979. Being a single parent wasn't easy. I worked for a logger, cutting timber in sub-zero temperatures and struggling to make financial ends meet. I'd do the grocery shopping and visit the laundromat with our dirty clothes when I finished work, taking the boys with me. Then, I'd come home and cook dinner for them. I wanted them to have real home-cooked meals, and I made them sit at the dinner table to eat so we could all talk about our day. Bathing the boys was an ordeal. The water heater held only ten gallons of hot water, so an hour in advance of their bath, I would start boiling water in every pot I could find and pour it into the bathtub.

Financially, I finally reached bottom and I knew I had to ask for assistance. With great humility, I applied for food stamps. After that, I went out of town to shop so no one I knew would see me using stamps to buy food for my children. We lived one day at a time, and I was determined that circumstances would eventually improve.

One afternoon that spring, I received a call that Davy had been injured at a Little League event and had been taken to Bassett Hospital. I rushed to the hospital's emergency room, where Davy was positioned on a table, his arm resting on a pillow. I could see his bone protruding through the skin on his arm, and it was obvious he was in great pain.

"It's a serious break," explained the attending emergency room doctor. "He'll have to be admitted to the hospital for a few days."

Davy was scared, and I grieved as I watched him trying to be brave, tears running down his face. The doctor administered pain medication and worked to repair the damage to Davy's arm. When the doctor finished, a nurse wheeled Davy to his room and I helped get him settled in for the night. Then I went home to be there for Donnie. While Davy was in the hospital, I worked to balance my time between working, being at the hospital, and keeping things under control at home.

One day when I arrived at Davy's hospital room for a visit, his nurse was in the room.

"Dad, this is Mary; she's my favorite nurse here," Davy said with a big smile on his face. "Mary, this is my dad!"

Mary and I looked at each other. She was a pretty brunette with hazel eyes and the most wonderful smile. Her positive energy was contagious. Watching how she lovingly tended to Davy, chatting with him the entire time about baseball and other things in which Davy was interested, I understood why she was Davy's favorite. She soon became my favorite, too.

After Davy was released from the hospital, I asked Mary for a date. She declined. Then, one evening I had arranged for a babysitter and walked to a local pub. Mary was there and when she saw me come in, she came over to me and asked about Davy's arm. We started talking; she told me that her fiancé had recently died in a motorcycle accident. I felt bad for her and asked if she's like to walk over to the park.

"It's been a long time since I've had someone to talk to," I said, not being able to remember the last time I felt so at peace.

"I'm still feeling a little fragile about dating," she responded, "but I, too, would love to have someone to talk to."

We walked over to the park and, sitting under the light of a million stars, talked until three in the morning.

"Let's walk back to my apartment and wake up Davy," I suggested on impulse. "I know he would love to see you again, and it would be a fun surprise."

Blinking his eyes, Davy sat up in bed as I nudged him. "Wake up," I said, smiling." "There's someone here who wants to say hello."

Davy opened his eyes, and when he saw his favorite nurse standing there, he cheered in delight and, jumping out of bed, threw his arms around her and hugged her tight.

After that, Mary and I became the best of friends and spent a lot of time together. We would ride in my pickup, listening to eight-track recordings of Elvis as I reminisced about my youth. When she came to my apartment to have dinner with me and the boys, after the boys were in bed, we'd sit and talk long into the night. Whenever we were together, the boys were with us. Mary and I spent our first night together in a tent at the Cooperstown Tent and Trailer Camp, with Davy and Donnie between us in the sleeping bag. Our time together and with the boys was filled with thousands of wonderful moments. The boys absolutely loved Mary, and she loved them. To Davy's delight, it was Mary who took Davy to the hospital when the time came for him to have the cast on his arm removed because I had to work that day.

Three months later, parked on Lake Road looking out at glimmering Otsego Lake and sipping chocolate milkshakes, I told Mary that I loved her with all of my heart and that I wanted to spend the rest of my life with her.

"Will you marry me?" I asked.

"Yes, I will," she answered.

I leaned over to her and kissed her.

Looking back, I realized that my entire life had actually been evolving through an extraordinary series of serendipitous events that took me from my beloved Cooperstown and returned me there, bringing me to this moment. I knew then that everything had happened just as it should, and I had no regrets. I knew that at this very moment, my life was right where it should be.

Then, one day I was talking to Karen Clark, a friend of mine who worked for Delaware Otsego, a corporation in Cooperstown that owned a handful of local short line railroads. Walter Rich, the corporation's president, was Karen's boss. Karen knew I was looking for a full time law enforcement position.

"Walter is recruiting for a railroad policeman," she said. "Why don't you apply?"

I did, and Walter hired me.

Chapter Six

The future was plump with promise.

— Maya Angelou,
All God's Children Need Traveling Shoes (1986)

"You look nice!" Mary beamed with pride when I walked into the kitchen that early Monday morning in September 1979 sporting the crisp casual shirt and slacks she had meticulously pressed the night before. I poured myself a cup of coffee while she inspected my appearance, gesturing her approval. Giving her one of my quirky little smiles signaling feigned annoyance with her fussing over me, I rushed out the door headed for the car. I've never been comfortable with maudlin gestures of attention, and from the beginning of our relationship, Mary somehow understood that part of me.

"Good luck," she called out as she blew me a kiss. I waved goodbye and drove away.

It was my first day on the job as a full-time police officer for the Delaware Otsego Corporation. The position of chief of railroad police did not exist then, and, at the time, there were no other railroad police officers employed by the Delaware Otsego Corporation. The railroad police officer who had preceded me had resigned.

"I'm back in law enforcement and the future holds so much promise," I thought, enjoying my sanguine mood as I headed toward Railroad Avenue.

The Delaware Otsego Corporation seemed to be a progressive company and the job paid very well by Cooperstown standards. Also, I would have a railroad police vehicle to drive, and, importantly, my employment benefits would include health insurance for me, my sons, and, after our marriage in October, my wife, Mary.

"My wife, Mary," I said to myself, liking the sound of those words. Mary brought so much joy into my life and she adored Davy and Donnie, upon whom she lavished the kind of natural and wholesome maternal attention that nourishes a child's soul and instills a sense of security. We were becoming a family, and it felt very good.

I turned left onto Railroad Avenue and into the parking area next to the railroad's offices. When I entered the building, I headed directly for Walter's office. Walter was sitting behind his desk talking on the telephone. I waited outside while he finished his conversation.

I would describe Walter Rich as a short, pudgy, abdominous man with short arms, small hands, and a double chin. He had a roguish grin that I thought made him look sinister.

Walter, I learned, was born in Oneonta, New York, a small town about twenty miles south of Cooperstown. He was about a year younger than I. He told me that he became interested in railroads as a child. Knowing that he had a law degree, I thought it strange that he chose to run a railroad rather than practice law. I learned later that it was while he was studying political science and law at Syracuse University that he began laying the foundation for making the railroad his career.

In written documents profiling his history with the railroad, Walter boasts his achievements.

"In 1971, the year he graduated from law school, he acquired a significant ownership interest in the Delaware Otsego Corporation, a publicly held short line railroad holding company located in Cooperstown, and its subsidiary, the Cooperstown and Charlotte Valley (CACV) railroad, a 2.6 mile steam-powered tourist excursion line between Cooperstown and Cooperstown Junction.

That same year, he became the corporation's president and a member of its board of directors. He wasn't more than twenty-five years old at the time.

Through a "very savvy" real estate deal, he then acquired another several miles of track to take the CACV line to Oneonta."

The "savvy" real estate deal that allowed him to expand the operations of the CACV, I later learned, involved a substantial amount of money provided through state and federal programs to maintain the CACV and preserve rail service in the area. Thereafter I presume is when the CACV began providing occasional rail service to the Agway store and the Bruce Hall Corporation in Cooperstown, both of which received no more than a single boxcar delivery once every few weeks. They were the only customers on the line.

Between 1971 and 1979, when Walter hired me as the company's police officer, Walter had added to the corporation's holdings (I surmised through the same scheme of public funding) the Central New York (CNYR) and the Fonda, Johnstown & Gloversville (FJG) short line railroad companies in New York, and the Lackawaxen and Stourbridge (LASB) short line railroad company in Pennsylvania. Rail service on the CNYR, the FJG, and the LASB was in no greater demand that it was on the CACV. But Walter was just beginning to build his empire.

As I stood there outside of Walter's office that first morning on the job, I felt confident and positive about my future as a law enforcement professional with what I believed to be an avant-garde, growing company. I also felt very fortunate to have found what appeared to be such a quality law enforcement position in Cooperstown, where well paying jobs were extremely rare.

When Walter finished his telephone conversation, I walked into his office.

"Good morning," I greeted my new boss cheerfully.

"Morning," Walter replied, then added, "Welcome aboard!" He handed me my railroad police badge, took me on a quick tour of the facility, introduced me to several employees, and then directed to me to my office.

My office was in the basement of the old railroad station building, down the hall from dispatch. It was a modest cubicle with a small, narrow daylight window near the ceiling. I looked around and thought, "I won't be here much anyway." I wasn't one who was content spending much time sitting behind a desk, and, as the only railroad police employee, I figured I'd be spending most of my time out of the office doing actual police work.

The first order of business was to fill out and submit the necessary paperwork to apply for railroad police commissions in New York, New Jersey and Pennsylvania, the states in which Delaware Otsego operated, and where I would be working. First, I had to obtain certified copies of records from Portsmouth relating to the indictments and the final disposition of all of the charges. Once again, it was discomforting to have to explain the indictments. But I knew I had done nothing wrong so I just went through the process. Because I was acquitted of each of the indicted charges, the records were not public and the City of Portsmouth would not release them to anyone except me personally. I had to provide to Portsmouth a written request on Delaware Otsego stationary, stating the purpose for which I needed the records. My signature on the request had to be notarized. Once I received the copies from Portsmouth, I provided them to the Delaware Otsego Corporation, which retained them as part of the background investigation related to my employment application. Walter Rich assured me that the records would be kept confidential and not released for any other purpose. Several weeks later, when the background investigations had been completed, I received word that my police commissions had been approved and I was certified as a railroad policeman in all three states.

My plan for the remainder of my first week was to visit all of the railroad's facilities in New York, New Jersey, and Pennsylvania. On Tuesday, I visited local facilities, intending to visit the facilities in New Jersey and Pennsylvania by the end of the week. However, on Wednesday my plans quickly changed. I was sitting in my office finishing some paperwork when the telephone rang.

"Butler," I answered.

"There's been a grade crossing accident between Honesdale and Lackawaxen," the dispatcher stated. "A vehicle-train collision…driver of the vehicle injured."

I jumped into my car and headed south to rural Pennsylvania.

Honesdale, Pennsylvania, is about 113 miles south of Cooperstown. Lackawaxen is approximately another fifteen miles southeast of Honesdale. That area of Pennsylvania has a rich railroad history that dates back to 1829. Heading south/southeast out of Honesdale, the railroad tracks parallel U.S. 6, intersected now and then by narrow country roads. Such rural crossings were commonly unguarded and posted by nothing more than simple white and black crossbucks signs. That's still the case today at many rural crossings.

The Delaware Otsego Corporation had an office in Honesdale, and Walter maintained a private railcar there for his convenience when he needed to stay in that area. The tracks between Honesdale and Lackawaxen were within the Delaware Otsego Corporation's jurisdiction. When trains approached the unguarded rural crossings along those tracks, railroad crews were required to stop and flag the intersection to alert motorists of the oncoming train. After dark, they were required to light flares.

The drive to the scene of the grade crossing accident between Honesdale and Lackawaxen took me almost three hours. It was late afternoon when I arrived. Walter and Malcolm Hughes, a member of the railroad's board of directors and the part-time district attorney for Delaware County, were at the Honesdale rail yard. They had traveled to Honesdale earlier in the day on other business. I greeted them both and told them I would report back to them after I completed my investigation. Because the Delaware Otsego Corporation was self-insured, the two of them were understandably concerned about the issue of liability with regard to the accident.

I checked the train and the damaged car and found nothing of substance in either related to the accident. Spent flares along the crossing evidenced to me the fact that the train crew followed procedures to alert motorists approaching the crossing of an oncoming train. The injured driver had been taken to a local hospital, so I drove to the hospital to interview him. His injuries were not serious, and the property damage was less than significant. I then retraced the driver's activities from the night before. Following my investigation, I reviewed all of the evidence and concluded that the accident was most likely the result of simple driver inattention. I walked over to Walter and Hughes and advised them of my conclusions.

"Any evidence of alcohol in the vehicle or that the driver of the vehicle had been drinking?" they both asked.

"No," I responded. "Nothing points to that."

"Are you sure?"

"Yes, I'm sure."

They seemed extremely disappointed with my conclusion. That puzzled me, and I was surprised by the leading questions they asked about the driver's state of sobriety. Nonetheless, I had conducted a thorough and impartial investigation of the accident and reached the only reasonable conclusion that could be inferred from the evidence. So, deciding to believe that they were just making sure I was thorough, I dismissed the thought that they were actually attempting to influence a different conclusion.

The local police were at the scene and also investigated the accident. They concluded that neither party was at fault.

Neither conclusion dissuaded the driver of the vehicle from threatening legal action against the railroad for damages. The railroad ultimately settled the case for an undisclosed amount.

The Honesdale accident was the first of many grade crossing accidents I would eventually investigate for the railroad. Some of those accidents would involve fatalities; many would not. Some would be the result of misjudgment or inattentiveness of the driver of a vehicle, and some would be the result of a train engineer's misfeasance. In each case, however, it was my consistent practice to conduct a thorough and impartial investigation and report conclusions based in their entirety on truthful information and credible evidence. That's how I functioned as a police officer.

After my investigation that night, I was required to leave my police vehicle in Honesdale and drive Walter and Hughes back to Cooperstown in Walter's Mercedes sedan. As I drove, Walter kept demanding that I drive faster so that he wouldn't be late for a meeting.

"I'm already driving over the speed limit; I don't want to get pulled over by the state police," I responded, annoyed.

Walter laughed.

"There's nothing to worry about," he said. "No cop is going to write you a ticket with Mal Hughes in the car with us!"

It was the first of what would be many instances I would experience and come to know all too well as Walter's proclivity for controlling people and situations to benefit his personal interests through blatant abuse of power and influence. The concept was foreign to the code of ethics to which I had always subscribed as a law enforcement professional. It caused me concern.

During the following weeks, I made an effort to acquaint myself with the various local police departments within the three states of New York, New Jersey, and Pennsylvania and to allow them to get to know me. Some of those police departments were familiar with the railroad police, and some were not. I wanted to establish a good working relationship with each department so that I could depend on their assistance and cooperation when I was engaged in railroad business in their jurisdictions.

After working for Walter during the first month, I began to wonder to what extent his self-serving directives would challenge my sworn duty as a police officer and encumber my efforts to build a credible railroad police department. Time would tell.

Meanwhile, my attention would be temporarily diverted by a very important event.

On Saturday, October 20, 1979, a month and ten days after I was hired by the railroad, Mary and I were married in the small white New England style steepled church at Cooperstown's Farmers' Museum. It was an unusually bright and beautiful fall day in upstate New York. Mary smiled radiantly as she walked toward me, elegant in her vintage ivory lace wedding gown, a halo of delicate white baby's breath encircling her soft dark brown hair. She held a nosegay of zinnias, chrysanthemums and bachelor buttons in brilliant fall shades of red, orange, and gold accentuated with creamy white stephanotis. I smiled adoringly as I stood there beholding her beauty and her joy. We vowed our love and commitment to each other before Davy and Donnie and a small congregation of family and friends, and then gathered for a reception dinner at the Hickory Grove Inn, my boyhood home, toasting our new life together with flutes of sparkling champagne. Following dinner and the traditional wedding cake ritual, I took Mary's hand in mine and, under a shower of rice, we dashed to our car and drove away. For the next five days, we blissfully honeymooned at Cape Cod, sipping pina coladas, dining on fresh seafood, and strolling along the beach. We drove home on Thursday, promising each other we'd return each year to celebrate our life together – a promise we've kept.

I returned to work the following Monday, determined not to be distracted by Walter's egocentricity and to keep my focus on establishing my credibility as a law enforcement professional and building a respectable railroad police department. It didn't take long for me to realize how big a challenge that would be. A couple of days later, I was in my patrol car driving to one of the railroad facilities when I was summoned on my police radio.

"Walter wants you to pick up a package A.S.A.P. and deliver it to Franklin," I was informed.

"That's interesting," I thought, knowing that Walter's parents lived in Franklin. "I wonder what's up."

I turned the car around and headed back to the office. When I arrived, I went to see the dispatcher. He looked at me, leaned to the side of his desk, and pointed to two full bags of dirty laundry.

"This is a routine thing with Walter," he explained. "There are no laundry facilities in his private rail car here, so his mother, who lives in Franklin, does his laundry for him. Now that you're here, Walter expects you to make the laundry runs to Franklin."

I looked at the dispatcher in disbelief, then, not wanting to create an issue so new into my career, I took the bags of laundry and left for Franklin in the patrol car. It was a forty-five minute drive south of Cooperstown, just beyond Oneonta. I was teeming with ire as I drove. After delivering Walter's dirty laundry to his mother, I turned to leave.

"Wait," she called. "You have to take this back with you."

I turned around and there she stood with several neatly pressed shirts on hangers and a stack of Walter's clean underwear and socks in her arms.

"How humiliating is this?" I thought as I drove off. "A uniformed police officer in his patrol car driving through the upstate New York countryside with Walter Rich's underwear neatly stacked on the back seat!" I prayed I would encounter no one on the drive back to Cooperstown.

When I arrived, I went to Walter's office, informed him in the most civil tone I could engender that his clean underwear was neatly stacked in the back seat of my patrol car, and then just stood there looking at him waiting for a response, or an apology, or even a simple "thank you." Instead, without even looking up, Walter waved his hand and, dismissing me like domestic staff, directed me to take the clean laundry to his private railcar and put it away.

Thereafter, just as the dispatcher promised, the laundry runs between Cooperstown and Franklin were expected and became routine. Frequently when I made the Cooperstown to Franklin laundry run, Walter would hand me an envelope and instruct me to stop at his bank in Franklin. The envelope always contained a number of Delaware Otsego payroll checks made payable to Walter and a deposit slip for his savings account. I supposed Walter was not dependent on his Delaware Otsego Corporation paycheck for his day-to-day living expenses like most of us were because, unlike most of us, his day-to-day living expenses were paid by the corporation, which provided his opulent living quarters, his luxury vehicle, and all of his other living expenses, right down to his personal toiletries. I surmised that made it possible for him to stash one hundred percent of his salary in his savings account.

"How nice for him," I mused sarcastically as I stood in line at the bank waiting for the teller.

As time went on, Walter increasingly expected me to be his personal driver and transport him and his friends in my patrol car whenever he called. I guess it gave him a sense of security or importance, or maybe even power, to be chauffeured around by the railroad police. But, I found it demeaning and incompatible with the duties and responsibilities of a railroad police officer.

Finally, after one of the Franklin laundry runs, I decided to speak to Walter and went to his office. Walter was sitting at his desk.

"Walter," I said, looking down at him, "I'm not comfortable with being required to transport your laundry back and forth between Cooperstown and Franklin and being your personal chauffeur. Not only do I find it demeaning, but it's unreasonable and outside the scope of responsibility of a railroad police officer." Then, I quoted for him the railroad law that stated a railroad police officer shall perform no function for the company other than police duties.

Walter sat in his chair behind his desk and stared at me for a moment. Then, his face red and his tone ruthless, he stood up, firmly planted his fists at his hips, looked straight at me, and shouted, "You will do WHATEVER I want,

WHENEVER I want, or you can look for another job. This is the last I want to hear about this subject! Go back to work."

Stunned by Walter's reaction to what I believed were reasonable comments and concerns, and needing to cool down, I left the building and drove off in my patrol car to think. "I can't afford to lose this job," I thought as I drove, thinking about Mary and the boys, and the baby we were expecting very soon. "Let it go," I told myself, deciding to keep my focus on police matters and, as much as possible, maintain a comfortable distance from Walter.

On September 23, 1980, just after I completed my first year with the railroad, Mary and I welcomed our new son, Daniel Kircher Butler, into the world. We were thrilled to now have three sons, and Davy and Donnie were thrilled to have a baby brother. Kircher was Mary's maiden name, and it worked perfectly to continue a wonderful family tradition – my three sons and I all have the same initials – D.K.B.

The work schedule Walter imposed on me at the railroad kept me away from home many hours a day and often at night, and I wasn't a lot of help to Mary with the new baby. I felt bad about that, but I knew that it made little difference to Walter. Knowing that I couldn't afford to lose this job – especially now – I worked the long hours and tried to keep my focus. It helped that the railroad had hired a second full time railroad police officer.

Just before the end of my first year, the Delaware Otsego Corporation purchased the bankrupt New York, Susquehanna and Westerns (NYSW) railroad and Walter decided the railroad needed another full time police officer in the New Jersey yard. On my recommendation, he hired Bruce Buffet, my brother-in-law. Bruce was an excellent candidate and available. He was married to Mary's sister, Kathy, and they lived in New Jersey. He was honorable, he had a clean record, and he was trustworthy, and those personal characteristics outweighed any nepotism concerns. Recruiting good people, especially for police work, is difficult in a small village like Cooperstown.

Before Bruce could be commissioned, he had to have police training, so I sent him to the regional police academy in Binghamton, New York. While he was attending the four-months of training, the railroad housed him in a motel near the academy.

With Bruce came a second railroad police patrol car. Both were a very welcome addition to what was becoming a very over-worked police department of one. However, it wasn't long before I realized that Walter viewed both Bruce and the second patrol car as additional accoutrements for his personal convenience and benefit. Now, both Bruce and I were on call twenty-four hours a day to chauffer Walter and his friends whenever Walter called.

That I desired personal time to spend with my family mattered not to Walter. In my opinion, his demands on my time ranged from the ridiculous to the absurd.

I was once driving Walter in my patrol car through New York City en route to the railroad complex in New Jersey. Walter was in the back seat. We were on Broadway and Walter spotted a Burger King.

"Stop the car," he ordered. "I'm hungry."

I pulled up to the Burger King and parked the car.

Walter started to get out the car, looked at the people entering and leaving the Burger King, and then turned and leaned over the front seat. "You have to go in with me and protect me from the niggers," he commanded.

Offended by his racial slur, I turned and glared at him. Then, as ordered, I got out of the car and stood beside him like a bodyguard while he ordered a burger, fries, and a soda. He grabbed the bag of food and we walked back to the car. As I drove, Walter sat in the back seat devouring his food. When we arrived in New Jersey, Walter got out of the car and walked over to one of the buildings in the rail yard, leaving the back seat of my patrol car littered with crumpled wrappers, food crumbs, and an empty paper beverage cup with straw sticking out through its plastic lid.

"What a slob," I thought to myself as I cleaned up his mess.

Although Walter had a luxury company car, he seemed loath to driving himself anywhere, relying instead on Bruce and I for his transportation. Walter often insisted that we use red lights and siren to get him through traffic and to his destination without delay. That it was a very inappropriate use of the patrol car's emergency equipment apparently was of no interest to Walter, and challenging him on such issues was occupational suicide. Frankly, I wasn't willing to risk my ability to provide for my family. Neither was Bruce. So, we'd accommodate his command. We learned to pick our battles with Walter very carefully.

Bruce and I were frequently required to transport Walter between Cooperstown and the New Jersey rail yard, a four-hour drive. It seemed his trips between Cooperstown and New Jersey were often in the evening or on a weekend, interrupting our time with our families. However, Walter didn't seem to care about anyone's time or convenience but his own. Bruce and I devised a plan. Since I was in Cooperstown and Bruce was in New Jersey, we implemented what we called the "Roscoe Relay."

Roscoe, New York, was just about exactly halfway between Cooperstown and the New Jersey yard. I would transport Walter in my patrol car from Cooperstown to Roscoe. Bruce would meet us at the Roscoe Diner and, after waiting for Walter to feed himself, Bruce would transport him to New Jersey. When Walter was ready to return to Cooperstown, Bruce would transport him to Roscoe where I would meet them and, after Walter fed himself at the Diner, I would transport him to Cooperstown. Each leg of the trip was about two hours. Walter would stretch out across the back seat of the patrol car and either sleep or eat, offering no conversation and leaving behind whatever trash he generated.

Walter used the railroad police department like his personal fleet of limousines and drivers, and he would sit in the back seat of the patrol car looking like he believed he was someone important. I often wonder if he ever realized that he was often mistaken for a detainee in transit by other law enforcement units who happened to see him sitting there in the back of the railroad police patrol car.

With one blatant example after another, I was becoming more and more aware of Walter's interminable use of power, intimidation, and fraud to control and manipulate employees, politicians, and the government to benefit his personal and financial interests and to satisfy his seemingly insatiable greed.

I learned that Walter had hand picked the corporation's board of directors from among his close friends. They included vendors of the railroad, business owners, public officers, and politicians. They all appeared to me to have something in common: each was beholden to Walter, and, consequently, Walter could strong-arm their individual and collective support and loyalty.

The board of directors re-appointed Walter as the corporation's president every year and set his salary at a handsome level. I reckoned that Walter had figured out how to work a system of state and federal railroad funding, capitalizing on the opportunity to provide himself and his directors with substantial benefits and an exorbitant lifestyle while using his employees to facilitate and perpetuate the scam. My suspicions would later be confirmed. I noticed that any director or employee who crossed Walter or challenged him was summarily removed. That's exactly what happened to Ed Browne, the company's Comptroller; Jim Maltese, the assistant purchasing manager; Andrea Novello, a department manager; and John Tobin, a member of the board of directors.

Ed Browne had been hired to replace Jerry Beasman, who resigned during my first year with the railroad. I never knew why Beasman resigned, but I often wondered. Beasman's title was Vice President of Administration, but his primary responsibility centered on the company's books. When Beasman left, Walter bestowed on his assistant, David Soule, Beasman's "Vice President" title.

David Soule came to work for the railroad a few months after I became the railroad's police officer. He was a young man in his twenties. Walter hired him and gave him the title "Assistant to the President," a new position Walter created. Prior to becoming Walter's assistant, Soule had worked in a restaurant in Cooperstown. I believe that the restaurant job was the extent of Soule's prior experience. Walter offered Soule a starting salary that exceeded mine, so I was curious about what exactly he was hired to do. From what I observed, he appeared to be nothing more than Walter's valet, carrying Walter's briefcase for him and accompanying Walter on trips. Perhaps he was Walter's personal bodyguard, I thought, after Walter sanctioned Soule's request that I submit paperwork for a New Jersey police commission for Soule so that he could carry a hand gun and a badge when he was with Walter in New Jersey. When Soule was later promoted to Executive Vice President (and given a company car and a hefty salary increase),

Walter hired a new young male assistant, Tony Osterdahl. Shortly after Tony became Walter's assistant, I asked him what he understood his duties to be as Walter's assistant. "Walter has plans for me," was his nebulous response.

In any event, I was sure Soule had no accounting qualifications or experience, so I wasn't surprised when Walter hired Ed Browne, a C.P.A., as the company's comptroller to replace Beasman.

Ed Browne had an affable manner but took seriously the ethical responsibilities of his profession. He championed a wholesome value system and maintained high personal standards of integrity. He and I became friends and our families often socialized together. He and his wife also had three children.

One night, there was a knock on our apartment door. When I opened the door, I was surprised to see Ed standing there. He was visibly upset.

"Can I talk to you?" he asked. He quickly looked around and then added, "Privately?"

"Sure," I said. "Come in." "What's wrong?"

"Walter has directed me to do some things with the company's books that I believe are illegal," he said. "I just can't do it, but it's been made clear that my failure to follow Walter's instructions will end my career with the company." Ed sat there looking completely defeated.

"What is it that Walter wants you to do?" I asked.

"It involves accounting for federal and state funds received by the railroad. That money is received for specific government-funded railroad projects." "Walter wants me to falsify accounting entries so he has a set of books for government audit purposes."

Ed walked across the room and, gazing out the window, succinctly framed the issue.

"This is a public company, I'm the company's accountant, complying with Walter's directives could result in very serious consequences – criminal, I believe."

Then, just as succinctly, Ed avowed the obvious. "You know Walter won't take the fall, he'll lay it on me."

We talked for a long time. Ed was struggling to find a way to reconcile two disparate principles – integrity and duplicity – something we both knew was impossible. Finally, I offered Ed the counsel I knew he believed he would hear when he came to my door.

"You need to do what you believe is honest and ethical and let the chips fall as they may," I advised. It was the same counsel I had dispensed to myself on many occasions. "If you stand firm on your ethical and professional principles, maybe Walter will wise up and back off."

But, we both knew he wouldn't. I felt helpless and concerned for my friend, remembering Walter's words to me about doing what he wanted, when he wanted, or looking for another job.

Less than a week later, Walter called me at home one night.

"I want to see you in my office right away," he commanded.

I hung up the phone and looked at Mary. We had been enjoying a rare opportunity to spend a quite evening together. "I know," she said with a heavy sigh and looking very disappointed. "The railroad. Will you be late?" she asked, clearly hopeful I'd say no.

I kissed her on the cheek, assuring her I would be home as soon as I could, but not knowing what Walter's emergency was this time.

When I arrived at Walter's office, he stood up and began pacing. "I'm going to fire Ed Browne," he announced. "He's incompetent." "Browne's in his office; go escort him from the building. Oh, and make sure that he doesn't take any files or papers – only his personal property."

I felt sick. Ed Browne had challenged Walter's impropriety and had lost his job. My heart was heavy as I walked to Ed's office. Ed was sitting at his desk, his head resting in his hands. He looked up when I walked in, his eyes reflected the despair I was sure he felt.

"I know why you're here," he said softly.

As I helped him box up his personal belongings, I said, "As far as I'm concerned, you can take anything you want."

Ed told me he had been offered several weeks' severance pay "to help him relocate." "Walter made it clear that if I caused any trouble, I would get nothing but a substandard employment reference. I need to think about my family."

There were no other jobs for Ed in Cooperstown, so he was forced to sell his house and move away. When I later heard from Ed, he said that he had moved his family to Rochester where he found a job as comptroller for a large corporation.

"Will you be willing to speak up later if necessary about what you know regarding the railroad's books?" I asked him.

"Only with a written guarantee of immunity from prosecution," he responded.

I rarely heard from Ed again.

Jim Maltese was a bright young man in his late twenties and good looking. He was tall and lanky with a head of thick black curly hair. His heavy black five-o'clock shadow defied his boyish looks.

As Delaware Otsego Corporation's assistant purchasing manager, Maltese participated in the company's contract bidding process on government-funded railroad projects. When the company was awarded such contracts, it was obliged to follow the government's sealed bid regulations. However, according to Maltese, Walter preferred to rig the bidding process to ensure that contracts were awarded to his cronies. Richard White, a member of the railroad's board of directors and owner of the Bruce Hall Corporation, a Cooperstown lumber company, was one of Walter's cronies who profited from Walter's bid rigging.

On behalf of the Bruce Hall Corporation, Richard White submitted a sealed bid to Delaware Otsego Corporation for a railroad construction project in Utica, New York. So did several other construction supplies companies in the general area. I learned from one of the secretaries in the purchasing department that following the deadline for submitting sealed bids for the project, as required by regulation, Maltese, in Walter's presence, opened them to determine the lowest bidder to whom the contract would be awarded. Bruce Hall Corporation wasn't the lowest bidder. Maltese later told me that after the bids were opened, Walter picked up the Bruce Hall bid and walked out to the secretary's desk and gave it to her to retype.

The Bruce Hall Corporation was awarded the contract.

Another one of Walter's cronies who profited from Walter's bid rigging owned a grade-crossing construction company called Safe-Tran. When the Delaware Otsego Corporation put out to bid a $200,000 contract for grade-crossing work, Safe-Tran and a number of other companies submitted sealed bids. Walter had apparently promised the work to Safe-Tran. However, when the bids were opened, Safe-Tran was not the lowest bidder. Walter instructed Maltese to have a secretary retype Safe-Tran's bid and back-date it. Safe-Tran was awarded the contract.

Maltese came to my office one day to talk. He told me that Walter's frequent bid rigging efforts made him very uncomfortable. "He's now ordered me to make false entries in federal rail accounting books," Maltese said looking very worried. "I talked to an attorney," he said, telling me that his attorney advised him that if he complied with Walter's order he would be committing a felony.

Maltese wrote Walter a memo informing him that he would not make the entries in the federal rail accounting books as ordered, advising Walter of his visit with his attorney. He showed me the memo before he delivered it to Walter.

"I heard Walter discussing my memo with Ned Wilkenson," Maltese told me a couple of days later. "And I heard Ned tell Walter that 'someone could go to prison for this.'"

A short time later, Maltese stopped by my office and told me that Soule told him that he wouldn't have to make the entries in the federal rail accounting books. "A mistake had been made," Soule told Maltese.

"I just want to do my job," Maltese said to me. "I don't want to get in trouble."

Maltese took some time off for vacation. When he returned to work, he found his office had been cleaned out and someone else occupied it. He no longer had a job.

Andrea Novello, a pretty, dark-haired, dark-eyed Oneonta native in her twenties, was one of Walter's department managers. She was outspoken, but very polite. She and I were talking one day and I asked her a question about the required timecard entries.

Under the timecard system, railroad employees were required to enter a code indicating in which state the hours were worked. Each state had a specific code. Cooperstown, New York, was 1430. Richfield Springs, New York, was 2430. Pennsylvania was 4430. New Jersey was 7430. When I was hired, Walter instructed me to code my timecard showing forty hours each week primarily in Pennsylvania whether I was working there or not. I learned that employees in other departments were also required to code most of their time in Pennsylvania.

Andrea told me that she was required to show that at least forty percent of the labor in her department was devoted to work in Pennsylvania when it was actually ten percent or less.

"The State of Pennsylvania reimburses the railroad for labor in its state, including overtime at time-and-a-half, as part of a program to keep rail service alive there," was Andrea's explanation. "It makes me angry that we are all required to submit false timecards," she protested.

The only exception that I recall to the forty-hour rule was when the railroad police department provided round-the-clock security for an extensive grade-crossing project on State Route 17 in New Jersey. In that case, I was instructed to use the New Jersey code on the railroad police department's timecards and show the exact amount of time each officer spent on the site, which was often in excess of seventy hours a week. The State of New Jersey reimbursed the railroad for our time, including the overtime. However, we received nothing more than our regular forty-hour weekly salary. Walter and the Delaware Otsego Corporation retained the excess, making a tidy profit off our labor.

Not long after my conversation with Andrea, Soule called me.

"Andrea Novello is being fired," Soule said. "I need you to be present when I tell her."

"Why is Andrea being fired?" I asked.

"She can't do her job," was Soule's response.

My instincts told me that Andrea probably complained to Soule or Walter about the phony timecards she was required to submit coded for labor in Pennsylvania.

Andrea received the usual severance pay for not making a fuss and I never saw her again.

John Tobin was a major stockholder in the corporation and a member of the board of directors. Tobin was Walter's nemesis on the board of directors, and I knew that Walter wanted to get rid of him. Apparently, the feeling was mutual. Tobin approached me one day.

"I want to take over the railroad," he stated. "I need your help. Once I'm in control, I'll make sure the police department is equipped with new cars and everything else the department needs."

At that point, the railroad police cars were hand-me-downs from a couple of company vice presidents who passed them on to the railroad police department when they were issued new vehicles. Although I had lights, sirens, and radios installed in the vehicles, they were really nothing more than ordinary used cars –

old and less-than-reliable diesel klunkers that spewed black smoke, would rarely exceed a speed of 60 M.P.H., and were mechanically deficient.

Tobin's offer was tempting, but I was skeptical.

"My plan is to buy out a majority of the corporation's stock, take over the company, and get rid of Walter," he continued.

"Why do you need me?" I asked cautiously, sensing great personal risk by getting involved.

"Walter keeps the list of stockholders locked in the safe in his office, and I need a copy of that list," he explained. "You have keys to everything."

To me, the whole plan had a bad smell to it. "Let me think about it," I said. "I'll get back to you."

Tobin's plan preoccupied me for a couple of days as I considered what to do. As much as my dislike for Walter was growing, and as much as the railroad police department really did need new police cars, I had little interest in jeopardizing my position with the railroad or in compromising my integrity. Finally, knowing that I needed to protect myself, I decided to test how far Tobin would go with his plan. That evening while sitting at home, I dialed Tobin's telephone number. As his phone rang, I pressed the record button on my answering machine.

Tobin answered.

"This is Butler," I said. "I don't have a key to the safe in Walter's office, but I know someone who does."

"Great!" Tobin responded.

I continued. "There's a catch."

"What's the catch?"

"The person who has a key wants two hundred dollars to get the list of stockholders out of the safe."

"I'll pay it!" Tobin responded without hesitation.

His enthusiastic response surprised me as I thought surely that would have ended it. I thought for a moment, and then continued.

"I'll need the money right away," I said, then added, "Send me a check," thinking nobody, including Tobin, would be that stupid.

"I'll put the check in the mail tomorrow; you'll have the check in a couple of days."

Tobin lived downstate in White Plains, about 30 miles north of New York City. I estimated it would take no more than two days for the check to arrive in my mailbox in Cooperstown, if Tobin actually mailed it.

Sure enough, a couple of days later the check arrived in the mail. I was amazed. I locked Tobin's check and the cassette tape from my answering machine in my filing cabinet at home and spent the night considering what to do next. The next morning, I drove to the office knowing that I had to go to Walter.

I went straight to Walter's office that morning and told him about Tobin's hostile takeover plan. I had decided to reserve the information about Tobin's check and the recorded telephone conversation for later.

"I don't believe it," Walter huffed. He sat back in his chair for a moment absorbing the significance of what I told him, and then said, "I'm calling a special meeting. I want you there," he said, leaning forward in his chair for emphasis.

The following day, before the select majority of board members, I explained Tobin's hostile takeover plan. The check and the cassette tape of my telephone conversation with Tobin were both in the briefcase I had with me, but I kept that evidence concealed pending their reaction.

"It's simply untrue," one board member stated.

"You've misinterpreted what Tobin said," suggested another.

"You should be very careful making an accusation like this against a board member," still another declared.

I looked at each of them as I pulled a tape player out of my briefcase, placed the cassette tape in position, and pressed the play button. At the end of the recorded conversation, I reached into my briefcase, pulled out Tobin's check, and handed it to the board member sitting closest to me.

They were speechless as they listened to the tape and looked at Tobin's check. Indignant, they immediately voted to call a meeting of the full board, including Tobin, at Malcolm Hughes' office the following day.

"Be there," Walter ordered me, "and bring the tape and Tobin's check with you."

The following day we all met at Malcolm Hughes' office. I arrived about an hour before the scheduled time and was instructed to wait in an adjoining room. Tobin had no idea I would be there. When everyone was assembled around the conference table in Hughes' office, Tobin was advised that I had met with a majority of the board members the previous day. Tobin was then confronted about his hostile takeover plan.

"Butler is setting me up," he yelled. "He's been pressuring me for weeks to take over the company so he could get new equipment for the police department."

I could hear him from the room where I was waiting.

"What a crock of shit," I thought.

When Tobin finished his tirade, Walter pressed the play button on a tape player, which was sitting on the table. While Tobin listened to his recorded telephone conversation with me, a board member showed him the check.

Tobin's face turned ashen. He sat there silently for a few minutes and then admitted his plan. Walter and Hughes seized the moment and offered him a deal. Tobin signed an agreement to sell back to the company all of his Delaware Otsego stock in exchange for the board's promise to not refer him for prosecution for commercial bribery, a misdemeanor in the state of New York.

Tobin was history. I watched the board members leave Hughes' office and walk to their cars, laughing and patting Walter on the back. No one said a word to me as they left.

"What will happen next?" I wondered as I drove back to Cooperstown, glad this ordeal was over.

Chapter Seven

It has been said that when one bases his life on principle, ninety-nine percent of his decisions are already made.

Early on, I based my life on principle. So did Walter, I believe. It's just that Walter's life principle appeared to be very different than mine.

The employees of the railroad seemed to recognize what happened with Tobin and, although the concept of loyalty may have been lost on Walter and the board members, their employees understood the underlying principle that neither my loyalty nor my integrity are for sale.

However, it seemed to me that Walter was systematically weeding out those in the company who ultimately held themselves to a standard of ethical principles and moral values, thus enabling him to practice a management style that continued to evidence the principle of rapacity on which it appeared his life was based. I worried about that.

Walter often called me on weekends and holidays to go to New Jersey and sit in the rail yards to secure them against trespassers and vandals. He refused to hire additional people, saying that I could do it. Bruce and I would have to leave our families and spend entire holiday weekends on railroad business at Walter's beckon call.

On one occasion, Walter arrived in New Jersey late at night after everyone was asleep. After settling into his private railcar, he discovered his favorite blanket was missing. At one o'clock in the morning, he walked up and down the crew car banging on everyone's door screaming that someone had stolen his blanket. The next morning he demanded that I conduct an "intense investigation" into the theft.

On another occasion, Walter called me and told me that a certain track employee was "stirring up the track crew and trying to start a union." "Get rid of him," was Walter's directive to me.

"How?" I asked.

"Arrest him!"

"For what?" I questioned.

"I know I can't fire him just for union activity, so it will be your job to find something on him so I can fire him."

I asked what exactly he had in mind.

"As a police officer, you have access to drugs," he said. "Get some and plant them on him; then call the local police."

A wave of cold fear ran through me as I realized that Walter wasn't kidding.

"I'm not doing that," I emphatically responded, wondering how Walter could be so cavalier about maliciously devastating another person's reputation and life. I ignored his ridiculous request.

It appeared to me that examples of Walter's lack of integrity were increasing in frequency.

After researching the availability of a suitable police car to replace the old diesel car I had been assigned, I learned one day that the Chrysler Corporation, through a local dealer, Warnock-Ryan, in New Jersey, had a state contract to sell vehicles for police and municipal use. With a railroad police department purchase order and a railroad check, I could acquire a new police-equipped vehicle through the state contract for a substantially reduced price. I talked to Walter about it, hoping he would approve the idea of replacing the inadequate hand-me-down cars we were using. At first, he resisted, reasoning that he wanted to continue using vehicles equipped with diesel engines. Most of the company's vehicles, including Walter's vehicle, had diesel engines. There was a reason Walter preferred cars with diesel engines – they could be fueled from the company's bulk diesel fuel tanks. I had often seen Walter's car and other vehicles owned by the company being filled up at the bulk tanks in the rail yards. The railroad was able to purchase diesel fuel in bulk at a special price with no fuel tax through a special state program reserved strictly for locomotive fuel. The police cars available through the state contract were equipped with gas engines.

Surprisingly, I was ultimately successful in convincing Walter to purchase new police cars through the state contract even though the cars were not equipped with diesel engines. Walter had apparently found another self-serving opportunity. Even though the vehicle price under the state contract required a certification that the vehicle was for police or municipal use, Walter soon ordered me to buy another car from Warnock-Ryan under the state contract. He instructed that the car be equipped with special comfort equipment "fit for a police chief" and that he wanted it in a color other than white. Under the state contract, such cars were available and widely used in law enforcement as unmarked police cars. However, Walter wasn't ordering a car for police use. He was ordering a car for a member of the company's board of directors, Ned Wilkenson. Walter instructed me to certify that the car was to be used for police use. I presented the dealership with a purchase order and a company check in the amount of $7,176.00 (the price of the car in the early 1980s), but I certified nothing. I asked the clerk who typed the check to indicate on its face that the money was for a car for Ned Wilkenson and he would reimburse the company. The company controller signed the check with the memo. I picked up the car the next day and delivered it to Wilkenson. I don't know if he ever reimbursed the company for his car, but, either way, in my opinion, the transaction fraudulently exploited a government program. However, my efforts to bring it to the state's attention have proved futile. I still have a copy of that check.

A few weeks later, Walter directed me to use police department purchase orders and company checks to purchase under the state contract a station wagon for Wilkenson's daughter and, a short time later, a pickup truck for Soule's father.

"Walter operates this railroad with no regard for the law," I thought. "I'm getting sick of him involving me in his scams."

Walter was still using as his residence the private railcar behind the company's offices in the old Cooperstown railroad station building on Railroad Avenue. He had a new air conditioning system installed by the company at what I was told was an outrageous cost. Then he had the company buy him a new luxury vehicle. It appeared to me that he spared no expense to the company when it came to his own comfort or when entertaining his political friends. That he was in the game for himself was obvious to me and many of his other employees.

The blatant lack of consideration and appreciation I saw him extend to the railroad's hard working employees disgusted me. In the winter of 1982, there was a train accident near Norwich, New York. A freight train had derailed. Although there were no injuries, there was a lot of damage. Box cars were strewn all over an area covering about a mile of track. The wreck crew would be on the scene for days clearing the wreckage and reopening the track. For security purposes, the railroad police were also on the scene round the clock. The weather was a frightful mixture of snow, freezing rain, and biting wind. Temperatures often hovered near zero. The crews, soaking wet and cold, worked diligently round the clock to clean up the wreck and restore the track. They had only short, infrequent breaks to warm up and get dry clothing. The hours were long and the men were weary from the heavy work in the frigid weather. Late on the third night, Walter appeared at the scene to check on the progress. There were no roads to the site, so he had to park his car down the tracks and walk in the same way as everyone else had to do. In his brand new bright and shiny yellow rain suit, complete with a hood, he was quite a contrast to the crew members who were covered with mud, slush, and grease.

About an hour before Walter arrived, and not knowing that Walter was on his way, the on-scene supervisor ordered hot meals from a nearby take-out restaurant to feed the hungry crew. One individual dinner had been ordered for each crew member working at the site. The food arrived after Walter arrived. There was a driving rain and the only shelter was that provided by a few trucks parked down the tracks. As the crew members lined up to get their hot meal, Walter suddenly pushed to the front of the line, reached into the back of the truck, and took not one, but two of the individual meals and walked away looking for a dry place to eat. I was standing next to a dump truck, my plate sitting on top of the tire under the fender. I had just started to eat when Walter walked up to me and held out his two meals.

"Hold these," he commanded.

Thinking he just wanted me to hold them while he got situated, I took the two meals from Walter and stood there holding them. Walter reached over and opened the lid on the top meal; then he started to eat.

"No way, Walter," I said in disgust, handing him his meals.

He looked at me and, without saying a word, took his food and walked back down the tracks to his car. He never came back that night.

Because of Walter's inconsideration, two cold and hungry hard working crew members were without a hot meal. Bruce and I walked over to the police car and drove to a nearby restaurant. We ordered two big Italian dinners to go, paid for them on our expense account, and brought them back to the work site for the two hungry and grateful crew members.

Walter's notorious eating habits earned him the nickname "Porky" from his employees. When we were at the New Jersey yard, we all ate in the diner car. The cook prepared the meals and bought the food, making sure all of Walter's favorites were on hand.

For breakfast, Walter apparently liked a certain brand of cereal. One morning as we all filed into the diner car for breakfast, Henry, a particularly hefty and rugged trackman with a keen sense of humor, was near the head of the line and right in front of Walter. Henry picked up a large serving bowl and then grabbed Walter's box of cereal. He poured the entire contents of the box into his bowl, sat the empty cereal box down, and walked away to one of the tables to eat. Walter picked up the cereal box and looked inside. He then looked over at Henry, but said nothing. He picked up a banana and left the diner car. After he left, everyone started to laugh.

The next day, the cook told me that Walter was furious about the empty cereal box and demanded that in the future his meals be prepared separately. Thereafter, Walter ate by himself in his private car, his table dressed with a white linen table cloth and silver utensils.

Walter knew how to play the political game, and I watched him play it well, greasing the palms of politicians and lavishly entertaining them to curry favor for some future *quid pro quo*. Using his employees to scam the political contributions laws, Walter practiced his political gamesmanship with abandon.

In 1981, the Delaware Otsego Corporation purchased Edgewater, an elegant brick Cooperstown mansion built in the 1800s by Isaac Cooper, the younger brother of novelist James Fenimore Cooper. The mansion sat majestically under old, ornamental trees on four acres of beautifully groomed grounds across Lake Street from Otsego Lake. A tall privacy hedge surrounded the estate.

The corporation purchased Edgewater ostensibly to use as a corporate conference center and offices. Walter's real plan, though, as he revealed it to me, was to move out of the railcar in which he lived and into the mansion where he could entertain in style. "Why should I buy a house when the company can buy me a mansion," he rationalized to me before the purchase was consummated.

After Delaware Otsego Corporation closed on the deal, an army of renovators, contractors, tradesmen, and decorators converged on Edgewater. For months, a fleet of construction trucks and delivery vans passed through Edgewater's gates bearing construction materials and equipment, a new HVAC system and an extensive security system, and a small fortune in appliances, antiques, rugs, furniture, decorative accessories, fine art and fine linens to furnish the renovated interior. The entire second floor was transformed into Walter's private suite and guest rooms for his important guests. In the new state-of-the-art kitchen, a full-time cook would prepare Walter's meals and create exotic fares for Walter's lavish parties. With top of the line appliances, domestic staff would clean the mansion and do Walter's laundry.

Among Walter's acquisitions for Edgewater was a stately antique grandfather's clock that Walter prominently placed in the mansion's new entry hall. Walter was especially intrigued by the special one-of-a-kind key that wound the vintage clock.

Since there was plenty of office space at the existing building on Railroad Avenue, there was little need for offices at Edgewater. However, when it purchased Edgewater, the railroad received government funds and special tax considerations for industrial development and the creation of more jobs. Since more office space was a part of the government funding deal, two small offices were obligingly constructed in the basement of the mansion.

Once Walter moved into Edgewater, he began hosting lavish parties and fund-raisers for various politicians. He encouraged each of his administrative employees to attend the fund-raisers and, with the understanding that they'd be reimbursed, to make personal contributions to the honored guest's political campaign. In the days or weeks following the party, each employee's political contribution was quietly reimbursed with a corporate expense account check. Those employees who did not have an expense account were asked to submit a voucher for mileage in the amount of their political contribution and the corporation would cut them a business expense reimbursement check.

Walter called me into his office one day and handed me an envelope.

"Take this to Congressman Gary Lee's office in Syracuse," he instructed.

The envelope contained several personal checks, including checks from Soule, Soule's father, Ned Wilkenson, Bill Lloyd (a company vice president), and others, mostly friends of Walter. Each check was made payable to Congressman Lee's campaign fund in the amount of $1,000, the maximum individual political contribution allowed by law.

I took the envelope containing the checks to Congressman Lee's office in Syracuse and handed it to his secretary. A few days later, Walter circulated through the office showing everyone a photograph of himself, Congressman Lee at his side and his arm around Walter's shoulder, an American flag in the background.

Congressman Lee was up for reelection. I have no doubt that Soule, Wilkenson, Lloyd and the others were all reimbursed for their "contributions" through bogus expense claims. In fact, Soule told me that was exactly what happened.

In 1982, Hank Nicols, the village of Cooperstown's chief of police, decided to campaign for the office of Otsego County Sheriff. The sitting sheriff was retiring at the end of his term. Nicols was a Democrat in a Republican town and had limited access to funding against the Republican candidate, Marty Ralph.

Walter was a loyal Republican, but he took a liking to Nicols and wanted to help his campaign. However, Walter was concerned about the political implications of supporting the Democratic candidate rather than the Republican candidate. Therefore, rather than openly contribute to Nicols' campaign, Walter found a more discreet way to provide Nicols with financial backing so that there would be no record of his political contributions.

In addition to being the village chief of police, Nicols ran a small private investigating business. Walter told Nicols to occasionally invoice the Delaware Otsego Corporation for "investigative and security" services, none of which, of course, were actually provided. I was instructed by Walter to approve the invoices for payment when they were received and deliver them to the accounting department for payment. Through this scam, Nicols discretely received a sizeable contribution to his campaign.

After Nicols ultimately lost the election, he came to Walter lamenting the fact that he still had $600 in campaign expenses he was not able to pay. I was in Walter's office at the time. Walter pulled out his personal checkbook and wrote Nicols a check for $600. Walter then began counseling Nicols on the fine art of political gamesmanship to prepare Nicols for his next campaign. I was shocked by the advice Walter gave Nicols.

"You have to start now building a power base," Walter advised Nicols, explaining to him that he needed the "right people" behind him. "For instance," Walter continued, "as chief of police, there are some people you just shouldn't arrest. You should make sure your men know who those people are, and when they see one of those individuals leaving a bar to drive home, your men should ignore them, busying themselves with other business someplace else."

Walter then provided several names as examples, including Soule, who frequently entertained railroad guests in local pubs and dining establishments.

"About as close to the suggestion of bribery as it gets," I said to Nicols as we left the meeting. "Walter should be prosecuted."

"I'd never do that to Walter; he's my friend," Nicols responded.

At Edgewater, Walter entertained his political cronies in extravagant style.

"It's a crime how much food is thrown away at Edgewater," the local garbage man once told me. "Sometimes entire cases of seafood are left for me to pick up."

Employees of the railroad began talking amongst themselves about what they thought of Walter's excesses. As they came to know me, they began to trust me. And, as their trust in me grew, they began confiding in me.

Referring to Edgewater and Walter's extravagant lifestyle there, employees began asking the question, "How can company afford all of this, especially since we've received no raises last year and we are constantly told to limit expenses?"

Karen Clark was an administrative assistant who worked closely with Walter. She had been employed by him since the beginning and Walter trusted her probably more than any other employee. Karen and I were good friends before I was hired by the railroad, and we had a good working relationship. I went to see Karen one day about my expense account. She was visibly upset about something.

"What's wrong?" I asked.

"I asked Walter for a raise, he denied it, and I'm pissed off!" Karen declared, and then she began talking about all of the money that was being spent on Edgewater.

"Where is the money coming from?" I asked.

"The son-of-a-bitch is stealing it from the state," she said giving me a doleful glance, and then explained that she was required to make entries in the books that showed state money being used for state projects when, in fact, it was being spent on Edgewater.

"How much are we talking about?" I asked.

"Well over $100,000," she said. "I'm mad and I'm scared."

Karen and I talked for some time. I had no doubts about her truthfulness. There was simply no way the few trains that ran on the company's short-lines could possibly produce enough revenue to maintain Walter's lifestyle and Edgewater.

After Karen's conversation with me, I thought back about the conversations I had with Ed Browne about accounting irregularities and with Andrea Novello about timecard codes. Then I recalled a conversation I had with my friend, Jimmy Briguglio, the company's superintendent of transportation.

Jimmy told me that he completed track safety reports from his desk and signed them. "I'm supposed to certify track safety reports from visual, on-the-scene inspections," he said. "But, Walter has instructed me to gun-deck them."

"Fabricated track records?" I shuddered at the thought.

I thought back to when I had learned that the codes I used to justify my railroad police time were, in fact, nothing more than a way for the company to be reimbursed by the State of Pennsylvania for work never performed. I thought about the police car purchases for Walter's friends and their family members. I thought about Walter's insistence on buying vehicles equipped with diesel engines being nothing more than an effort to avoid paying fuel taxes. I thought about all of the things that were beginning to come to my attention. I was gravely concerned, but nothing I had learned yet would compare to what I was about to learn.

Ron Bonfardice, the senior purchasing agent, came to talk to me on a cold December day in 1983. Bonfardice was a young man in his early twenties, tall and slender with black curly hair. He was always impeccably dressed and well groomed. He was Maltese's boss. What Bonfardice told me was beyond anything I could have imagined about the extent to which Walter would go to exercise power and control over an employee. The following excerpt is his statement:

"About three months ago, I wanted to sell back my three weeks' accrued vacation to the company. Bob Pierce told me I would have to get Walter's okay to do that, so I grabbed my time sheet and went over to Edgewater to see Walter. Walter was upstairs in his suite. I walked in and asked him to approve my pay in lieu of vacation request.

Walter told me to close the door and asked me why I wanted to sell three weeks' vacation time. I told him I needed the money to buy fuel oil for my trailer. Walter said he'd been meaning to talk to me and told me that he had been thinking about firing me because he was unhappy with a few things I had done in the past. He said that on a return trip from Pennsylvania with Tovey and some others, he'd invited me to Edgewater for cocktails and I'd said 'no' because I wanted to get home. It was ten o'clock at night. He said he had just wanted to compliment me on what a good job I'd done in Pennsylvania and that I shouldn't have refused his invitation. Then Walter said he likes me a lot, even though people like Ned Wilkenson have told him to fire me. He said he didn't have time to talk to me then, but he wanted me to meet with him again. He had me worried about my future with the company, so I agreed to meet with him a couple of weeks later, on a Sunday morning at Edgewater. I thought that was a little strange, but I didn't feel I had a choice.

When I got there that Sunday, Walter took me upstairs to the center room at the top of the stairs and we both sat in chairs. He told me that he was thinking about firing me and wanted to know where I thought I'd be if that happened. He kept telling me he liked me a lot, kept making that comment. But then he said one of the secretaries could do as good a job as me, but for less money, and maybe the secretary should replace me. He talked about firing me and about liking me a lot at the same time. Then he put some other guys down, saying that Lou Tovey was a total idiot and that Bob Pierce had no judgment qualities.

Then he stood up and walked behind me. He started to rub my neck and shoulders. He said he wanted to know everything about me so he could help me. I said that I might have done some things wrong in the past and that maybe some of my work wasn't getting done, but I had two departments by myself at the same time and I was really backed up with work. You know that yourself. He was still rubbing my neck and shoulders and then told me to take off my shirt. At the time, I figured he saw I was upset about my job and future and he was trying to help me. I was totally unaware of his real intentions. Then he told me to lie down on the couch. I started to, but it was too small, so he told me to go to the room across the hall. He told me to lie down on the bed and he...he laid down next to me and kept rubbing my shoulders and neck and back. He told me to relax and calm down. I asked him what he wanted me to say. He said he wanted me to talk, but I didn't know what he wanted me to talk about. He said he liked me a lot and he wanted me on his team. He wouldn't explain what the team was. Then he took me over to his bedroom suite. He closed the door and locked it. He told me to lay on his bed. Christ! I didn't know what to do! He started to rub my shoulders. I asked him again what he wanted me to talk about. He said he wanted me on the team. Then the phone rang and he got up to answer it. I tried to get away from the situation, without implying he was making homosexual advances, so I got up and sat on the chair.

I was really worried about my job and future with the company. I asked him why he was doing this and what he wanted. He said it was his way of helping me. He told me if I wouldn't go along with him, he didn't think he could help me in the organization. He made me get back on the bed again and talk. He told me to think about something to talk about, to relax. I was concerned about my job and I didn't know how to get out of the situation. He told me to lay on my back and he started to rub my chest and stomach and then my legs. He told me again that he liked me and wanted me to talk to him. I said I didn't know what to say to him anymore. He began to get really free with his hands and he started to rub my penis. He tried to unbuckle my pants. I put pressure on my stomach so he couldn't. I wanted out, but I didn't know what to say or do, and he was becoming very aroused. He got up, then knelt between my legs and started to rub my legs again and tried to unbuckle my pants again. He laid on his side, facing me, propping his head up with his hand, and he began rubbing my penis again. I guess he felt I wasn't interested. I sat up on the edge of the bed and he sat next to me. He told me again that he wanted me on his team. He said I was just being nervous. I was...very nervous. He reached out and held my hands. Thank God the phone rang again and I got up.

I stood by the door and he came up to me and put his hands on my shoulders, with his face very close to mine. I told him I'd always been loyal to the company and worked really hard at my job. He said we'd talked enough today and he wanted to set up another meeting with me...at Edgewater again. I put on my shoes and shirt and we walked down the stairs. He told me to report anything I thought he should know about at the office, because he couldn't be everywhere. I told him I had a lot on my mind, that I was concerned about my job and future."

As shocked as I was by what Bonfardice told me, I knew by his demeanor that he was being truthful.

"What can I do about this?" Bonfardice asked.

"Let me see if I can find out what action may be appropriate," I offered. "Will you be in your office later?"

"Yes," he responded, and then left.

I contacted the State Human Rights Division in Binghamton on behalf of Bonfardice, relating his story to the agency representative in hypothetical language. I was told by the agency that to process a sexual harassment complaint, they required a written statement from the victim of the harassment.

When I saw Bonfardice later, I told him that he would have to provide a written statement about the incident if he wanted to file a complaint against Walter.

"I need to think about whether I want to put this in writing," he said, knowing the consequences to him would be grave.

I didn't blame him.

After a week or so passed, I asked Bonfardice if he filed a written complaint.

"No," he said, adding "I'm worried about losing my job and my future, and I'm worried about what Walter will do to me if I put this in writing."

I sensed his embarrassment and humiliation and reluctance to talk about the matter.

"I don't know what else I can do to help you with this," I said, "unless you're willing to give me a written statement."

He said he'd think about it.

As I walked back to my office, the things I was learning about the principles to which Walter apparently subscribed lay heavy on my mind. Then I thought back to the Poolville accident the month before, and Tom Charette.

Chapter Eight

"Mr. Butler's honesty and integrity are above reproach."

— E. R. Boone, Assistant Chief of Police,
Portsmouth, Virginia (June 30, 1975).

Iron on iron made a soul-piercing screech followed by the tearing of sheet metal, the dripping of blood, and the final groans of a dying man as the train slammed to a stop several yards beyond the grade-crossing. I didn't witness the Poolville grade-crossing accident, but in my mind I could envision and hear it as I stood there observing the aftermath. "The inevitable," I thought.

It was a cold, gray November afternoon in 1983 when I received the call on my pager: "Call dispatch…emergency."

I had been enjoying the second day of my long-overdue two week vacation, which had been canceled too many times before because of Walter's railroad "emergencies." Perched in a tree stand at the edge of the seven acres of land Mary and I had recently acquired with our rural Cooperstown home, I was looking out over the adjacent woods and farmland, watching for coyotes while visualizing the week-long camping trip I had planned with Davy and Donnie and the projects I would finish at home the week after.

"I can't believe it," I muttered as I reluctantly climbed out of the tree stand and ran toward the house. I dashed into the house, picked up the telephone, and dialed railroad dispatch.

"This is Butler."

"Get to Poolville immediately," the dispatcher ordered in a grave voice. "There's been a serious grade-crossing accident."

I knew from experience that a call like that meant a train had collided with a vehicle.

Hanging up the phone, I called to Mary, who was busy upstairs with the boys packing for our camping trip.

"Gotta go…" I shouted as I grabbed my keys. "There's been a grade-crossing accident in Poolville."

Sensing my urgency, Mary and the boys hurried downstairs.

"But you're on vacation and you promised to take us camping," Davy and Donnie protested when I turned to leave.

As I drove away, I looked back at them and saw disappointment once again washing over their faces. It broke my heart.

Heading out of Cooperstown, I took a series of back roads all the way to Sherburne, in Madison County, where I turned north on State Route 12. While daylight was quickly changing to dusk, I raced through the pastoral upstate New York countryside. At Brooks Corner, I turned left onto Willey Road and headed west toward where the road crossed the railroad tracks just outside of Poolville. I crossed a small bridge and the road banked to the left, crossing Tackabury Road and then curved sharply to the right just before the tracks. As I rounded the curve, I could see the crossing ahead. A large vacant building that had housed Ogdon Farm Supply before it went out of business occupied the entire southwest corner of the intersection. The building was engulfed in the swirling red and blue police lights and the flashing lights from other emergency vehicles.

I pulled off the road to the right just before the tracks, got out of my patrol car, and walked toward the tracks. The train was sitting on the tracks north of the crossing, its engine idling. State troopers were on the scene writing reports and collecting information. A group of curious onlookers, who lived close enough to hear the crash, had walked up from their houses down the road and stood off to the side talking excitedly. A wrecker was busy preparing to haul away the debris. I looked south down the track toward the crossing. Chet Tybrinski, a twenty-seven year veteran with the railroad, was standing off to the side. With him was Tom Charette.

Charette was in his early twenties at the time and cocky as hell. He'd been with the railroad about a year longer than I had – hired personally by Walter Rich. Charette flagrantly, arrogantly and with impunity, flaunted a complete disrespect for the law and the rules and regulations to which railroad employees are subject. He overtly dealt drugs on railroad property. He frequently raged in violent anger and screamed obscenities. He exploited railroad equipment and property for personal benefit and pleasure. Nevertheless, railroad employees pretty much left Charette alone, fearing that messing with Walter Rich's "golden boy" would accomplish nothing but getting themselves fired.

Charette didn't intimidate me. I considered him nothing more than a punk, but I took seriously my responsibility as railroad police chief to enforce the rules and the law. By the time of the Poolville incident, I was very familiar with Charette and his disreputable comportment. I knew he was trouble. I also knew that Walter Rich aggressively protected Charette. I just couldn't understand why.

I first encountered Charette in the first week or two I was with the railroad. He was nineteen years old then. I was traveling near the railroad's short-line yard in Gloversville, New York, one warm late fall day when I heard a burst of obscenities over my police radio. The railroad track department and the railroad police shared a radio frequency.

"This fucking piece of shit truck...!" reverberated from the radio's speaker.

"Obviously a Gloversville track department employee," was my immediate thought.

Knowing that such language was a blatant violation of company rules, not to mention F.C.C. regulations, I drove to the Gloversville yard to investigate.

The Gloversville yard was a dreary old freight house with bunks for transient railroad work crews. I parked my patrol car and approached the scruffy yard crew on foot. They eyed me with a mixture of curiosity and scorn. Seeing my patrol car drive in the yard got their attention.

After asking a few questions, I soon identified the offender as a nineteen-year-old track laborer named Tom Charette. I walked over to talk to him. Charette was filthy; his appearance was seedy. "Looks like a street corner thug," I thought as I approached him. The entire track crew was a rough bunch in general, but Charette stood out as the most unsavory and belligerent of the group.

"Your string of obscenities on the radio violates company rules and F.C.C. regulations," I admonished. "I'm writing you up; your behavior will be reported to Walter Rich."

He snarled some derisive comment, using a smarmy tone of voice that made me fume inside. His every movement and each expression exuded attitude. I maintained my composure, but thought to myself, "What a cocky little son-of-a-bitch." I listened to his disdainful response to my verbal reprimand and thought, "He'll be nothing but trouble for me." As I left, I felt confident that the smart-assed little punk with no regard for rules would be history when Walter learned of the incident.

Later that afternoon I delivered a complete investigative report to Walter and briefed him on the incident.

"I'll take care of it," he sneered as he snatched the report from my hand and summarily dismissed me.

I never heard another word about Charette and the Gloversville incident, and Charette's employment seem to continue with no consequences for his misconduct.

"No action was ever taken against Charette for the Gloversville incident," I commented to Walter a few weeks later. "Why?" I inquired warily.

"That's none of your business," Walter snapped as he turned and left.

Several months later, in the summer of 1980, when Walter's Delaware Otsego Corporation acquired the New York, Susquehanna and Western (NYSW) railroad line in New Jersey, Walter immediately rewarded Charette with a promotion to track supervisor at the New Jersey yard. The veteran New Jersey track foremen, who with over twenty years' experience should have been in line for the promotion, were incensed.

"Just like that," I thought when I learned of Charette's promotion. "In the blink of an eye, the trashy little kid goes from unskilled and inexperienced track laborer on the FG&J line to boss of the NYSW crew in the New Jersey yard." I was astounded. "What the hell is going on?" I wondered. I learned later that Charette's employment as a track laborer on the FG&J line had been arranged personally by Walter.

In the summer of 1982, Walter summoned all of his railroad executives and me, his chief of police, to the New Jersey yard for a couple of days for a special event.

The New Jersey yard was located in the borough of Little Ferry near the bank of the Hackensack River. It was a huge dismal and dirty facility consisting of acres and acres of flat land bordered on one side by the river's tall reedy grass. Industrial New Jersey and metropolitan New York surrounded the yard and were visible in the distance. A long, dusty dirt road led from the locked entrance gate to the big old roundhouse that enclosed the railcar turntable. Railroad tracks laced in and out throughout the facility and past old brown weathered buildings that housed the engineering shop and warehouses. It was a depressing sight.

I arrived in New Jersey a day early, as did most of Walter's vice presidents and department managers, anticipating Walter's arrival late that night. Walter's newly-appointed vice president of operations, William Lloyd, nervously walked around checking for anything amiss that might upset Walter when he arrived.

"Walter's bed isn't made…someone has to make it before he arrives," Lloyd announced frantically after inspecting Walter's private car. The full-time cook would normally attend to Walter's bed, but he had been away getting food and supplies for meal preparations. Lloyd looked in my direction.

"I'm not making *anyone's* bed," I stated resolutely. My response infuriated Lloyd, but he didn't challenge me.

"I guess I'll have to do it myself," he snapped. Lloyd was really pissed by my comment, but he went about readying the private car for Walter's arrival.

I couldn't believe he was serious. "The vice president of operations rendering maid service for Walter, including turning down his sheets," I thought as I watched in amazement. "I wonder if he'll hang around and tuck Walter in when he finally arrives!" After Lloyd left Walter's car, I peeked in to see if he left a mint on Walter's pillow.

There was a lot of activity in the New Jersey yard the next day, and Walter, in his usual manner, barked orders and ranted vociferously about the most unbelievably petty matters. I found ways to keep busy and maintain a comfortable distance from the sphere of commotion he created.

I was amused when Charette strutted by me, laden with the spoils of an obviously successful shopping spree.

"Walter is taking me to a Boston Pops concert," he bragged in his typical cocky manner as I skeptically eyed his shopping bags. "Gave me his company credit card and sent me off to get some nice threads to wear!"

Walter donned a grin of satisfaction as Charette later paraded around in front of him modeling his new attire.

"Shit!" Charette quickly bellowed. "These damn shoes don't fit!"

I watched Walter's air of satisfaction quickly turn to irritation.

"Bob Kurdock!" Walter shouted to the vice president of the New Jersey office who was standing with a group of other railroad executives. Walter always used first and last name when he was shouting like that at one of his underlings. "Take Charette's shoes back to the store and get him a pair that fit," he ordered.

The other executives snickered amongst themselves as Vice President Bob Kurdock, embarrassed and humiliated in front of his peers, snatched the shoes from Charette's outstretched hand and, like an annoyed but obedient servant, left to execute Walter's order.

"Walter has this entire railroad, executives on down, kissing his pompous ass and catering to that snotty kid, Charette," I marveled, silently vowing to avoid such denigration.

In New Jersey, Walter maintained a railroad dining car, complete with a full-time cook. The dining car was connected at one end to Walter's lavish personal car and at the other end to a more utilitarian car for the yard crew. We were all gathered in the dining car for our evening meal the night of the New Jersey railroad event. I was seated in a booth near one end of the dining car quietly eating my meal and observing others dining and engaging in subdued conversation. Suddenly, someone moving at the far end of the car caught my attention.

"What the hell?" I muttered.

Everyone turned to look, reactions changing quickly from astonishment to outrage. Charette, obviously fresh from the shower in Walter's personal car, arrogantly sauntered stark naked down the middle isle of the dining car past everyone and then disappeared into the crew's car. I looked at Walter for his reaction. The sly little grin on his face as he eyed Charette's naked body disgusted me. I was beginning to get the picture.

Late one night a couple of months later, I got a call from dispatch informing me that a Delaware Otsego pickup truck had been involved in an accident in New Jersey.

"It's Charette," the dispatcher said, adding, "He asked that the local police NOT be called."

I sent Bruce Buffett, my sergeant, to investigate.

Charette stepped out of the truck when he saw Bruce arrive, an open beer bottle in his hand.

"I was trying to turn into this bar," Charette began to explain, taking a big swig of beer before continuing. "I missed the turn, so I went back."

Actually, after missing the turn, Charette "went back" on the wrong side of the road, driving against traffic, striking another vehicle, and causing $3,000 worth of damage to the railroad's truck.

Notwithstanding Charette's violation of the railroad's specific guidelines regarding the use of company vehicles, including the prohibition against drinking and driving a company vehicle, endangering lives, and putting the railroad at risk, Walter once again ignored the police report and summarily dismissed the matter with no consequence to Charette. Charette was behind the wheel of a newly-assigned company vehicle the following day.

On one of my trips to the New Jersey yard a few weeks later, Jim Champlin, the head of the maintenance unit, approached me when no one else was around.

"We're missing a whole bunch of electrical material from the yard," he stated gallingly. "I have some information that may help your investigation of the theft."

Champlin proceeded to blow the whistle on Walter's golden boy. "It's no secret that Charette regularly loads material from the yard into the trunk of his car," he affirmed.

I interviewed several yard employees about the missing electrical material. Each of them confirmed Champlin's statements. I learned that the missing electrical material was the same type of electrical material used for residential electrical service. I also learned that Charette was helping his father build a house in Pennsylvania, about a two-hour drive from the New Jersey yard, and was told that the missing electrical material could be found on the construction site. I telephoned Walter at the Cooperstown office to advise him of the situation.

"I'm going to drive to Pennsylvania and visit the Charette construction site," I informed Walter after explaining the situation. "If I find the missing electrical material there, I'm going to arrest Charette for possession of goods stolen from the railroad yard; and, if I determine that Charette's father knew the electrical materials were stolen from the yard, I'll arrest him, too."

"Don't do anything until you hear back from me," Walter responded. "I'll call you back in a few minutes," he said as he hung up the phone.

A few minutes later, the telephone at the New Jersey yard rang. "It's for you," announced the crew member as he handed me the receiver.

"Butler," I stated, talking into the receiver.

Walter, in his familiar despotic voice, responded, "I'm satisfied that Tom Charette is not involved in that theft, and your investigation is terminated."

I was furious. I saw Bill Lloyd across the yard, and I walked over to him.

"This is outrageous," I complained to Lloyd as I detailed to him my conversation with Walter.

Lloyd simply looked at me, shrugged his shoulders, and responded, "It's Walter's property; don't worry about it."

"That little bastard can do anything he pleases," I fumed as I walked away in frustration.

On a hot weekend in the late summer of 1983, the New Jersey crew, including Charette, was gone for the weekend, leaving the yard vulnerable to trespassers. Walter directed me to spend the weekend in New Jersey protecting the yard from vandals and other miscreants. Although he didn't seem to be concerned about the theft of railroad property in general, he was very protective of his private railroad car and its contents. So, notwithstanding that there was pressing police work that required my attention, the job of protecting Walter's decadent lifestyle in the New Jersey yard while the crew was gone fell to me by his order. I would be the New Jersey yard's security guard for the weekend.

"What a waste of my time," I thought to myself, annoyed with the assignment. I called Bruce.

"I'll be at the New Jersey yard for the weekend," I informed him. "Meet me there."

During the last year, I had learned that incidents of theft of railroad property and vandalism in the New Jersey yard were not unusual. The two most recent occasions involved two crew radios that had been stolen from the yard and a police badge that had turned up missing from one of the railroad police cars. Bruce and I had successfully tracked down and recovered the crew radios from a couple of young punks, but my investigation of the missing police badge seemed to be stalled.

Bruce was waiting for me when I arrived in New Jersey. I parked the patrol car and looked around, visually scanning the yard. I saw nothing unusual, so Bruce and I walked toward the private railcars. Bruce walked around outside, and I entered the crew's car. I immediately noticed a jacket hanging at the entrance.

"That's unusual," I thought, not recognizing the jacket as one that a member of the crew would wear. I reached my hand in one of the pockets to check for some identification.

"Son of a bitch!" I muttered as I pulled out the missing railroad police badge and enough information to conclude that the jacket belonged to Charette.

I poked my head out the door and called for Bruce. "Guess this weekend assignment was worth our time after all," I reflected, holding out my hand with the badge displayed in my palm. Bruce walked toward me.

"I found it in Charette's jacket."

"Why am I not surprised?" Bruce asked, shaking his head in disgust.

The following Monday morning, I marched triumphantly into Walter's office. "I found the missing police badge this weekend," I reported as I entered, "in the crew car in Charette's jacket pocket. I'm going to arrest him for possession of stolen goods."

Lloyd was in Walter's office and the two looked at each other, then back at me.

"How did you find the badge?" Walter huffed.

"In the pocket of the jacket," I responded.

"How do you know the jacket belonged to Charette?" Lloyd continued the grilling.

"Overwhelming evidence in the jacket's pocket along with the badge," I assured him with as much patience as I could muster.

"You're not arresting anyone!" Walter shouted indignantly and concluded, "If anything, you've conducted an illegal search in violation of Tom's rights."

I was dumbfounded by Walter's reaction. When I later questioned Charette about the badge in the pocket of his jacket, he told me he didn't have to talk to me and arrogantly walked away, knowing that he, Walter's golden boy, would suffer no consequence. He was right.

By now, Charette had very few friends on the track crew in New Jersey, and he was as cocky as ever about the level of protection he enjoyed from Walter.

A couple of months after I returned from my weekend in the New Jersey yard, I started getting word from the track crew there that Charette was selling cocaine out of the New Jersey yard. I also learned that he was running cocaine to Cooperstown every Friday. With the help of some of the New Jersey yard employees, I initiated a sting operation using the employees to buy drugs from Charette with marked money I provided to them. A short time later, two railroad employees provided me with written and signed statements affirming that Charette had sold them cocaine for eighty dollars a gram.

During the sting operation, a member of the crew asked Charette, "Aren't you afraid of getting caught?"

"Absolutely not!" responded Charette. "I have Walter Rich wrapped around my finger, and he won't let the railroad police touch me!"

He was right.

Armed with evidence of Charette's drug activities, I contacted the Bergen County Drug Task Force and they immediately initiated their own investigation to identify Charette's supplier, knowing they could bust Charette at any time based on the information I provided to them.

The following Friday, when I had solid information that Charette was carrying drugs with him to Cooperstown, I called Hank Nicols, chief of the Cooperstown Police Department. When Charette crossed the line into the village of Cooperstown late that afternoon, he was stopped by the Cooperstown Police, who found cocaine in his possession and arrested him on drug charges.

I was traveling from the New Jersey yard to Cooperstown that Friday, about an hour behind Charette. "Charette's been arrested for possession of cocaine," Nicols' voice came over my radio.

When I arrived in Cooperstown, I drove straight to the police station.

"When we searched Charette after his arrest, we found some marked money on him," Nicols said. I identified the money as that I had marked for the sting operation.

The arrest was huge for the quiet little village of Cooperstown. I was talking to Nicols in his office when the desk sergeant walked in.

"Walter's on the phone," he said. "Wants to talk to you."

I picked up the phone.

"What the hell in going on?" Walter yelled at me when I answered. "Who authorized you to arrest Charette? Why wasn't I informed?"

"I didn't arrest him," I informed Walter. "He was arrested by the village police. I was on my way back to Cooperstown from the New Jersey yard when I learned of the arrest."

"Where did they get the information?" demanded Walter.

"Beats me," I responded. "He doesn't have a lot of friends, so it could have been anyone."

"What's his bail?"

"A couple of thousand dollars, I believe."

"Report to me at my railroad car as soon as possible," Walter ordered and hung up.

I stalled around the police station for a couple of hours, and then finally went to see Walter. His face was red with rage and he was pacing in circles, his small, pudgy hands fidgeting in front of him. He looked at me as I entered his railcar.

"I don't have a large amount of cash lying around; I'm calling around to local businesses to find cash that can be exchanged for company checks so I can make Charette's bail."

"That's interesting," I thought. "Aloud I asked, is Charette blackmailing you or something, Walter; what's he got on you?" I was curious about why Walter seemed to believe he had an obligation to bail Charette out of jail.

"No," he answered. "I have that relationship under control."

"What the hell does THAT mean?" I wondered.

Later that night, Walter had succeeded in pulling together enough cash and he sent his executive vice president, David Soule, and me to the county jail to bail out Charette. We brought Charette back to Walter's railroad car where he spent the night. The following day, Walter informed me that Charette was now going to live with him in the railcar. "I'm doing this to keep Tom out of trouble," he explained.

Walter then directed me to write a statement for Tom to sign. "By signing the statement, Tom will agree to be back on my railcar by eleven o'clock each night unless he has permission otherwise directly from me or you."

"Great," I thought. "Now Walter and Charette are living together, and I'm Charette's babysitter!"

"There's another small problem, Walter," I interrupted and candidly broke the news to him about my investigation of Charette's drug activity at the New Jersey yard and the investigation being conducted by the New Jersey Drug Task Force. "They'll likely arrest Charette on felony drug charges for selling cocaine," I said in a serious tone. Walter looked vexed.

"Charette's not worth it," I tried to persuade him.

He stood there for a while without speaking. Then, matter-of-factly, he retorted, "Tell the New Jersey people you lost the evidence."

"I can't do that," I shot back. "I'm not going to lie," and then added, "They wouldn't believe it anyway."

Walter's solution was incredible. "I'll just keep Tom in Cooperstown; I don't think New Jersey will extradite him."

"Good God," I thought. "This is unbelievable."

Then Walter abruptly announced, "You no longer work for Lloyd; you work directly for me, and I am to be kept advised of all investigations." He looked at me with great disdain and said, "If you value your job, get rid of the charges in New Jersey against Charette."

I went home. The next day, I called my contact at the New Jersey Drug Task Force and told him that I had determined my informants were unreliable and that I didn't think their testimony would hold up in court. It wasn't exactly a lie. I knew Walter would make every effort to persuade the New Jersey crew to recant their statement. At my request, the task force dropped the charges against Charette.

I had a strong interest in self-preservation: my family depended on my continued employment. But I felt awful. "No one should have to choose between their integrity and their job," I silently fumed. I worried about the ultimate ramifications of all of this on the railroad. In my opinion, Walter was flirting with destiny and I didn't like being a part of it.

Charette skated free of the New Jersey drug charges, but within a couple of weeks he was at the defendant's table before the Cooperstown Village Court judge. The judge read the charges against Charette associated with his arrest for possession of cocaine.

The judge directed himself to Charette. "How do you plead?"

"Guilty," responded Charette.

The judge found Charette guilty of a misdemeanor and fined him $1,000. Charette now had a drug conviction on his record. I'm sure Walter paid the fine.

In Cooperstown, there was little for Charette to do other than strut around the railroad office and do as he pleased. Cooperstown didn't require a track supervisor, and it was clear that Charette wasn't going to be sent back to New Jersey. So, Walter created a position for him.

"Tom Charette has been appointed chief dispatcher in the Cooperstown office." Walter's announcement was circulated to all railroad employees.

"There's never been such a position," protested the railroad dispatchers who had successfully worked their own shifts for years with no need for a "chief." "Besides, Charette isn't qualified to be a dispatcher, let alone the 'chief dispatcher'…he has no experience," their protest continued.

Their concerns fell on deaf ears.

"Tom's a fast learner," was Walter's response.

"That's for sure," I thought to myself. "He's learned quickly that he can do as he pleases and Walter will protect him."

It wasn't long until Charette became bored with his dispatcher duties and Walter indulged him in something more substantial and more exciting.

Among my responsibilities as chief of the railroad police was that of "safety officer" with regard to train operation and the railroad crossings. Not long after Charette had been appointed "chief dispatcher," I got word from the train crews that he was acting as engineer on some of the scheduled train runs. I went to see Lloyd, who was still the railroad's vice president of operations.

"Who authorized Charette to be assigned as a train engineer?" I demanded. Lloyd knew I was livid.

"Walter," he responded matter-of-factly. "Let it go."

"How am I supposed to let it go?" I was furious. "I'm responsible for train safety. Charette has no training to be an engineer. The track crews, with twenty or more years of experience are complaining. Some of them are being bumped to brakeman, for God's sake, so that Charette can engineer the train and, look at Charette's history!" I snapped back at Lloyd in a staccato manner.

It was futile. Indulging Charette's whims apparently trumped my concerns about railroad safety. "Incredible," I thought.

It wasn't long before Charette was on my radar screen again. One day while he was engineering a train, he ran over a cow that had wandered onto the tracks. The owner of the cow angrily confronted Charette at the scene. Charette, smiling, backed the train over the cow's remains, and then he laughed at the farmer. The farmer's complaint was forwarded to me. When I notified Walter of Charette's behavior, he simply responded, "You're picking on Tom again."

In the fall of 1983, just before the Poolville accident, I received a letter from the New York State Department of Transportation complaining of the railroad's trains exceeding the speed limits in the Madison County area. The complaint listed specific days and times, indicating that the trains had been clocked going 45 mph in a 10 mph zone. I checked the train logs against the days reported in the complaint. Charette was the engineer on each of the offending trains. The consequences could be serious, so I immediately confronted Walter.

Walter exploded in rage. "You're harassing Charette again," he shouted. "Tom is trying hard to straighten up; he just needs your help."

Then Walter quickly changed his tone, and with his characteristic little smile said, "Tom and I are having dinner tomorrow night at the Horned Dorset; I want you and Mary to join us so we all can get better acquainted."

It wasn't an invitation, it was an order. I was dumbfounded.

The Horned Dorset Inn is an exquisite French restaurant located in a converted Victorian-era building on Route 8 in Leonardsville, New York, about 40 miles west of Cooperstown. Its cuisine, wine list, and ambiance attract the New York City affluent, who make the 4 hour drive to Leonardsville simply to dine at the Horned Dorset.

I called Mary and told her to arrange for a babysitter the following night and explained the obligatory dinner we were to attend with Walter and Charette.

"Please make up an excuse and tell Walter we can't go," she protested. But, when I told her Walter would make my life hell if we didn't go, she agreed to do it for me.

Walter and Charette were just walking into the restaurant when Mary and I arrived. We sat in the car for a couple of minutes, anticipating the awkward evening ahead, and then walked to the entrance. I opened the door and Mary walked in ahead of me. Walter greeted us nervously, while Charette stood back watching as if waiting for his cue.

An impeccably dressed maître d' ushered us through the dimly lit vestibule to one of three formal dining areas and directed us to an intimate table in the corner Walter had reserved. A crisp white linen table cloth covered the table, which was set with what looked like fine china and silver place settings for several courses. A lovely bouquet of fresh flowers adorned the table's center. On one wall of the dining room, a fireplace flickered with softly dancing flames. Large Palladian windows on another wall overlooked an artistically lit formal garden. Classical music played softly in the background and candlelight washed the room with a romantic glow.

The mood was lost on Mary and me as we awkwardly sat there feigning congeniality, listening to Walter making insufferable small talk in an obvious attempt to engage us all in conversation, as though we were best of friends enjoying an evening out together. Charette sat across from me chatting as though he and I were old buddies. I sensed he had been coached on his behavior for the evening.

As uncomfortable as we were, Mary and I sat there and played our parts in the bizarre charade as we sipped fine wine in fragile crystal goblets and dined on multiple delectable courses, between which we delicately rinsed our fingertips in lemon-laced water placed before us in little porcelain finger bowls, the purpose of which had to be explained to Charette.

I thought the evening would never end. The Horned Dorset is an establishment where you go for an entire evening of fine dining; a fast-food restaurant it's not. About three hours later, when the evening did finally end, Walter waxed lyrical about friendship as we walked toward our cars, apparently believing he had pulled off his scheme to convince me of Charette's virtue. He should have known it wouldn't work.

"As far as I'm concerned," I commented to Mary as we started to drive back to Cooperstown, "Charette is still a thug and Walter is still a bully." We laughed all the way home as we thought about the absurdity of the evening.

Now as I arrived on the accident scene a state trooper approached me.

"David Butler, railroad police," I identified myself.

"Two victims dead; a third is critical; they've all been taken by ambulance to the hospital in Hamilton," the trooper stated without emotion. "Everything was left in place pending your arrival."

"Thanks," I said and walked over to the pile of twisted metal on the side of the tracks.

"That was the pick-up truck struck by the train," the trooper called to me. "Train hit it broadside; completely crushed it," he continued.

I looked down. Dark red blood was still trickling out of the bottom of the crumpled mass and puddled at my feet. A wave of nausea washed over me as I visualized the impact and thought about the victims.

Earl Johnson, his younger brother Calvin, and Tom Flummer were all in their twenties and good friends. Earl and Tom were both married and had small children. On that cold, gray November afternoon in 1983, the three friends climbed into the cab of Earl's small blue Datsun pick-up.

"We want to go with you, dad," Earl's and Tom's children pleaded, sensing their dads' excitement about wherever they were going. But there was no room in the cab of the small pick-up, and so the children were left at home.

Calvin had just sold his Jeep, and the three young men were off to pick up the money. Cash in hand, they stopped by the garage where Calvin worked to see his fiancée and, from there, drove up the road and paid for the 1960's Plymouth Barracuda Calvin had had his eye on for some time. After that, the three headed east on Willey Road. The vacant Ogdon Farm Supply building blocked their view of the tracks to the right as they approached the crossing. The familiar white reflective crossbucks sign, with "Rail Road" printed in black on one arm and "Crossing" printed in black on the other arm, marked the intersection. They had seen it hundreds of times in the past as they approached the tracks, being flagged to a stop when a train was approaching.

That day, there was nothing that warned them of the approaching train. Just as the cab of the truck was centered over the tracks, the train barreled out from behind the Ogdon Farm Supply building and slammed into the passenger side of the small Datsun pickup, hurling it off to the side of the track in a crumpled heap, the broken and bleeding bodies of the three young men inside. They never saw it coming.

With a great thud, the twisted heap of metal hit the dirt and slid to a stop. Earl opened his eyes. There was blood and glass everywhere. Calvin and Tom were underneath him, flesh torn from their bodies and blood pulsing from the wounds. They gurgled as they tried to breathe, their lungs filling with blood. Earl writhed in pain from several broken ribs and other internal injuries as he tried to move. Shards of glass and torn metal were protruding from his legs and arms. Slowly, he pulled himself out of the mangled mess through the shattered windshield, staggering away from the carnage and screaming in agony. Charette approached him.

"I didn't mean to hit you...the others are gone; they're dead!" Charette blurted impassively, and then asked Earl if he wanted a cigarette.

In shock and overcome with pain and grief, Earl began sobbing uncontrollably. Someone led him to the fire truck, where he sat alone shivering and sobbing until the ambulance arrived. When the paramedics strapped him onto a backboard, his pain became unbearable and Earl begged for relief. The paramedics loaded him into the ambulance and, with sirens screaming, sped off for the hospital.

I looked up from the puddle of blood at my feet and toward the train sitting several hundred feet up the tracks from the intersection, the engine still idling. It was a short-line diesel train carrying farm products and grain. It had been headed north. Wheels and debris were strewn in a trail along the tracks behind the train.

I walked down the tracks to the intersection where Tybrinski and Charette were standing.

"Who was operating the train?" I asked Tybrinski.

"Charette," he responded.

I looked at Charette.

"I gave a statement to the trooper," Charette said, looking scared but acting cocky. "I was only going ten to fifteen miles per hour," he added, and then asked, "Is Walter on the way?" I didn't answer.

"This is an unguarded stop-and-flag crossing," I thought as I stood there trying to estimate the distance from the crossing where the train collided with the vehicle to the spot where the train had finally stopped.

At a stop-and-flag crossing, railroad policy requires the engineer to signal by a series of long and short blasts of the train's whistle when approaching the crossing and stop the train prior to entering the intersection to allow another crew member to get off and flag motorists down so the train could safely go through the intersection.

When the accident occurred, the Poolville crossing was a blind approach for cars traveling east on Willey Road, and there were no warning devices other than the white railroad crossbucks sign.

"I'll have to interview local residents," I thought. "To determine if anyone heard the train's whistle as it approached the crossing."

Dusk was quickly disappearing into the dark of night. I wanted to get to the hospital, hoping that the one victim who was still alive could talk.

"Open the road to local traffic, but leave the truck and the train where they are," I instructed before leaving. "I'll be back."

Hamilton was about four miles north of Poolville. My mind was focused on the accident scene as I drove toward the hospital, my internal maelstrom of thoughts raging.

"Charette had to have that train close to full speed going through that crossing," I thought, estimating in my head the distance the train traveled after the impact before coming to a stop. "The train was too far up the tracks after the impact, and the damage was too severe, for it to have been going only ten or fifteen miles per hour."

I was anxious to do what I needed to do at the hospital and get back to the accident scene. "Charette's story just doesn't make any sense," I concluded.

The hospital was at the south end of Hamilton, near Colgate University. I drove around to the emergency entrance, parked the patrol car, and walked inside.

I identified myself at the front desk and asked about the victims.

"Two fatalities and one critical," the nurse on duty responded.

Calvin and Tom had died; Earl was in a nearby room, his body mangled from the accident.

I asked for the victims' identification. Handing me the information, the nurse pointed in the direction of a small waiting room and said, "Some family members of the victims are in there; they've been told of the deaths."

I looked across the hall and saw two women and two small barefoot children wailing with grief. It was heartbreaking.

I walked over to the women and identified myself.

"I'm David Butler, chief of the railroad police," I said, looking at each of them.

One of the women spoke, telling me she was Earl's and Calvin's mother and the other woman was Earl's wife. The two little barefoot tots stood in the corner crying, fear in their little eyes reflecting the chaos of the moment.

Just then, two more women arrived. At the front desk they identified themselves as Tom Flummer's wife and Calvin Johnson's girlfriend. The nurse walked them over to the waiting room where I was standing with the other family members.

I introduced myself and then, with as much sensitivity as was possible, I said, "Tom and Calvin died in the accident; Earl's in critical condition." One of the women immediately collapsed to the floor screaming in agony. The younger woman tried to console her while her body heaved in great sobs.

I told them each how sorry I was for their loss and promised them I would conduct a full investigation of the accident.

I walked over to the pay phone and called Walter, who had been informed of the accident and was waiting to hear details.

"Two fatalities and one victim in critical condition," I said as Walter answered. "Charette was the engineer," I continued.

"Tell Charette not to say anything until Gozigian and I get there in the morning," Walter ordered. Ed Gozigian was a Cooperstown attorney who often worked for Walter on various legal matters.

"Charette gave a statement to the state police before I arrived at the scene," I informed Walter, and then stated, "I want to test Charette for drugs."

"Absolutely not!" Walter bellowed. "I won't allow it!"

I hung up the phone and left the hospital to drive back to the accident scene. I felt a great sadness for those innocent victims and their families, whose lives were now forever changed. I also felt trepidation about Walter interfering with my investigation of the accident.

I stayed at the accident scene late into the night photographing the area, taking preliminary measurements, and talking to about a dozen or so witnesses. I then released the remains of the truck to the wrecker and told the train crew to leave the train where it was so I could take some more measurements and photographs in the morning. I also asked the train crew to be on site when I arrived in the morning, and then I went home.

"Something's not right," I thought to myself as I drove back to Cooperstown. Charette's story just didn't jibe with what I saw.

When I arrived at the accident scene the following day, I measured the distance the train traveled from the point of impact to where it finally stopped. The train traveled 900 feet after impact before it came to a stop.

The train crew then helped me reconstruct the accident.

"Back up the train to the point where it is approaching the crossing," I directed Charette, telling him to go exactly the same speed that he had reported he had been going the night before and to apply the emergency brakes at the same spot he did the night before. I set up a portable radar gun to record the train's speed.

The first time through, the radar gun recorded the train's speed at exactly 10 mph. Charette hit the brakes at the point of impact and the engine stopped within the limits of the crossing. We repeated the exercise two more times with the same results. The train stopped within the limits of the crossing every time. It was obvious that if the train had been going only 10 mph the night before as Charette stated in his report to the state troopers, the train would have stopped in the crossing, not 900 feet up the tracks.

"Are you aware that this is a stop-and-flag crossing?" I asked Charette. "Did anyone get out of the train last night and flag the crossing?"

"Uh, no," Charette responded.

Just then, Walter and Gozigian arrived and walked over to the tracks near the place where the pile of twisted metal that had been the small Datsun pickup truck had come to rest the night before. They looked around and talked for a while. I walked over to join them, and as I approached, I noticed something floating in the puddle of blood that remained after the vestige of the pickup truck had been removed by the wrecker the night before. Using a stick I picked up off the ground, I fished a wallet out of the puddle of blood.

"It's not looking good for Charette," I said to Walter, who was standing at my side.

Walter nudged me in the side with his elbow and, with a little smirk on his face, said, "Tom tells me he has no idea how fast he was going." I simply looked at him, astonished.

"I want Charette to submit to a drug test," I said after a few minutes.

"Absolutely not," was Walter's response. Then he added, "We're not looking for trouble here."

Then he asked, "Any evidence that the driver of the truck had been drinking?"

"No," I responded indignantly. "There's not a shred of evidence to assign responsibility for this to the victim."

"What a despicable bastard," I thought as I walked away to continue my investigation.

I had Charette test the train again at various speeds. At 40 mph, it took the train 900 feet to stop. I surmised that hitting the truck would have slowed the train slightly, so Charette must have had the train running at a speed in excess of 40 mph when the accident occurred.

Realizing the significance of the reenactments, and knowing that the sworn statement he gave to the state trooper the night before was not going to hold up, Charette began to change his story in an attempt to explain how the train might have ended up 900 feet down the track after the accident. I'm sure he was being coached by Walter, who had explained to the state trooper that Charette must have gradually applied the brakes after the impact to avoid a derailment. In one of his latest versions of his story, Charette commented, "The damage was done, so I stopped the train slowly."

The trouble with Charette's latest version of his story was that Tybrinski stood by his statement that Charette had "dumped the air" (railroad terminology for applying the brakes) at impact.

"Lying son-of-a-bitch," I thought as I completed the report of my investigation concluding that the accident was a result of Charette running the train in excess of the speed limit and his failure to stop and flag the crossing. As it turned out, I later learned, the state trooper's report and my report reached the same conclusion. I submitted my report to Bill Lloyd, the railroad's Vice President of Operations.

Apparently, my report disappeared from the railroad's files after I submitted it to Lloyd. I suspect it never went any further than Walter. The railroad's "official" version of the accident report was clearly written by someone other than me and contained fabricated information regarding the train's speed, the number of cars the engine was pulling, and warning devices at the crossing. It's no surprise, therefore, that the report the railroad submitted to the FRA reached an entirely different conclusion than did the report of my investigation.

The state trooper's report was submitted to the Madison County district attorney, who reviewed it for evidence on which he could bring criminal charges against Charette. However, there was no evidence of intent in either report, an essential element of a criminal charge, and no statute over which Madison County had jurisdiction that prohibited reckless driving of a train. Furthermore, the state trooper's report included a statement from a Federal Railroad Administration official asserting that there was no way to prove the train's speed. I was surprised when I learned that the FRA had taken that position, since during my investigation immediately following the accident, I had conclusively demonstrated the train's speed to have been in excess of 40 mph using the same train, the same weight, and the same engineer and brakeman, and no representative of the FRA ever appeared at the site of the Poolville accident.

Because the stop-and-flag order was the railroad's policy, not state law, and there was no expert testimony available to prove the train's speed, the district attorney concluded that the accident occurred as a result of Charette's carelessness and declined to bring criminal charges against him. Charette was directly responsible for the death of two people and severe injuries to a third and he would not face criminal changes.

Charette may have once again escaped consequences for his behavior, but this time his behavior would significantly affect Walter and the railroad.

About two weeks later, Walter received a letter from Patrick Joyce, an attorney in Sherburne, New York, the small village about eight miles south of Poolville.

"I have been retained by the families of Earl and Calvin Johnson and Tom Flummer," the letter began. After the introductory formalities and references to the Poolville accident, the letter got right to the point. "Please provide this office with the name of your liability carrier." It was clear what would come next.

After reading the letter, Walter scribbled a note on it, stating, "Since we have no liability, there is no need to furnish this information." He then forwarded the letter to me.

When I saw the letter and Walter's hand-written note, I exploded. "No liability? Good God, if EVER there was liability, this was it," my thoughts raged, directed by my moral compass. "The engineer was convicted of drug possession; he was suspected of selling drugs; he had no training to be an engineer; he had a poor safety record; he lived with, and was protected by, the railroad's president, and there's no liability?"

I took the letter to Larry Malski, the railroad's in-house corporate attorney. "Malski needs to deal with this, not me," I thought as I laid the letter on his desk.

Sure enough, in a matter of days, Walter was served with notice that the victims' families had filed a wrongful death lawsuit against the railroad. The railroad was self-insured.

Walter came into my office, the notice of claim in hand, and shut the door. He looked nervous and upset and started talking about the accident and the lawsuit. He paused and then looked directly at me. "You'll have to lie for us on this one," he declared. Without saying another word, he turned and walked out.

My reaction was automatic. "There's no way I'm going to lie, there's no way I'm going to perjure myself in court, and there's no way I'm going to cover for Charette," I thought to myself after Walter left. "It simply is not going to happen."

I knew what the consequences would be.

Mary looked at me when I walked in the door that evening. "What's wrong?" she asked, knowing by the way my head was cocked that the news was not going to be good.

"Walter expects me to lie about the accident," I began. I looked into her eyes and said, "You know I can't do that." Tears welled up in Mary's eyes, and I knew she understood the inevitable.

"Well, that's the end of this job," I continued.

I had objectively investigated the accident and provided Walter with an accurate and honest report of my investigation. However, it was now clear that Walter wasn't interested in the truth.

"We'll be okay," Mary said, sensing my fear, tears streaming down her face.

We sat on the sofa and talked until almost dawn.

"I've proven myself in the past to the board of directors," I said to Mary, her head resting on my shoulder and her arms gently embracing me. "I'm going to go talk to some of them; I think I'll go see Niles first thing tomorrow."

I gently pulled myself away from her and rose from the sofa. "Let's try to get some sleep," I said. Emotionally drained, we walked upstairs to our bedroom.

"I shouldn't have to choose between my job and my integrity," I thought as I drifted off to sleep.

Chapter Nine

He has honor if he holds himself to an ideal of conduct though it is inconvenient, unprofitable, or dangerous to do so.

— Walter Lippmann,
A Preface to Morals (1929)

Niles Curtis lived in Cooperstown and owned the local Agway store on Railroad Avenue just up the street from the Delaware Otsego Corporation offices. I was a frequent customer at the Agway store and knew Niles to be fair and reputable. He and his wife had a daughter about the age of my son, Don. They both attended Cooperstown Central School. Niles had been a member of the railroad's board of directors for some time.

I stopped at the Agway store the next morning. It was Wednesday, January 18, 1984. Niles was behind the counter when I walked in. A customer had just walked out with his purchases, and there was no one else in the store.

"Hi, Niles," I greeted him. We engaged in customary small talk, and then he asked, "What can I do for you this morning?"

"If you have a few minutes, Niles, I'd like to talk to you about the railroad," I responded.

"Sure," he said. "What's up?"

In detail, I told Niles about the Poolville accident, Charette's history with drugs, and statements I'd received from other railroad employees. Niles listened without saying much. When I finished, he suggested that I go see Deane Winsor, the chairman of the railroad's board of directors.

I was disappointed not to get some reaction from Niles, but understood his inclination to defer to the board's chairman. I went back home and called Deane Winsor.

Winsor was also a local resident and a long-time member of the Otsego County Board of Representatives. I explained the same information to him that I had explained to Niles, but unlike Niles, Winsor reacted with concern and anger about Walter's instruction that I lie about the accident.

"We need to take this to Malcom," he said, referring to Malcolm Hughes. "I'll call and set up a meeting with him tomorrow morning."

"I'll pick you up and we can drive there together," I offered. "There's hope," I thought to myself after Winsor and I concluded our conversation.

The next morning, I picked up Winsor for our hour-and-a-half drive to Margaretville. As we drove, we talked about Walter Rich and issues concerning the railroad.

"I'm a little concerned about exposing any of this to Hughes," I remarked. "Hughes and Walter are good friends; he's Walter's frequent legal advisor," I continued.

"Don't worry about that," Winsor reassured me. "He's a member of the board and we need his legal expertise on this."

"I'm concerned that Walter will find out what's going on and try to fire me," I finally said.

Winsor did his best to reassure me with comments about Walter's credibility now being on the line with the board and the vast amount of evidence against me that he'd need to get rid of me. I wasn't exactly convinced and I was stressed about the meeting with Hughes.

We arrived in Margaretville, parked the car, and walked a short distance to Hughes' law office. The office consisted of three small, cheaply furnished, fluorescent-lit rooms, the walls of which were paneled with sheets of thin spurious wood. Hughes greeted us curtly and then ushered us to the small conference room near his office. He motioned for us to sit down in two chairs situated near an oval table. Hughes, a middle-aged, paunchy man with thinning gray hair and not terribly well-groomed, began to pace back and forth across the room.

"Well?" he finally asked, glancing back and forth at me and Winsor.

I detailed for Hughes the same information about the railroad, Charette, and Walter that I had presented to Niles and Winsor the day before. Hughes was sweating as he angrily paced back and forth across the room. As I spoke, he would snap, "How do you know that?" or "Can you prove that?" I began to feel very uneasy.

"You need to do more of an investigation," Hughes finally suggested.

"I'm a witness," I protested. "The result of any investigation I conduct on all of this will, therefore, be suspect; so, I think you should probably ask the state police to investigate this matter."

"No; I want you to do it…that's why we pay you," Hughes' rebuffed.

His response troubled me. "How am I supposed to do that right under Walter's nose without his finding out and having me fired?"

Winsor leaned forward in his chair, and with an unmistakable tone of authority, stated, "If Walter finds out, you don't have to talk to him; just tell him you're working at the direction of the chairman of the board." He then sat back in his chair and folded his hands in his lap.

"I agree," Hughes said, and then added, "I want the investigation completed in twenty-four hours!"

"Twenty-four hours?" I repeated. "A proper investigation will take me at least a week!"

Nonetheless, I was given twenty-four hours to investigate.

On our drive back to Cooperstown, Winsor told me not to worry, calling Walter a "spoiled brat who has had his way too long and needs to be brought down a notch or two." Winsor looked directly at me and said, "He can't fire you."

I wasn't so sure.

I realized later the next day that as soon as Windsor and I left Hughes' office, Hughes had picked up the phone and called Walter.

Back in Cooperstown, and having only twenty-four hours to complete the investigation that Hughes and Winsor authorized, I immediately collected all of the written statements I had previously received from railroad employees complaining about corruption, spurious bookkeeping, and other wrongdoing. That night I called my friend, Peevers.

John Peevers was a trusted and loyal friend. He had a law enforcement background and sometimes accompanied me on railroad patrols and business when I needed assistance. He was born and raised in Cooperstown, but had left as a young man to go out west. He moved back to Cooperstown in the summer of 1979 and purchased the local Western Auto store. I met him shortly after that. He and his wife, Nancy, and Nancy's two daughters, lived in the charming Dutch Colonial style house on Fair Street directly across the street from Edgewater. Nancy helped John run the store and also worked for a while as a legal secretary at Gozigian's law office. She had been working at the railroad as an administrative assistant for about a year or so. Our families had become good friends over the past four years, and John and I spent many weekend afternoons hunting woodchucks on my property, coming back to the house in the evening to a wonderful meal Mary and Nancy had prepared. Our kids played together and rode the boys' ATV's around our property.

It was a cold January night. I knew Peevers would be home. When he answered, I told him about my discussions with Curtis and Winsor, and my meeting in Margaretville with Winsor and Hughes that day. Then I said, "I have less than twenty-four hours to complete this investigation; I don't know what's going to happen."

"I'm here if you need me," Peevers responded.

The next day was Friday. When I got to my office that morning, I called Nancy Peevers and asked her to come see me. She was the only one in the company who could take shorthand and I trusted her. I asked her if she would be willing to assist me by recording and transcribing signature statements from various people that I would bring to her. She agreed.

I then called Bonfardice and asked him to come to my office. I told him I was involved in an investigation authorized by the board's chairman and I needed him to provide a written statement about his previous complaint to me about Walter's homosexual advances toward him. "The time has come for you to take a stand," I said. "You can dictate your statement in private to Nancy Peevers, who will type it up for your signature.

"I want your promise that I won't get in trouble over it," he said.

I explained to him again that the chairman of the board had authorized the investigation, promising there would be no problem with Walter.

"Can I call Winsor first?" he asked.

"Sure," I said and handed him the phone.

Winsor assured Bonfardice that the investigation was authorized and it was okay for him to give me his statement. Satisfied, Bonfardice agreed to dictate his statement to Nancy on the condition that no one else would be in the room.

I took Bonfardice to the room where Nancy was waiting. He went in and shut the door. As Bonfardice spoke, Nancy silently recorded each word verbatim in shorthand. When he had finished, Nancy told him to give her time to type it and then return so he could sign it. He agreed and left.

Next was Jim Maltese. Nancy recorded Maltese's statement about the memo he had written to Rich refusing to make false federal accounting entries, and his personal knowledge about the railroad's bid-rigging activities. Maltese hung around while Nancy typed his statement and, after he read it, he signed it.

Meanwhile, I was busy asking a lot of questions of a lot of people, reassuring them that my investigation was authorized by the board's chairman and they had nothing to fear from Walter Rich by talking to me. Or so I thought. Twenty-four hours wasn't a lot of time, and time was quickly running out.

Nancy brought Bonfardice's typed statement to me, ready for his signature.

"Bonfardice hasn't come back to sign his statement," she said, handing it to me.

I tried to locate Bonfardice so he could sign his statement, but he was nowhere to be found.

Then, I tried to talk to Karen Clark to get some information from her regarding the state money spent on Edgewater. Karen was noticeably apprehensive and refused to talk to me.

I was beginning to believe that Walter had gotten word of the investigation and was raising hell.

Then my phone rang.

"This is Lloyd; Walter wants to see you right away."

I ignored the summons and I continued my quest to find the elusive Bonfardice so I could get his signature on his statement. I talked to anyone who was still willing to talk to me.

Several times I was told by different people that I was wanted on the phone or that Walter wanted to see me at Edgewater. I continued to avoid any contact with Walter, Soule, or Lloyd. Time was running out much faster than I had hoped, and I hadn't finished my investigation.

Lloyd called again. "Walter wants you at Edgewater at three o'clock," he said.

The pressure for me to go to Edgewater was increasing. I hung up the phone and called Winsor at his home. After three or four rings, the recorded message on his answering machine began to play. "Damn," I said under my breath waiting for the beep so I could leave a message. I was beginning to panic.

"Deane, this is Butler; call me as soon as you get this message; Walter wants to talk to me and has summoned me to Edgewater; I need to know what to do; call me!" I hung up the phone and waited. After what seemed like forever, Winsor called back.

"David, this is Deane...I got your message."

"Walter wants me at Edgewater."

"Yes, I know."

The tone of his voice indicated to me that Walter had gotten to him, too.

"Since you authorized this investigation, I'm going to refuse to attend the meeting," I told him.

"If you don't show up," he said, "he'll accuse you of insubordination. You'd better go," he said somberly.

I hung up the phone and called Hughes at his office in Margaretville. His secretary informed me that he was en route to Cooperstown for a meeting at Edgewater.

The cards were on the table, and it was obvious that I was in a no-win situation. If I didn't go to the meeting at Edgewater, I'd surely be fired for insubordination. If I did go, the result would surely be no different.

I gathered the information I had been able to collect and removed all sensitive documents from my office files. Then, I called Peevers at his store.

"Western Auto..."

"It's Butler," I interrupted him. "Everything's coming to a head...Walter wants me at Edgewater and Winsor's tone has completely changed since I met with him and Hughes yesterday...I think Walter's going to fire me and the board's not going to challenge him."

"Get Mary and the boys and come over to the house," he responded without hesitation. "I'll arrange for my mechanic to mind the store...meet me at the house."

I picked up Mary and the boys and drove to the Peevers' home. It was early afternoon on Friday, January 20, 1984. John and Nancy greeted us warmly. Davy and Donny took Danny upstairs with Nancy's daughters to watch television so Mary and I could talk to John and Nancy. I tried to remain positive as we sat in the living room waiting for the appointed hour and talking about the statements and information I had been able to marshal in such a short period of time. But the air was heavy with despair and anxiety.

75

From the windows in the dining room, we watched board members' cars drive one after another into Edgewater. I feared the worst. I looked at Mary and saw in her face fear about the future and grave concern for me.

At just before six o'clock, I opened the front door, walked out, and looked across the street, hoping that Hughes and Winsor would be true to their word.

"We'll all be waiting here for you after it's over," John said, giving me a firm pat on the back.

I learned later from Mary that as I crossed the street to Edgewater, John, Nancy, and Mary watched me and once I was out of sight, the three of them walked into the living room and sat on the sofa and in the two big chairs that faced it. They joined hands and closed their eyes, and Nancy and Mary listened as John prayed aloud for my welfare, Mary's welfare, and the boys' welfare. Then they hugged each other and began what would be a seven-hour vigil waiting for me to return.

It felt like I was walking to the gallows as I crossed Fair Street and passed through the gates of Edgewater. Entering the property, I was struck with how the long line of sedans parked in front of the mansion gave the appearance of a mafia family meeting. A chill ran through me.

As I walked up the long driveway, I saw Buffett standing in the main courtyard by the steps leading up to the mansion's grand entrance.

"Were you summoned here, too?" I asked.

"Yep," he responded.

Together we walked up the steps and entered the mansion's lobby. Walter's precious antique grandfather clock flanked the door to the central living rooms on one side of the lobby. The clock's one-of-a-kind key rested in its one-of-a-kind keyhole, and its pendulum swung back and forth as it ticked off the minutes. Nicols, Cooperstown's police chief, stood next to the clock.

"What are you doing here?" I asked.

"Walter wants me here; he thinks you'll be upset at the conclusion of the meeting," Nicols replied coldly.

The shit was clearly about to hit the fan, but at my expense, not at Walter's as Winsor and Hughes had led me to believe the day before when they ordered me to conduct an investigation. I'd apparently been set up and my fate was now pretty clear.

I looked right into Nicols' eyes and said, "You whore; how much did he pay you for this?"

He didn't answer.

Nicols directed Bruce and me into the kitchen, a spotless, stark, and substantial workplace for nameless kitchen staff hired by Walter to cater to Cooperstown's elite and New York state politicians. Just off the kitchen was the boardroom.

Through the swinging doors from the kitchen to the boardroom, I could hear muffled sounds of a meeting in progress. While Bruce and I waited, Nicols remained in the kitchen, ashen-faced and certainly cognizant of my growing anger.

I looked at Nicols and walked back out into the lobby. I looked around, my eyes resting on Walter's precious antique grandfather clock. I walked over and stood in front of it.

"Walter and his material possessions," I thought. "That's all that matters to him."

I reached up, took the one-of-a-kind key out of its one-of-a-kind keyhole, dropped it into my pocket, and walked back into the kitchen.

Shortly after six o'clock, the boardroom door opened. Winsor stuck his head out and looked at me. "They're ready for you," he said and motioned at me to go in.

As I entered the boardroom, I felt all eyes on me. It looked like about half a dozen or so of Walter's hand-picked directors were seated around the long boardroom table, which was scattered with empty and half-empty cocktail glasses. I supposed that some of the out-of-state directors couldn't make the meeting on such short notice. Walter was seated at the head of the table. To his right sat Ed Gozigian. Malcolm Hughes was sitting next to Deane Winsor. Next to them was Ned Wilkenson.

"Ned Wilkenson," I thought. "The lawyer who received two vehicles from the state bid for police cars, one for him and one for his daughter. Everyone here has received substantial favors and personal benefits from Walter," my thoughts continued. "They all owe him."

I was directed to a seat at the opposite end of the table facing Walter. As I took my place, Walter, with his characteristic little smile, and everyone else except Deane Winsor silently glared at me. Deane Winsor wouldn't even look at me.

I looked around the room and saw no clerk or anyone taking minutes of the meeting.

"If this is a legitimate board meeting, I want minutes taken." I said.

"Minutes aren't necessary," Hughes huffed.

I saw David Soule and Bill Lloyd standing toward the back of the room.

"Why are Gozigian, Lloyd and Soule in the room?" I asked. "They're not board members."

"The board authorized them to be here," growled Hughes. "Now, get on with your charges."

I was beginning to get some real dirty looks. It was clear that nothing I had to say was going to make any difference.

Just then, Richard White, a member of the board of directors and the owner of the local Bruce Hall Corporation, rushed in and sat down.

"Another one," I thought to myself. It was White's company that was awarded a federally-funded contract by the railroad after the sealed bids were opened. Walter had directed that White's bid be adjusted to qualify as the winning bid so that the contract could be awarded to the Bruce Hall Corporation.

"This is an unfair forum," I protested. "Walter has substantially benefited everyone here, and everyone here will back Walter no matter what is presented."

"I will support Walter Rich no matter what," announced Wilkenson.

"Exactly the problem," I thought to myself.

There was no question that earlier in the day, Walter had personally contacted each and every one of his hand-picked directors and reminded them of the benefits they had received, and could continue to receive, from him.

I took a deep breath and began my presentation. When I told them about the bid rigging schemes and the written statements I had to support my information, Richard White glared at me, but never denied that his company was involved in the matter. The other members of the board sat there stone faced, asking no questions and making no comments.

I talked about the Poolville accident and Walter's directive to me to falsify the investigation. Again, no questions and no comments.

I told them about my experiences with Charette, about his drug conviction, and about his drug sales alleged in written statements from railroad employees. I talked in detail about the cases developed by the railroad police department against Charette involving theft, drunk driving, and rule violations. I discussed the protection Charette consistently received from Walter and their living arrangements following the drug case. Once again, no questions and no comments.

I talked about the phony time cards Walter ordered employees to keep. No questions and no comments.

Finally, I read Bonfardice's statement about Walter's homosexual advances.

"Did Bonfardice sign that statement?" Walter asked, his tone arrogant and indignant.

"No," I responded.

Walter smiled. "You fabricated it."

"Nice try, you bastard," I thought, knowing that Nancy's original shorthand notes from the statement Bonfardice privately dictated to her were safely in my files.

For two hours I sat there presenting them with detailed information about corrupt railroad activities condoned, if not mandated, by Walter. During that entire time, not one director asked for any proof, not one director asked any questions, and not one director made any comments. They simply deferred to Walter, who asked only one question – whether Bonfardice's statement was signed. When I finished, I was ordered out of the room and told to wait in the kitchen.

Buffet was called in next and made a similar two-hour presentation. No questions, no comments. Bruce was then ordered out of the room to wait in the kitchen.

Minutes turned into hours. Food was taken in to the boardroom. Buffet and I were offered nothing.

Finally, shortly after midnight, Winsor opened the boardroom doors and walked in to the kitchen where Buffet and I were waiting.

"I know I told you that you wouldn't get fired, but this is a board decision; you've both been terminated effective immediately."

"On what grounds?" I asked.

"Incompatibility with management," he answered then turned and walked back into the boardroom.

Then Soule came out of the boardroom and handed each of us a letter signed by Walter. The letters stated that we were fired, our commissions were revoked, we were to turn in all police equipment, and we were forbidden to enter upon railroad property.

Just like that, it was over.

I passed by Nicols as I was leaving. He started to say something to me.

"Save it!" I snapped without looking at him and I kept walking.

He shut up and moved out of my way.

I walked across the street to Peevers' house where Mary, John and Nancy were anxiously waiting. We all sat down and I told them what had happened. I then collected my family and we drove home.

Once the boys were in bed, Mary and I talked, trying to convince ourselves that everything would be alright. Neither of us believed it. I was unemployed. How would we survive? I had been fired, so finding another law enforcement job would be virtually impossible, not that there were any in Cooperstown anyway. How could I explain it? "I was fired, but it was all bullshit...I didn't do anything wrong." Oh, sure, and everyone would believe that!

On Sunday morning, I drove to the offices on Railroad Avenue and turned in my keys and all of my equipment. Soule was there to escort me to my office so that I could remove my personal items. I was glad I had removed what I needed to on Friday before going to Edgewater.

I left the railroad office and drove to Otsego Lake. At the Lakefront Motel, I parked my car and walked out on the dock. It was a cold January day. Most years Otsego Lake is frozen by the end of January. But on Sunday, January 22, 1984, the cold water of the Glimmerglass reflected the gray cloudy sky overhead as it washed up gently on the sandy shore. I walked out to the end of the dock and stood there in the cold air for a few minutes, my hands in my pockets. Then, in total defiance, I took the one-of-a-kind key that wound Walter's precious antique grandfather clock out of my pocket and flung it as far as I could out into the lake. I felt a deep satisfaction as I watched the key hit the water and disappear into the lake's depths, leaving only a spreading circle of ripples on the surface of the Glimmerglass. When the ripples subsided, I took a deep breath and then turned and walked back to my car and drove home.

In the following days, I read in the newspaper that Nicols was offered and accepted the railroad police chief position. I also learned that he was temporarily staying at Edgewater to protect Walter. The word was that Walter was afraid of me!

Nicols immediately hired George Crippen as a railroad policeman.

"Good God, I thought…Crippen is just the type Walter needs! He'd agree to do anything in order to keep a job like that."

I was puzzled about why Nicols and Crippen had sold me out. In the past, we had all been friends. Or, so I thought. They could have stayed out of the whole affair and still been hired by the railroad. I presumed Walter manipulated them like he did everyone else. It was all about power, money and influence.

I still had some friends in the company that sympathized with me, and they kept me posted on what was happening. However, for the most part, railroad employees were afraid of losing their own jobs and kept silent.

Bonfardice told everyone that I fabricated the statement concerning his little incident with Walter at Edgewater. Walter promoted him to assistant comptroller – a new position – and gave him a hefty raise.

Maltese was fired. He had taken a vacation, and when he returned, his office had been cleaned out and someone else occupied it. No warning; no explanation. They bought his silence with some severance pay. I heard that he moved to San Francisco. I felt bad about Maltese because he had put his faith in me that this wouldn't happen. Unfortunately, my faith had been based on Winsor's and Hughes' false promises.

Charette was transferred back to New Jersey.

The railroad's routine continued, and everyone understood that Walter was in charge.

Buffet and I received a letter from each state police superintendent revoking our police commissions. I wrote a letter to each state explaining the circumstances and requesting an official investigation. They weren't interested, stating it was a "civil matter."

I never received my final paycheck from the railroad.

A couple of days after I was fired, Nicols came to see me at home.

"I have some questions I need to ask you," he stated with authority. "But first, I need to advise you of your rights."

"Just what in the hell do you want?" I asked him.

He said he needed to question me about a theft that had occurred several weeks ago in the New Jersey yard. I was stunned! He was actually attempting to make me a suspect.

"Just a few days on the job and Nicols is allowing himself to be a part of Walter's intimidation tactics," I thought to myself.

I looked Nicols square in the eye and said, "If you have a charge to bring against me, then present it; if not, get the hell out of my face or I'll slam your teeth down your throat!"

Without another word, Nicols left and I never heard from him again.

With absolutely no income, Mary and I struggled to figure out how we were going to survive. Mary took a part-time job as a private duty nurse and I started taking on odd jobs anywhere I could find them. I pulled together some equipment and started a firewood business. Some friends let us cut wood from land they owned, and although it wasn't much, every bit of income helped. I borrowed money from family and friends.

Frustration and anger pulsated through me. I had worked hard and done my job well. I had done nothing wrong. I insisted on telling the truth because it was the right thing to do.

"How could this happen? How on earth am I going to clear my name and get my life back?" Those thoughts permeated my consciousness.

I shared the facts about my experience with bureaucratic officials, but no one was the slightest bit interested in the fact that a police officer had been fired because he would not lie and falsify an accident report. Everyone offered essentially the same response: "It's a civil matter."

The legal system being my only apparent recourse, Mary and I borrowed the money to retain an attorney without knowing how we would pay it back. We were determined to right this wrong.

Chapter Ten

"This is the Court of Chancery; which has its decaying houses and its blighted lands in every shire; which has its worn-out lunatic in every madhouse, and its dead in every churchyard; which has its ruined suitor, with his slipshod heels and threadbare dress, borrowing and begging through the round of every man's acquaintance; which gives to monied might the means abundantly of wearying out the right; which so exhausts finances, patience, courage, hope; so overthrows the brain and breaks the heart; that there is not an honourable man among its practitioners who would not give – who does not often give – the warning, 'Suffer any wrong that can be done you, rather than come here!'"

— Charles Dickens (1812-70),
Bleak House (1852-53)

"FIRED RAIL CHIEF FILES $3M SUIT." The headline appeared in the Oneonta Daily Star on February 22, 1984, the day after my attorney, James Featherstonehaugh, filed a lawsuit on my behalf in Federal District Court against the railroad, Walter Rich, and Dean Winsor. The story was less than complimentary toward Walter.

The lawsuit was the beginning of what would become over twelve years entangled in the American civil legal system – a system I naively believed would vindicate the truth and, ultimately, serve justice. Instead, it worked to avoid the truth and evade justice through a web of legal maneuverings by the railroad and its high profile attorneys intended to bleed dry my very limited financial resources and effect my surrender.

The railroad's appointed spokesperson, David Soule, responded to the news story on behalf of the three defendants. "The railroad considers the allegations unfounded and without merit."

"No shit," I thought. "What else was he going to say?"

Just before the lawsuit was served on the railroad, Soule called me with an offer of "severance pay" in the amount of one year's salary and "relocation assistance." The offer, of course, was contingent upon my signing a waiver and release of all claims against the railroad. Soule said the railroad would also sign a waiver and release. I had never expressed an interest in "relocating" and Mary and I had no intention of moving away. However, I was curious about the railroad's offer to sign a release of claims against me. I asked Soule to explain.

"Well," he began arrogantly, "what if we find improprieties in your expense account, or equipment funds, or something like that?"

"Go to hell," I said, thinking, "Nice try!"

A couple of days later, I called Patrick Joyce, the attorney in Sherburne who was representing the victims of the Poolville accident. The lawsuit Joyce filed against the railroad was also making headlines. I told Joyce I was no longer employed by the railroad and discussed with him what I believed from my investigation caused the accident. Following our conversation, Joyce's case against the railroad advanced quickly. Joyce subpoenaed Walter's deposition. Afterward, Joyce provided me with a copy of the transcript and I brought to Joyce's attention the numerous inconsistencies and outright lies in the testimony Walter gave under oath. One of those outright lies was Walter's answer to Joyce's question about whether Walter knew Charette socially. Walter responded that he did not know Charette socially.

"My God," I said to Joyce. "Before the accident, Walter and Charette lived together in Walter's private railcar, Walter took Charette to see the Boston Pops perform and Mary and I were forced to have dinner with Walter and Charette at the Horned Dorset Inn. If that's not 'knowing him socially,' I don't know what is!"

The following week, on the day that I was scheduled to be deposed, the railroad settled the lawsuit with the families of the Poolville accident victims for $290,000, a very substantial pre-trial settlement in those days.

Then, I got a call from a representative of the ABC television network, which aired the new weekly investigative show, 20/20. They had heard about my case and wanted to feature my story along with two others in a segment they were doing on whistleblowers in the workplace.

I didn't consider refusing to lie to cover up an accident as "whistleblowing," but I guess in essence that was what it was. So, after speaking with the representative of 20/20, I agreed to be on the show, thinking, "Why not?" I wasn't paid for my appearance on the show, but I believed exposing all of this on national television certainly couldn't hurt.

By then, the railroad, through its high-profile attorneys, began aggressively defending my lawsuit against the railroad, filing motions and pleadings asking the federal court to dismiss the case.

Mary and I had borrowed $5,000 to retain Featherstonehaugh based on his assessment that our case had real merit and his assurances that everything would go well. We believed him. Now my attorney's fees were mounting and my personal economic situation was critically declining. Mary and I put our house up for sale.

While I was waiting to be filmed for the 20/20 segment, I contacted the local United States Navy recruiter. I had heard that Navy veterans with subsequent civilian experience, including law enforcement experience, were being recruited back into active duty through a master-at-arms program called the NAV-VET.

Although I otherwise qualified, I wasn't sure I'd be eligible because of my disability discharge from the Navy about sixteen years ago. But I was desperate for an income and health benefits for my family, so I applied.

At age 40, I was the oldest NAV-VET candidate the recruiter had encountered. He scheduled me for a physical examination in Albany, which I passed. Aside from some scars, there were no obvious signs of the dreadful injuries I received in Vietnam; and I could walk, run, and pretty much function like anyone else. The examiner certified me physically fit for active duty.

I completed the forms outlining my employment history and documenting my experience as a police officer, four years of which was with the railroad. I wondered how Walter would respond to the request for verification of my employment from the United States Navy, so I told the recruiter the whole story about the railroad. I had nothing to hide. The recruiter responded nonchalantly and sent out the employment verification forms. I returned home hoping I'd know soon about my reenlistment.

I checked the mail every day for news from the Navy. Instead, I received devastating news about my lawsuit against the railroad. Without hearing any evidence on the merits of my case, the Federal District Court dismissed the lawsuit on jurisdictional grounds, a technicality I didn't understand based upon Featherstonehaugh's optimism when he took the case.

"What had gone wrong?" I wondered. "There's no question I can prove everything to a jury; I just need the opportunity." I called Featherstonehaugh.

"There's nothing more we can do in Federal Court," he said.

"What about state court?" I asked.

"There is no state law provision under which we can file," Featherstonehaugh responded. "As far as I'm concerned, it's over." His voice sounded terse.

Legally, I was apparently screwed. It was as simple as that.

"What about the five thousand dollar retainer I paid you?" I asked, hoping some portion of it would be refunded to me based on the lawsuit's short life. My financial circumstances were dismal.

"The retainer is nonrefundable; it's been exhausted," he responded unsympathetically.

Interestingly, just eight months later, the state of New York enacted whistleblower statutes which, had they existed earlier, would have provided me civil relief in state court. The statute was not retroactive.

In all of my years as a policeman, I had always tried to make the system work for others. Now, when I needed it to work for me, it was a miserable failure.

"How can it be fair that we could not at least have our day in court over something that is so patently unfair?" I wondered, feeling deeply depressed and desperate about how I was going to support my family and provide for our future.

The local newspaper reported the news that my lawsuit had been dismissed. Walter and his cronies took every opportunity to bloviate about the dismissal, opining that the case was "obviously unfounded" because the court "threw it out." The belief that once again his power and money had successfully defeated another decent human being appeared to elevate Walter's unjustified sense of self-importance to an even higher level.

I had to let it go and focus on survival. Mary and I were behind on our mortgage payments, and we were having no luck selling the house. Being without health insurance, our family medical bills were mounting, and our creditors were beginning to threaten legal action against us. I called the Navy recruiter to check the status of my application and was told that the railroad had not yet verified my prior employment. Knowing that the railroad's failure to verify my employment would thwart my chance of being accepted for re-enlistment, I called Soule.

"Has the railroad received a request from the United States Navy to verify my prior employment?" I asked, and without waiting for a response, I added, "If so, please complete the verification form and send it back."

Soule said he'd check into it and call me back later that day. When he called, he asked if he could stop by our house that evening "to talk about it."

Although I was suspicious about what he and Walter had in mind this time, I had no choice but to agree. After supper that night, Soule showed up with one of the railroad's attorneys. After exchanging some small talk, I was told that they were aware of our overdue account at Bassett Hospital, which was then approaching three thousand dollars.

"George Crippen!" I thought to myself. Crippen had worked at the hospital as a security guard for several years, and it was my guess that he was the railroad's informant of this personal information.

Soule handed me a document. I took it from him and started reading. In essence, the document stated that I released the railroad from future claims arising from my employment termination and that I had "made up" everything I had said about Walter Rich and that none of it was true.

I looked up at Soule. "No way will I sign a paper saying I made up anything about Walter...there's no point in even discussing it!"

Soule pulled $3,600 is one hundred dollar bills from his jacket and said, "If you'll sign the release, this money is yours and the railroad will send the employment verification to the Navy."

Mary and I went into another room and discussed our options. We had no choice. Financially, we were desperate, and Walter knew that. I had to feed my family and pay our medical bills. I needed the employment verification from the railroad. I signed the release and took the cash, but I ignored the document that stated I "made up" everything I said about Walter Rich.

It was coercion, pure and simple. I asked Soule for a copy of the release, noting to myself that the document made no mention of the cash I was paid in consideration for the release. In my mind, the coerced written release of claims, which, on its face, provided no consideration for the release, was unenforceable. I vowed to myself that I would spend the rest of my life seeking justice for the egregious wrongs and indignities Walter had inflicted on me.

Out of frustration, I wrote to the Federal Judge who had dismissed my case, outlining what had happened to me and asking for a suggestion on how I might have my day in court. Featherstonehaugh had had no suggestions, nor did he have much interest in me after consuming my five thousand dollars. I didn't really expect an answer from the judge, nor did I receive one. Judges don't simply communicate with individual litigants, but I wanted him to understand the impact of his decision. It seemed to me that right and wrong apparently didn't matter in our legal system.

I initiated a letter writing campaign to television stations, newspapers, magazines, politicians, and anyone else I could think of, hoping to stir up some interest in my case. By writing the letters, I believed I was doing something positive and it made me feel better.

Finally, the Navy notified me that I had been accepted. I would leave the first week of February 1985 and report to the Great Lakes Training Center in Illinois for two weeks of re-indoctrination training followed by ten weeks at the criminal investigation school in Alabama and then sea duty for some period of time, leaving Mary and the three boys alone in Cooperstown. Danny was just four years old and didn't understand why I had to go away. His agony over my leaving devastated me. Mary and the two older boys tried to be positive, but none of us were happy. The anger inside of me was like a dead weight.

A few weeks before I was to leave, a filming crew for 20/20 arrived in Cooperstown to film the segment of their program concerning my case. Our little house was filled with cameras, lights and people. They took footage of Mary and I walking down the street in Cooperstown and standing beside the for-sale sign in front of our house. They filmed us in our living room with all three boys. The final footage showed me packing my bag to leave for active duty, Danny standing beside me watching solemnly. When the 20/20 crew left, they told us the program would air in a few months. It did.

On the eve of my departure, Mary and the boys gathered around me for our last night together, none of us knowing for sure when we'd see each other again. Little Danny crawled up in my lap and cried, "Oh, dear, I don't want you to leave, daddy!" It destroyed me.

The next morning, tears streaming down all of our faces, I got in the car and, waving goodbye, left to drive to Illinois. There was nothing more to say, and for two hours I drove down the highway shuddering in great sobs and blinded by uncontrollable tears. I hated Walter Rich, and I reaffirmed my personal vow to some day expose him for the vile and loathsome bastard I knew him to be.

Two days later, I arrived at the U.S. Naval Training Center in Great Lakes, Illinois. As a sense of déjà vu washed over me, I drove through the entrance gates. Twenty-three years ago, at age seventeen, I drove through those same gates to attend Navy boot camp, and the place still looked the same. However, this time I was there as a veteran for the short, two-week indoctrination into the NAV-VET master-at-arms program.

When I located the building where I was to report on arrival, I walked inside and identified myself. As a veteran re-entering as a petty officer, I was well received and treated respectfully by the Navy personnel who assisted me. After I had been processed in, I was told to relax the rest of the day and orient myself to the facility. My first class would be at four o'clock the following morning.

"Good grief – four o'clock in the morning?" I muttered to myself. "The Navy hasn't changed one bit!"

As I drifted off to sleep that night, I thought about Mary and the boys and felt very homesick.

My experience this time at Great Lakes was very different from my experience as a seventeen-year-old recruit twenty-three years prior. This time, as the most senior re-entering petty officer, I was placed in charge of our class, I ate in a private dining room with the company commanders, and I was served by Navy recruits attending boot camp. Displayed on my uniform were eleven ribbons – three full rows topped by the Bronze Star and the Purple Heart I was awarded for my service in Vietnam. Everywhere I went, my ribbons were noticed and I felt very proud. None of my supervisors and no other person of any rank at Great Lakes was decorated with more ribbons across their chest, and I was treated by everyone, including my supervisors, with great respect. It was good for my bruised self esteem.

While I was in Great Lakes, the HBO cable television network contacted me, wanting to do a special program on my situation. I thought it was a great opportunity for my case to get more exposure, but I belonged to the United States Navy and, for whatever reason, they declined permission. I was disappointed, but I knew enough about the Navy to not argue.

Just before the end of the two-week indoctrination program, I filled out my "dream sheet" requesting shore duty anywhere or, in the alternative, sea duty aboard a battleship or a destroyer out of New York or Florida when I completed the ten-week criminal investigation school in Alabama. I absolutely did not want to be assigned to an aircraft carrier, with its crew of 6,000 men, or any other ship out of Norfolk, the largest Navy base.

However, just before receiving orders to leave Great Lakes, I learned that after I completed the school in Alabama, I would be assigned to the aircraft carrier, USS Nimitz, based in Norfolk and currently deployed in the Mediterranean for seven months. There was no hope that I could be reassigned to other duty, and I knew that my assignment to the Nimitz guaranteed that I would be away from home for several months.

I left the bitter cold of Great Lakes in my winter dress blue uniform and drove south to Alabama. When I arrived, the temperature was ninety degrees. Overwhelmed with the heat and humidity, I was very uncomfortable and very homesick. I called Mary from a pay phone just to hear her voice.

For ten weeks, I was instructed on everything related to criminal matters, from homicide investigations to brig operations. I also attended courses to become certified in the Navy corrections process. Having been a civilian police officer, I knew the material well and breezed through the classes.

I graduated in April, 1985, and was given leave for a week before I had to report to Norfolk to fly to wherever the Nimitz might be at the time. I left Alabama without delay and drove nonstop to Cooperstown, and home.

Early spring in Cooperstown is lovely. When I arrived in the village my eyes, hungry to behold the place that for most of my life I called home, feasted on its wonderful storybook-like charm. Tulips and daffodils, nature's vibrant harbingers of spring, were in full bloom under hardwood branches tinged with that fresh new green that, after the barren winter, exalts nature's resurrection. How good it felt to be home, and I was excited to be with Mary and the boys again.

They all ran out to greet me as I drove into the driveway. Mary and I held each other, afraid to let go, as our three boys surrounded us, Danny with his arms wrapped around my leg.

Our time together was short and we wanted to spend that time enjoying each other and creating memories to carry us through the long periods of time we would be apart. But, while I was home, we also had to address the issues Mary lived with daily while I was gone. The house still had not sold, but Mary and I made arrangements for her and the boys to move into a small rental house in nearby Fly Creek once it did sell, where they would stay until Navy housing in Norfolk was available. Finances were an ever-present problem for which there was never enough money to fix. Mary shouldered the enormous burden of parenting three boys every day. It wasn't easy, and there were no simple answers. Without my Navy salary, things would have been even worse. But the truth was that our married life, our family life and our financial security were all in turmoil and while I was at sea, mail would be the only means of communication between us.

The night before I left, the boys and I said our goodbyes and I asked them not to get up the next morning when I had to leave. I simply could not bear to see their tears again. The next morning, Mary and I held each other until it was time for me to leave. There was nothing more I could say or do.

I arrived in Norfolk late that afternoon and reported directly to the Military Flight Command at the air station. About an hour later, I was on a flight to Italy in an old passenger jet marked "Arrow Airways" on its tail. The plane was filled to capacity. I sat down in an aisle seat so I would be able to get up and move around easier. After takeoff, I pushed the button on the seat to recline. Just my luck, the seat was broken and no other seats were available. For the nine-hour flight, I had to sit in an upright position with the seat in front of me reclined practically in my lap. By the time the pilot announced we were approaching Italy, I was tired and stiff. The passenger sitting by a window lifted the shade, and bright sunlight washed over me. I looked at my watch, which was still set for Eastern Standard Time in the United States. My watch indicated it was two o'clock in the morning; but in Italy, it was high noon. I felt sick.

I walked off the plane and into the terminal and told the officer on duty at the transit desk that I needed transportation to the USS Nimitz.

"The Nimitz is at sea; you'll have to stay here a few days until we can arrange transportation."

"Where do military transfer personnel stay?" I asked.

"The barracks are full; I'll have a driver take to you a hotel," he responded.

A short time later, the driver dropped me off at a dismal hotel not far from the barracks. No one at the hotel spoke English. I was hot and irritable. In the room, the water barely worked and there were no screens in the windows. After one night at the hotel, I returned to the transportation office.

"Please find some other means to get me to the Nimitz," I begged.

Taking pity on me, the transportation officer was able to arrange quarters for me on board an old ammunition ship leaving that evening for the area where the Nimitz was located. I was on board the ammunition ship for five days until it arrived where the Nimitz was operating. A helicopter plucked me off the old ammunition ship and deposited me aboard the Nimitz. I was assigned petty officer in charge of the ship's brig.

The USS Nimitz was like a floating city. Six thousand men, including the air crew, were on board, but I was lonely and very homesick.

In the mess decks there was a map showing the ship's current location. It was marked "Benoville."

"What's 'Benoville'?" I asked a sailor standing nearby.

"'Benoville' is where we are," he said with a grin on his face. "Where we are, there will be no liberty, there will be no women, and there will be no fun!" "Therefore, we're in 'Benoville.'"

"Seems like an appropriate name," I agreed with a chuckle. (I later sent that little bit of military humor to *Reader's Digest*, and they published it.)

I received news by telegram from Mary that our house had sold. It was bittersweet news. Financially, we had to sell the house, but I felt like our life was being dismantled. Mary and the boys moved into the house we rented in Fly Creek.

A few weeks later, I was directed to report to sick-bay for a routine medical evaluation.

"Any complaints?" the doctor asked as he proceeded with his examination.

"I've been having pain and cramps in my right leg," I explained.

"Hmmm," the doctor murmured. "We'll take some x-rays.

The x-rays revealed that twelve pieces of shrapnel were still lodged in my right leg from the injuries I received in Vietnam. I was surprised. I had always thought that all of the shrapnel had been removed years ago when I was hospitalized after my injuries.

"I'm going to prescribe some mediation; report back to sick-bay if the pain in your leg continues."

I took the medication and continued my routine. But, for the most part, the medication just made me sick and the pain and cramping in my right leg intensified. Life on the Nimitz required me to be on my feet constantly, walking around the ship and climbing up and down the ladders. When the pain become more than I could bear, I reported back to sick-bay.

"I'm sending you back to Portsmouth Naval Hospital for an evaluation," the doctor concluded after his follow-up examination.

I didn't protest.

I sent Mary a telegram telling her to meet me in Norfolk and then, for the next two days, I readied myself to leave the Nimitz. The day of my departure, I expected to board a helicopter, but I was in for quite a surprise. Instead, I boarded a "COD," which is the largest plane that can fly from an aircraft carrier. It's the aircraft that was used for transporting the ship's mail, but it also could carry four passengers. I was strapped in a seat facing the rear of the aircraft. Looking out a small port hole, I saw the flight deck officer salute the pilot, the final act before the plane is launched.

Suddenly, I was slammed into the straps holding me in my seat and I heard a loud bang as the aircraft went from zero to 160 knots in two and a half seconds, struggling to gain altitude.

The aircraft made stops in Greece, Italy and Spain before returning to the Norfolk Air Station. When we landed in Norfolk, I disembarked the plane and took a cab to the motel just outside the base gates. Mary, Donnie, and Danny were waiting for me. Davy wasn't able to come because of his after-school job.

After a brief but excited greeting at the motel, I went to the base hospital and checked in. I was then told I could leave and return the following morning when the doctor would be available to see me. I spent the night at the motel with Mary and the two boys. Mary and I held each other close as I drifted off to some much needed sleep.

The following day, I met with the doctor who would handle my case. After evaluating my condition, he said that there was little they could do other than operate on my leg in an attempt to remove the shrapnel. But there was a risk that such an operation could do more damage to my leg.

"I'm putting you on two weeks convalescent leave," the doctor said, "after which I want you to return for a final evaluation."

I was elated. In less than an hour, Mary, Donnie, Danny and I were headed home.

The house we were renting in Fly Creek was at the end of a dirt road, surrounded by dense woods. As we pulled up, Davy ran out of the house.

"Dad!" he shouted, surprised to see me getting out of the car.

"Finally," I thought as everyone was talking excitedly, "we're all together again."

"We call ourselves 'The Wilderness Family' out here," Mary informed me. The boys all laughed and nodded their heads in agreement. "It's been an adventure!"

I was home, but uncertainty continued to permeate our lives. I still had my Navy income and benefits, but I had no idea what was ahead. For two weeks, I relaxed and helped Mary transform the rental house into our home. Then it was time to return to Norfolk.

I reported to the Naval Hospital and was immediately scheduled for a medical evaluation, after which the doctor sat down with me to discuss the options.

"You have two options," the doctor began. "The first is surgery on your leg; however, there's great risk of further damaging your leg by attempting to remove the shrapnel."

"What's the second option?" I asked.

"Discharge from the service."

It wasn't a difficult decision. I signed the discharge papers and was sent home – this time for good.

When my military discharge was final, my military salary would be replaced, once again, with a lesser disability pay. In the meantime, I had time to think about our future and how I would support my family. I continued my letter writing campaign about my experiences with the railroad, but in return received nothing more than form "thank you for writing" letters.

When I received my permanent discharge papers from the Navy, I also received my final paychecks and a small severance, and I was approved for the same disability pension I had previously received. Essentially, I was back to square one and had no time to waste finding employment.

Mary and I talked about our options. Finding a well paying job in Cooperstown was next to impossible, and we weren't willing to move away.

"I've decided to start my own business," I told her, "as a building contractor." I was a good builder and good builders were hard to find in Cooperstown. I knew if I worked hard, I could get the business up and going quickly.

I traded in a car that we owned and used some cash to buy a van and some tools to supplement those I already had. I had the words "THE WOODSMEN BUILDERS" painted on the sides of the van, along with "General Contractor" and my telephone number. It was important to me to present a professional image.

"Now, I just need to find a customer or two," I thought as I started marketing myself around town.

I called Bruce Buffett. Since we left the railroad, he had been doing small jobs around town. I told him about The Woodsmen Builders and asked him if he was interested in working for me.

"Yes," he said, adding, "as long as you have some work lined up."

Later that week, we started a remodel of an old farmhouse. As we worked, the owners kept adding to the remodel and it looked like the job would carry us through the winter. Indoor work was hard to find, and I felt fortunate to have this job.

After we finished, the owner gave us a nice reference and we were able to line up even more work for spring. I hired another man.

The more people noticed us, the more work we got.

I was on my own with a new career. I liked working for myself, and I was encouraged by the number of jobs that I was able to schedule.

In the midst of a job to build a garage, I was contracted to build another one and hired another man. While working on the second garage, I was hired to completely remodel a large house in Cooperstown.

Woodsmen Builders took off quickly, but I admonished everyone I hired that they would be employed only so long as we were busy. Then, each time I hired another man, it seemed that we'd get busier. My oldest son, David, quit his job as a mechanic's helper for a local motorcycle dealer and began working for me, scheduling his hours around his high school schedule. I instructed all of my employees that I expected the highest quality work.

"Do it right, or do it over," I would tell them.

We were a team, and we all took pride in our work. To bolster our professional image, I purchased T-shirts and baseball style hats embossed with "Woodsmen Builders." At each project was a Woodsmen Builders team attired in gray shirts with blue lettering and blue caps with gray lettering. In a short period of time, we earned the reputation as one of the area's quality builders.

When the lease on the house Mary and I were renting was within a few months of expiring, Mary and I decided to build our own home. My mother and stepfather helped us buy a small parcel of land and we acquired a construction loan from a local bank. In March, 1986, as soon as the frost was out of the ground, we began construction.

While building our home and working to get The Woodsmen Builders up and going, I continued my letter writing campaign and checked the mail every day, hoping someone would respond. Then, that spring, I pulled out of the mailbox a letter from the Office of the President of the United States.

Chapter Eleven

Every violation of truth is not only a sort of suicide in the liar,
but is a stab at the health of human society.

— Ralph Waldo Emerson (1803-82),
Essays I, Prudence (1841)

The letter was signed by a presidential aide and suggested that I present my case to the National Railroad Mediation Board. A booklet was enclosed outlining the lengthy and confusing process to petition the board to hear a grievance involving a railroad. I couldn't afford to hire another attorney, so I undertook the process of preparing and filing the petition myself.

"It's worth a try," I thought, "and will send a message to Walter that I'm not going to go away."

I worked on the petition every spare minute I had. Our kitchen table was strewn with papers and books, and I sat there night after night researching the process and preparing the complicated petition. I was determined to do it right and not make a fool of myself. I labored at my old manual typewriter, typing and retyping the thirty-six page petition until each page was error free. Mary and I then visited the local copy shop where we made seven copies of the lengthy petition and placed them in a large envelope addressed to the National Railroad Mediation Board in Chicago. We then delivered the envelope to the post office to be mailed by certified mail. I prepared the requisite notice to the Delaware Otsego Corporation that I was filing a petition with the board and mailed it to the attention of Walter Rich, advising him that the railroad was required to respond. If nothing else, I figured it would drive Walter nuts!

A week later, I received a notice that my petition had been received in proper form and was accepted. I was ecstatic! After the railroad responded to my petition, the matter was set for a September hearing before the National Railroad Mediation Board in Chicago.

That September, the day before the hearing, I left for Chicago, my briefcase in hand. It was filled with all of the documents that supported my case, a copy of my petition, and the presentation I had drafted to present to the board. I checked into a hotel that night and, in preparation for the following day, studied my presentation.

I got word that the railroad's new in-house attorney, Lester Sittler, was also in town for the same reason.

The next morning, I appeared at the designated place and was seated in a chair at a conference table in front of the seven members of the Mediation Board. Sittler was seated to my left. A stenographer sat off to the side of the board members to record the hearing.

As plaintiff, I presented my case first. I laid out the entire case, outlined everything I knew, and concluded with the information about the train accident. I had stacks of documents to support everything I said.

Sittler appeared stunned. He presented little defense and had nothing to discount or discredit my testimony. I almost felt sorry him; obviously, Walter had provided Sittler limited information and, because he had been employed by the railroad for a relatively short period of time, he didn't have the benefit of knowing the whole story.

"I'm new to the company and know only what I've been told about the case," he sheepishly explained.

It was obvious to me that what little he had been told about the case came from Walter Rich. It was even more obvious to me that neither Sittler nor Walter had any idea of the amount of documentation I had. That was valuable information then, and would be even more valuable over the coming years.

When the hearing concluded, I felt good that I had overwhelmingly proven my case. However, I learned at the hearing that to have standing to bring a complaint before the board, an employee was required to be a union member. I was not, but until the hearing, I didn't know about the union requirement.

Sittler left immediately following the hearing to catch a plane. I stayed around for a while to ask questions. One of the board members walked over to me.

"That is the worst case of employee abuse that has ever been heard by this board," he said, suggesting a lawyer he knew in California that might be willing to represent me in the future. Then he told me about the jurisdictional problem.

"Without jurisdiction, the board cannot award you damages; but, if they could, it would have been a new record."

He complimented me on a well-presented and well-documented case and wished me well, telling me that I would receive the official determination of the board in a few weeks.

I went home to wait for the board's determination. When it arrived, I was disappointed, but not surprised.

"The board is without jurisdiction to consider the complaint."

Just like the lawsuit, the case was dismissed, not on its merits, but on a jurisdictional technicality. I had done my best and I was satisfied that I had given Walter and the railroad a run for their money.

Interestingly, during the hearing in Chicago, I caught the railroad in another lie. During his presentation, Sittler produced what he claimed were "minutes" of the Board of Directors meeting at which my employment was terminated.

"That's interesting," I thought. At the time of the meeting, I had twice requested that minutes be taken, and both times my request was denied by Walter and the Board of Directors.

Soule, as acting secretary, had signed the purported "minutes," which consisted of a pithy one-and-a-half pages.

"That, too, is interesting," I thought, since the meeting the "minutes" purported to memorialize had lasted almost seven hours.

The "minutes" Sittler produced stated that the meeting had been called by Mr. Walter Rich because of an "unauthorized internal investigation by David K. Butler, superintendent of railroad police." They went on to state that the Board of Directors "concluded that Mr. Butler's allegations were without foundation." With no specific details, the "minutes" summarily ended, "After a full and lengthy discussion, it was the collective opinion of all members of the board present that Mr. Butler's services should be terminated for reasons of his self-state incompatibility...Mr. Deane Winsor informed Mr. Butler of his termination."

"'*Unauthorized*' investigation?" I wanted to shout in disbelief after reading the document. Winsor and Hughes *ordered* me to conduct the investigation.

"If ever there was a fabricated string of blatant lies, these 'minutes' are it," I thought.

When I returned to Cooperstown, I called a secretary at the railroad that I knew and asked her what she knew about the purported "minutes."

"Soule came to me about six months after you were fired," she began. "He had the 'minutes' written out on a yellow legal pad and instructed me to type it."

I taped my telephone conversation with her.

"This is outrageous," I grunted after hanging up the phone and then, once again, vowed that somehow, someday I would get someone to hear the merits of my case.

June, 1967 - Dave on patrol in Vietnam

July 11, 1967 - U.S. Navy "Monitor" Riverboat. This is Dave's boat.
Photo taken two hours before he was ambushed and wounded.

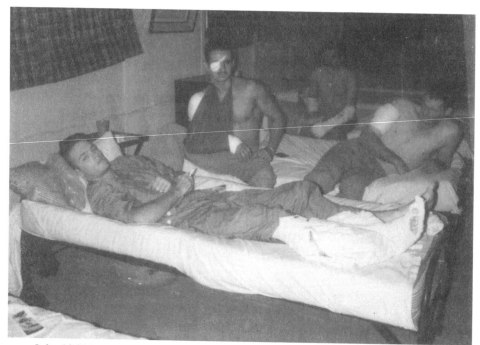

July, 1967 Long Binh, Vietnam - Dave (on bed) after being wounded in Vietnam

Summer, 1971 - Dave as Portsmouth, VA, Policeman

Summer, 1976 - Dave as Cooperstown, NY Policeman. Oldest sons, Dave, Jr. and Don

Summer, 1982 - Dave's oldest sons Dave Jr. and Don with Railroad Police Car

Spring, 1988 - Dave's oldest sons with
THE WOODSMEN BUILDERS dump truck

Deane Winsor,
Railroad Board member
who ordered Dave to
investigate accident
allegations and then
voted to fire him.
Photo by: Oneonta Daily Star

NYS&W Corporate Headquarters in Cooperstown.

Walter Rich's Edgewater Mansion in Cooperstown

Walter Rich in his luxurious home that includes a large double staircase.
Photo by: Oneonta Daily Star

April 2005, - "6 DKB's..." Dave, his three sons and two grandsons

June, 2005 - Dave and Mary Butler

October, 2005 - Dave works on the book in his "War Room"

NAME (Type or Print)   Butler   David   K.   85 Chestnut St. Cooperstown, N.Y.
                        Butler   FIRST   MIDDLE INITIAL   (RESIDENCE-NUMBER-STREET-CITY)

STATE OF NEW YORK
COUNTY OF Otsego   } ss.:   I do here by pledge and declare that I will support the constitution of the
United States and the constitution of the State of New York, and that I will faithfully discharge the duties of the
position of

(Title of position)   Railroad Policeman   (Salary Grade)

(Department or other Agency where employed)   Delaware Otsego Corporation

according to the best of my ability.

                                        (SIGNATURE OF APPOINTEE)
                                        Sept. 6, 1979
                                        (DATE)

I hereby acknowledge receipt of a copy of Public Officers Law Sections 73 through 78, have read the same, and
agree to conform to the provisions thereof.

G 110-665 (8/71)   Sept. 6, 1979
                SIGNATURE OF APPOINTEE   DATE

Copy of Dave's Railroad Police Oath Including Public Officers Law
(Required of all railroad policemen)

At Left:
Earl Johnson,
Poolville railroad crash survivor,
Sherburne, NY

The Daily Star

Vol. 93, No. 209   Copyright 1984 The Daily Star   Oneonta, N.Y., 13820, Wednesday, Feb. 22, 198   2 sections   20 pages   Suggested Price 25¢

Fired rail chief files $3M lawsuit

Freeholders Seek Rail Investigation

By MARGARET D. McGARRITY

Town seeks money from rail president's mansion

The Daily Star

©Copyright 1992, The Daily Star   Oneonta, N.Y. 13820, Saturday, Feb. 1, 1992   3 Sections   36 Pages   Suggested Price 5¢

Good deed haunts man for 18 months

By TIM GRACE
Cooperstown News Bureau

CHARLES CRIST

Ex-cop fights mudslinging
Long-time Otsego councilman battles smear campaign

Court denies ex-policeman DO line suit

Ex-councilman fights mudslinging

Pataki to attend Cooperstown fund-raiser

Rich named to state transportation board

DO official says suit unfounded

Company settles defamation feud with contractor

*Collected clippings from various New York State
newspapers show the history of Dave's lawsuit*

1983 - Tom and his mother center, family in background
- See Supplement -

Scott Lewis
- See Supplement -

Chapter Twelve

An honest politician is one who, when he is bought, will stay bought.

— Simon Cameron
US financier & politician (1799 - 1889)

By late fall, 1986, the construction of our house was essentially complete, and, although the counter tops and floors were plywood and the walls bare sheetrock, we moved in. It was home, and it was ours; and, we could finish the rooms one at a time, working whenever we had available time.

My construction business was doing very well, and I hired a couple more men. After finding a bank to finance a spec house, we began what would be the second house constructed from the ground up by The Woodsmen Builders. Timing was perfect. Finding winter construction work in upstate New York is a challenge, and the spec house allowed me to keep my crew busy all winter.

My letter writing campaign regarding the railroad issue was beginning to produce a trickle of mail, including a response from Sherwood Boehlert, a U.S. Congressman from the district in which I resided. Boehlert's letter assured me that he took his job "seriously" and made every effort to provide to his constituents "the most personal service possible." "In that regard," his letter continued, "I make no compromise."

"How noble," I thought.

Boehlert acknowledged that he knew that my lawsuit has been unsuccessful in Federal Court and suggested that I pursue the case in "a court that has jurisdiction."

"Cute," I said to myself. "He knows very well there is no such court."

Then his letter suggested, "If you have documented evidence that criminal acts have taken place, contact the Securities and Exchange Commission of the U.S. Attorney's Office."

When I had first written to Boehlert, I had accumulated enough information to justify an investigation, and I asked that he arrange for one. Now, it appeared, he expected me to have all of the documentation needed to prosecute, knowing that I had been cut off from such information when I was fired.

I penned a letter back to Boehlert.

"I am writing this letter to take you up on your offer to connect me with the U.S. Attorney," I wrote, continuing that I had also received one of his constituent mailings offering to veterans the assistance of this office. "I am a veteran," I advised. My letter concluded, "All I want is some type of fair, impartial hearing," and then I added, "I intend to pursue this matter in any way possible."

A few weeks later, I received a letter back from Boehlert. "Your service to your country and your career as a police officer are noteworthy," he stated, adding, "All citizens, no matter what their background, receive the same consideration under the eyes of the law." Once again, he suggested that I should take my case to the U.S. Attorney, "if you feel it is appropriate." Boehlert concluded his letter declining to involve himself or his office in a "judicial matter," and opining that my situation was a matter for the courts to decide. Boehlert further advised me that he could not present my case to the Justice Department for me.

I was infuriated by what I interpreted as Boehlert's condescending, self-serving, and politically motivated rhetoric. I knew he and Walter were good friends, and it seemed to me that his letter was designed to try to appease a constituent while not offending his friend, Walter Rich, and interfering with the hefty campaign contributions he was accustomed to receiving from him.

Just a week later, I had the good fortune to see Congressman Boehlert in person on Cooperstown's Main Street. He was apparently in town to perform some official function. As had been the case on many occasions in the past, he was staying at Edgewater as Walter's guest. Determined to stay on him regardless of his relationship with Walter, I stopped him on the street.

"You're Congressman Boehlert, aren't you?" I asked him.

All smiles, and likely sensing a political moment with a constituent, Boehlert replied, "Yes."

I held out my hand and introduced myself. "I'm David Butler."

Boehlert stood there for a moment looking puzzled. Then, from the look on his face, I knew he recognized my name and was aghast that I was standing there before him.

"What can I do for you?" he finally asked.

I explained to Boehlert that I had spelled out exactly what he could do for me in my recent letters to him, and then said, "I'd like to meet with you in your office in Utica next week."

Stuttering, Boehlert said he'd arrange a meeting with me the following Tuesday. "I'll have someone from my office call you with a time."

"Thank you; I'll see you Tuesday," I said and walked away.

A couple of days later, before our Tuesday meeting, I received a letter from Boehlert. "I believe I am familiar with your case and do not feel that meeting with you so as to determine the validity of your situation would be any value to you," he wrote.

I wrote back immediately, referring to his recent letters. "First," I began, "I'm surprised that you have changed your mind about meeting with me, especially after promising me you would do so. Secondly," I continued, "in your letter you stated that my case 'was a matter for the courts'. WHAT courts?" I asked emphatically. I then mentioned his comments about my "noteworthy" background and told him I agreed with his opinion that, as a veteran, I deserved no more consideration than any citizen. "All I want is AS MUCH consideration as any other citizen," I told him, reminding him that, as yet, I had received no consideration. Then I called him on what I believed to be his motivation.

"It's obvious to me that, because of your friendship and relationship with Walter Rich, you simply do not want to see any proof of wrong-doing involving the railroad or Walter," I wrote, suggesting things might be different if I were able to match the financial contributions to his campaign provided by Walter and the railroad. "I assure you that the true story will one day be made known."

I never heard from Boehlert again. But, as is obvious by the content of media stories over the years, he remains cozy with Walter and the railroad, who continue to lavishly entertain Boehlert and host his campaign fund-raisers at Edgewater. In a media story about federal funding received by Delaware Otsego, Boehlert was quoted. "I have been working hard to see that these dollars go to the D.O.," he boasted.

To me, the relationship between Boehlert and Walter smacked of political cronyism.

As part of my letter-writing campaign, I also wrote to the federal railroad administrator, John Riley, asking for an investigation of the Poolville accident. In his response, Riley said that his office had "reviewed" the accident.

"Apparently without any input from me or the state police," I thought.

Riley's letter continued, "The review has not shown evidence of a violation of federal regulations." It concluded, "Your interest in railroad safety is appreciated."

It was no surprise when I later learned that Riley was a personal friend of Walter Rich.

The next letter I received was from New York's Senator D'Amato. D'Amato told me that as a United States Senator, "I have no jurisdiction over this matter, because it involves private, non-governmental individuals."

I was amazed. "Maybe he doesn't know how much state and federal money goes into that railroad – money that he voted for," I thought.

"Bastards – all of them!" I raged, frustrated as hell.

I wrote a letter to Colonel Clinton Pagano, the superintendent of state police in New Jersey, informing him that David Soule had a railroad police commission issued by the state of New Jersey, and that Soule's purpose in obtaining the commission was for no purpose other than to carry a gun when he was in New Jersey. I explained that Soule was employed by the railroad as executive vice president, that he was not a railroad policeman, and that he had no affiliation whatsoever with the railroad police. To me, it seemed straightforward – Soule had no legitimate reason to be commissioned a railroad policeman in New Jersey, or in any other state for that matter. Colonel Pagano never responded to my letter.

One day, I saw an article in the local newspaper about Deane Winsor's position in the community and his activities as an Otsego County representative. The article quoted Winsor. "I've tried to build up a degree of credibility, so I'm not used to getting a runaround...Nobody is going to tell me black is white, when I know better...I'm an individual who does his homework; I don't go into a situation half-baked."

I couldn't stand it; I had to write Winsor a letter and let him know what I thought of him. Referencing the specific newspaper article, and alluding to his involvement in my termination from the railroad, I said, "The article gives the reader the impression that you are a no-nonsense, straight shooter, which we both know is not true." I went on to suggest that the only time he was a "straight shooter" was when the target was someone other than the person responsible for putting money in his pocket. "Because you failed to keep your word and stand up for what you said, my family has suffered incredible hardship," I reminded him. I then asked him how he could look at himself in the mirror and pat himself on the back in a effort to lead the public to believe that he was "his own man," knowing that he, like many other politicians, bowed to influence and money, without regard for moral principle. Concluding my letter, I told Winsor that in spite of what has happened to me, I would make the same decision again, choosing integrity and honor over fraud and corruption.

For whatever it was worth, writing the letter to Winsor made me feel better. Of course, he never responded; but, then, I really didn't expect that he would.

When I contacted the New York State Department of Transportation, two investigators showed up and were very interested in what I told them. Then, suddenly, I never heard from them again, nor was I able to even get them on the phone.

In response to each letter I wrote to a public official, I received either non-responsive lip service or no response at all. The more I pursued the system, the more I wondered about the kind of a political system under which we the people live. Not one person in state or federal government seemed to know where I should take my case.

In early 1987, I received a call from Mike LaRose. LaRose identified himself to me as a freeholder in New Jersey, the equivalent of a New York county representative.

LaRose asked me if I would come to New Jersey, at his expense, and provide to New Jersey officials information I had about the Delaware Otsego Corporation's railroad operations in New Jersey.

"You bet I will," I responded, and made arrangements to meet with him later that week.

LaRose explained to me that authorities in New Jersey were constantly having problems with Delaware Otsego's railroad operations involving everything from administrative issues to issues of railroad safety.

"Maybe the ice is finally beginning to crack," I thought.

A few days later, I met with LaRose in his New Jersey office. I told him everything I knew about the railroad and about my experiences as the railroad's police chief. LaRose told me that the railroad had very little credibility in New Jersey and that what I was saying carried a lot of weight with him. At his request, I agreed to provide my information to other officials at various levels of government in New Jersey.

"Before I have you meet with others, though," LaRose said, "I want to ensure that your credibility is squeaky-clean. Will you take a polygraph regarding what Walter Rich said to you after the Poolville accident?"

Because of what I had experienced so far from so many other government officials, my first response to LaRose's request was defensive.

"I'm not on trial here and I don't want to continually feel like a defendant," I said, looking LaRose in the eye. "Perhaps Walter Rich might want to take a polygraph test, too."

LaRose explained to me that he just wanted me to be a "notch above" any response that the railroad might have. I agreed to the polygraph test and LaRose made the arrangements.

A couple of days later, I walked into the building on West 57th Street in New York City where Certified Polygraph was located. Not having a lot of faith in polygraph examinations, I was somewhat apprehensive. But this company appeared quite reputable; they regularly conducted polygraph examinations for major banks and financial institutions.

After I was interviewed for almost two hours and administered at least three polygraph "pre-tests," the examiner administered the material test. Four of the questions I was asked were particularly pertinent.

"Were you directed by Walter Rich not to have Thomas Charette tested for drugs after the 11/83 Poolville accident?"

My answer was, "Yes."

"During your investigation of that 11/83 Poolville accident, did Walter Rich tell you 'you'll have to lie for me on this one'?"

My answer was, "Yes."

"Prior to that 11/83 Poolville accident, had you already reported to Walter Rich that Mr. Charette had sold drugs to railroad employees?"

My answer was, "Yes."

"Prior to that 11/83 Poolville accident, were you told by Walter Rich to notify Bergen County that you had lost the drug evidence against Mr. Charette?"

My answer was, "Yes."

Following my polygraph examination, the examiner opined in writing, "Based upon the polygraph examination of Mr. Butler, he is telling the truth to his pertinent test questions."

I felt that I had established my credibility with LaRose and his colleagues and had proven that I had nothing to hide.

"I wish Walter would take a similar polygraph examination," I thought, thinking that it would certainly expose him and his lies.

Following my polygraph examination, LaRose arranged a meeting between me and Congressman Florio of New Jersey.

Pleased that I finally had an audience with someone at the federal level, I thought, "Maybe now something will begin to happen."

"You can tell a lot about a man from his handshake," my father once told me. When I walked into Florio's office the next day, his limp handshake spoke volumes. I was not surprised, therefore, when neither Florio nor the aide to whom he finally referred me seemed to have a lot of interest in the information I was instructed to provide to them.

"We'll get back to you if we need further information or have anything to report," Florio's aide said as I was leaving his office.

I never heard from Florio or his aide again.

After my meeting with Florio, LaRose and I spoke at length and I gave him copies of everything I had. LaRose and his secretary compiled all of the information I gave them into small subject notebooks, creating a well-organized summary of my information.

Then, as time went on, I heard less and less from LaRose until finally I heard nothing at all. I called his home and spoke to his wife.

"Mike has retired from politics," she explained, promising to give him the message that I had called. I never heard from LaRose again.

While I was in New Jersey, I had the opportunity to meet Margaret McGarrity, who wrote for the *The New York Times*. I gave her a lot of information, and she used it in articles she wrote for some of the local newspapers.

In the late summer and early fall of 1987, McGarrity called me.

"I'm writing a story for the *Times* based on your allegations and those of other former Delaware Otsego employees," she said, and then requested certain background information for the story.

McGarrity asked who she should call to verify Charette's conviction in Cooperstown for possession of cocaine. I told her that the conviction was public information and that she should call the Cooperstown Police Department who had made the arrest. George Crippen's brother, Michael, was then Cooperstown's police chief.

Thanking me for the information, McGarrity said, "The *Times* will carry the story in a few weeks in its weekend section."

During the first week of November, 1987, I received another call from McGarrity.

"I've just received an anonymous package in the mail," she said, explaining that it was a plain brown envelope, mailed to her home address. "The package contains court records of your indictment in Portsmouth years ago."

McGarrity was already aware of the indictments, since I told her about them during our earlier meetings in New Jersey.

"There's no return address on the envelope," McGarrity continued.

"Is there a postmark?" I asked.

"Yes; it was mailed from Cooperstown. The only person in Cooperstown, other than you, who knows my home address is Michael Crippen at the Police Department; I gave him my home address and asked that he mail the confirmation of Charette's conviction to me there. I didn't receive the confirmation of Charette's conviction; just the court records on you from Portsmouth."

The contents of the anonymous envelope mailed to McGarrity were court records from Portsmouth that I had furnished to the railroad when I applied for my job there. The only people who had access to those records were those with access to the railroad police personnel files.

Nicols had since left the railroad for another job. George Crippen had taken his place as the railroad's police chief.

Chapter Thirteen

Oh what a tangled web we weave,   When first we practice to deceive.

— Sir Walter Scott, Scottish author & novelist
(1771 - 1832) *Marmion, Canto vi. Stanza 17.*

Things were beginning to add up.

From Margaret McGarrity's inquiry of Mike Crippen, Cooperstown's police chief, about Charette's drug conviction, George Crippen, the railroad's chief of police and Mike's brother, learned that McGarrity had received information from me for the story she was writing for the *Times*. It was an obvious attempt by the railroad to surreptitiously discredit me with McGarrity.

I asked McGarrity to send me the envelope that she received. She read to me the postage meter number from the envelope, and I quickly determined it to be that of Cooperstown's main post office. I went to the post office and, throughout the day as shifts changed, asked each clerk at the counter the same question.

"Do you remember anyone mailing an envelope over the counter around the third of November that was addressed to a residence in Andover, New Jersey; the postage was seventy-four cents?"

Thomas Redding was the last postal clerk of the day. He responded to my question.

"It wasn't seventy-four cents; it was seventy-three cents, and it was George Crippen, the one who works for the railroad."

I asked Redding if he thought he could identify the envelope if he saw it.

"Yes, I probably could," he answered. "Crippen handed it to me at the counter to be weighed."

Then I asked Redding if he would give me a written statement as to what he had just told me.

"I'll have to ask Roger," he said.

Roger Smith was the postmaster in Cooperstown. I had known him for a long time.

When I stopped by the post office later, Redding told me that the postmaster would not allow him to give any written statement to anyone regarding his work at the post office.

I went to see Roger and explained to him why I needed Redding's statement.

"It's an invasion of privacy for any employee to 'notice' things about the mail," Roger responded.

"It's not as if Redding opened someone else's mail. What if someone paid for a stamp with a one hundred dollar bill? Wouldn't it be reasonable that a clerk would remember that? For Redding to remember weighing an envelope, and who sent it, is not unusual." I tried to convince Roger to be reasonable, but he wouldn't budge.

"There will be no statement from Redding without a subpoena," Roger assured me.

The following day, the envelope arrived from McGarrity, and I took it to the post office during Redding's shift and asked him if he could identify it.

"Yep," he said, "that's the envelope Crippen brought in to mail."

I wrote down the details of my interaction with Redding so I'd have it for future reference if I needed it, and I gave a copy to Redding.

Then I started thinking about what action I could take against the railroad.

I contacted the state police, but they weren't interested. Even though Section 74 of the New York Public Officers Law stated that "an employee should not disclose confidential information acquired by him in the course of his official duties nor use such information to further his personal needs," and Crippen had taken an oath to comply with those provisions, the state police said nothing I provided established a criminal offense. The Superintendent of State Police had statutory authority, at his pleasure, to revoke Crippen's police commission. But, he did nothing.

I spoke with an attorney, who told me it would be difficult to prove that the railroad knew anything about Crippen's action.

So, I decided to make the railroad, and Walter Rich, aware of Crippen's action.

First, I called Soule. He said he'd look into it and get back to me. Two weeks passed and I heard nothing.

So, I wrote a letter addressed to Walter Rich at the railroad. After outlining Crippen's action, I told Walter that I was not interested in an "eternal feud" with the railroad. "Further," I wrote, "I don't particularly want to litigate again, but I'm prepared to do so if necessary."

About a week later, I received a letter from Les Sittler, who was still the railroad's in-house attorney. Sittler informed me that Walter had "no knowledge" of any confidential information about me being released by the railroad. He went on to say, "If you allow your personal irritation with Mr. Crippen to embroil into litigation involving the railroad, such efforts will meet with vigorous opposition and any claims that the railroad can assert against you will be brought to the light of day." Sittler concluded with, "I trust that this letter answers any questions that you might have."

I responded to Sittler's letter, essentially explaining that the purpose of my letter had been to inform him of the actions of the railroad's police chief and advising him that I would pursue any necessary litigation with the same vigor.

On November 22, 1987, McGarrity's story appeared in the *Times*. She never received the information about Charette she had requested from Michael Crippen, but her story was interesting.

McGarrity's story began with the information that New Jersey officials had requested an investigation of the railroad. According to the story, there had been "two dozen derailments and several grade crossing accidents, including three fatal accidents, in three years," all in New Jersey. The story went on to say that six employees of the railroad had quit or been fired, "including David Butler, the former railroad police chief, and James Briguglio, a former superintendent of Transportation." "The former employees," the story continued, "allege that the company has been involved in improper or fraudulent activities. A cavalier approach to safety, cover-ups of accidents, drug use by employees, improper bookkeeping of public funds and money owed to other railroads for shared railroad shipments." A spokesperson for a New Jersey Congresswoman was quoted as saying, "Serious questions remain, especially about irregular and haphazard safety procedures and the use of public money." McGarrity's story then listed several other allegations, including:

Sums owed other railroads were usually held back to improve cash flow (a federal accounting violation); Workers' hours were charged to subsidized portions of the railroad even when no work was performed; Job titles were falsified to get higher salary subsidies from New York on-the-job training programs; Certain shippers were favored on bills, in spite of Federal regulations; Little or no rehabilitation was done on the railroad even though state and federal funds were provided for that purpose; Track safety inspection reports were routinely filed, even when no such inspection had taken place.

Soule responded. He said that the allegations were "groundless" claims by disgruntled former employees and that the railroad "categorically" met all safety standards. Soule went on the say that "Mr. Butler and his band of merry men have been at this for years, and have been written off...Mr. Butler has become a nuisance for trying to resurrect already disproven allegations."

I read McGarrity's story and Soule's response.

"When," I wondered, "had these allegations been 'disproven'?"

After McGarrity's story appeared in the *Times*, I received a telephone call from Frank Larkin, chief engineer for the railroad.

"I read the story in the *Times*; I wanted to tell you that I, too, am constantly required to falsify safety inspection reports for the locomotives," Larkin told me.

That was right in line with what other railroad employees were saying. The railroad required its employees to do whatever Walter wanted, regardless of whether it was legal, ethical, right or wrong.

Malcolm Hughes was running for re-election as Delaware County district attorney that fall, and I learned that he was scheduled to appear at the Delhi Business and Professional Women's Club "Meet the Candidates" night shortly before the November election.

"How appropriate," I thought.

I attended the meeting and sat in the back of the room. Hughes saw me, and, as he spoke, he glanced nervously at me. He knew I wasn't there as an interested voter because I lived in Otsego County. Hughes was the Republican candidate, and Delaware County was a Republican county.

The question and answer portion of the evening followed the candidates' short speeches. When I raised my hand, I saw the color drain from Hughes' face, and I took delight in watching him sweat.

"Yes, you in the back of the room," the moderator said signaling to me. "Do you have a question for one of the candidates?"

"I have a question for Mr. Hughes," I said; and then, looking at Hughes, I asked, "Mr. Hughes, have you ever intentionally concealed evidence of criminal conduct in order to protect your personal or business interests?"

He stared coldly at me and snapped, "No!"

"Thank you," I said politely and sat down.

Everyone in the room seemed to wonder what that was all about. At the reception that followed, I explained my question to everyone who expressed an interest. The media reported it the following day, and Hughes was furious.

Someone suggested to me that I should be careful talking about Walter Rich and Malcolm Hughes. "They might sue you for slander," was their point, to which I responded, "Truth is the defense to slander, and the last place Walter or Hughes want me is in a courtroom with an opportunity to prove the truth."

Hughes was re-elected in the November 1987 general election. Shortly after the election, I learned about an agency in Albany that was responsible for investigating improprieties concerning government officials, the Commission on Government Integrity. I called them and spoke to one of their investigators.

"Is Malcolm Hughes, the Delaware County District Attorney, considered to be a government official?" I asked.

"Yes," he responded.

So, I told the Commission's investigator that I had made Hughes aware of documented evidence of criminal conduct and other information that would probably have led to criminal action had there been an investigation. I told the investigator of what had taken place when I was fired by the railroad and the part that Hughes played in my termination.

A few days later, I received a letter from the Commission on Government Integrity asking me to come to Albany to give sworn testimony before the Commission.

"Finally," I thought. "If Hughes is exposed, surely it will lead to more."

I testified before the Commission on Government Integrity in Albany in January 1988, beginning with my investigation concerning John Tobin early in my railroad career and pointing out that Hughes was aggressive in that matter, using the threat of criminal prosecution against Tobin to force him to resign. I also pointed out how Hughes directly benefited by Tobin's resignation. I talked about the similarities between that case and the case that I investigated against Walter Rich. In both cases, Hughes had instructed me to conduct the investigation. However, unlike the Rich investigation, no one ever claimed that my investigation in the Tobin matters was "unauthorized." The difference, I said, was that in the Rich investigation, I was investigating Hughes' friend, Walter Rich, and Hughes had something to lose. I made it clear that Hughes had direct knowledge of criminal conduct by Walter Rich, and I provided documentation, including names of witnesses. I suggested that Hughes insisted that I conduct the Walter Rich investigation even though I had requested that the state police investigate because Hughes knew he could not have controlled the outcome of a state police investigation. I talked about the special meeting of the railroad's board of directors at which my employment was terminated, and told the commission that at that meeting, Hughes made no attempt to ask questions or contact witnesses. Instead, the meeting was orchestrated by Walter Rich as "damage control." I testified all day, providing information and answering the commission's questions. When I finished testifying, the commission took a recess. I walked out of the room and the court reporter who had been recording my testimony came over to me.

"I don't usually comment on, or show an interest in, the matters that I report, but I want to tell you that this is one of the most interesting cases, and one of the best documented cases, that I have ever witnessed," she said. "I wish you luck in the future."

To me, her opinion had value. I hoped that the commission would view it in the same light.

When I received a copy of the transcript of my testimony, I was astonished by its length – 110 pages.

For the next several months, I waited to hear about what action the commission might take based upon the testimony I provided. Then I heard that because of state budget cuts, the commission had been abolished.

"If the state's going to abolish an agency, you can bet it would be the commission that investigated official impropriety," I though to myself, disappointed.

I added the lengthy transcript to what was becoming an enormous file on the railroad in my attic and turned my attention back to The Woodmen Builders.

By now, I had nine full-time employees, including Davy, who had graduated from high school. We now respectfully called him David. I purchased a building near our home and converted it into a shop, fully equipped for everything relating to woodwork. I had three company trucks, a back-hoe, and a trailer. The building provided ample storage for tools and materials, and the land surrounding the building provided ample parking for the vehicles.

After a major fire destroyed a downtown commercial building, The Woodsmen Builders was selected as the contractor to rebuild it. The owner's insurance company paid all of our bills.

The Woodsmen Builders had a good crew, and I continued to receive a number of employment applications every week from individuals interested in working for us. The company's reputation was excellent, and we had plenty of work. Customers were willing to wait until we were available to work on their projects. The respect that The Woodsmen Builders enjoyed was earned by hard work, attention to detail, and a supreme effort toward customer satisfaction.

I built a second-story office in my garage at home with the same expertise and craftsmanship that The Woodsmen Builders put into the homes we built, so, when customers came to my office, they could see the quality of my work.

I incorporated the business and installed a second telephone line dedicated to the facsimile machine. Mary volunteered to attend to the corporation's paper work, and she was an invaluable asset.

I felt good about the reputable business I had built, and my future seemed secure, but I regretted that frustration plagued my continuing efforts to find justice against Walter and the railroad.

I was reading the newspaper one day and noticed an advertisement for the Rural Legal Aid Society. The ad described the association as a group of attorneys who represented the legal interests of those who could not afford an attorney. I contacted them and arranged to meet with one of their attorneys.

I found the office of the Rural Legal Aid Society located in one room of a cluttered farm house. The staff of attorneys consisted of a man and his wife – both attorneys. Nothing about the office or the attorneys even whispered legal competence, but I explained my case to them anyway, hoping they could provide some legal assistance or at least suggest some alternative course I might pursue. But, by the expressions on their faces as I talked, and the questions they asked, it was my impression that my case was beyond their realm of experience and expertise. When I mentioned the release I had signed for Soule before I re-enlisted in the Navy, they balked and said the release prevented me from doing anything. I told them that I certainly wasn't an attorney, but I was familiar enough with the law to believe that because the release was without consideration and had been coerced, it could likely be successfully challenged. The attorney confessed that he had never challenged such a document and wasn't sure of the procedure. I thanked them and left, sure that there was little chance they could be of help to me and not wanting to waste any more time with them.

"They've probably never even been in a courtroom," I thought as I walked to my car.

Every so often I would talk to friends who happened to still work for the railroad, although they wouldn't talk to me in public for fear Walter or one of his spies would see us talking. It appeared that nothing had changed. After all that had happened, Charette still worked for the railroad and was back in New Jersey again as a track supervisor. I found out that even after the Poolville accident, the railroad was using Charette as an engineer when they were shorthanded. It seemed pretty clear to me that Walter did as he pleased, confident that no one would penetrate the wall of protection he had built around himself with money, political influence and sheer intimidation.

"I will never lose my resolve to break through that wall some day," I thought.

The railroad continued to needle me whenever they had an opportunity. Once, while The Woodsmen Builders were working on an addition to a house in the village, I had one of our trucks parked alongside nearby railroad tracks. The railroad hadn't used the tracks for a long time, and people often parked their vehicles in the clearing alongside the tracks with no problem – until the Woodsmen truck was parked there. I received a letter, signed by one of George Crippen's deputy railroad police officers, that my truck was "within the railroad right-of-way" and if found parked there again, it would be towed. From my experience as the railroad's former chief of police, I knew that the right-of-way in that area extended fifteen feet in both directions from the center line of the tracks. So, after that, I parked the Woodsmen truck exactly sixteen feet from the tracks' center line. Neither Crippen nor the railroad bothered me again on that issue.

Meanwhile, Woodsmen Builders, Inc. continued to grow. By the end of 1988, I had fourteen employees and we had contracted another big job, this time to convert an old car dealership into a baseball card museum. My crew and I survived with work to see us through another winter. As with our past projects, the owner was happy with our work when we finished, and I added a significant commercial project to the company's list of references.

In the spring of 1989, The Woodmen Builders gave back to the community by sponsoring a Cooperstown Little League baseball team.

"How appropriate," I thought. Cooperstown is home to the Baseball Hall of Fame, and I was proud to sponsor a team of budding young baseball players. It was great to see the team wearing their "Woodsmen" uniforms at the Little League games. It was also great advertising for the company.

I also joined the local volunteer fire department in Fly Creek, just outside of Cooperstown. We lived in that district, and the fire department was shorthanded. I knew my experience with the Portsmouth Fire Department would be valuable to the small volunteer company. I spent time with fire department activities, and I liked the excitement when there was an emergency. I also liked just being able to help people.

Through it all, Mary dedicated herself unselfishly to me and the boys. She kept the house immaculate, our laundry was always fresh, and she prepared wonderful home cooked meals for us each evening. Often I would come home to the aroma of freshly-baked cookies. Mary involved herself in the boys' activities and school functions and was active in the community. She volunteered her nursing skills at the hospital one day a week and did hospice volunteer work a couple of times a week. But the boys and I were always her first priority. She was always there for all of us, and all of us depended on her love and joyful enthusiasm. For a couple of years, she was a Cub Scout den mother, weekly welcoming into our home the entire Scout troop as they climbed off the bus after school. Mary always had homemade treats for them to enjoy as she helped them with their Scout projects. Afterward, Mary loved to visit with the parents when they came by to pick up their Scouts.

About mid-year, I decided to involve myself in local politics and was successful in being nominated by the town caucus to run for the office of Town councilman. The local town government consisted of a town supervisor and four councilmen. It was an interesting process. There were plenty of local issues (land use, preservation of the lake, taxes, town ordinances, and overall protection of the town), and it was a hotly contested race with four candidates for the two open seats. I was invited to participate in the League of Women Voters "Meet the Candidates" night, and almost expected Malcolm Hughes to show up. I stated my position on each of the issues and answered questions from the audience.

Unlike most politicians, I always believed that it was best to be honest about my position on a matter, regardless of its popularity, rather than just say what I thought people wanted to hear. As far as I was concerned, those who didn't support my views could vote for someone else. That was democracy.

Apparently, my honesty was well-received by the voters. In November, 1989, I was elected to a seat on the Otsego Town Council, and on January 1, 1990, I was sworn in as a town councilman.

The Woodsmen Builders continued to be a Little League sponsor that spring, and Danny joined the team. Mary and I went to all of the games.

Les Sittler was also a regular spectator at the local Little League games that year. After leaving his position as in-house counsel for the railroad, he opened a private law practice. At first, Les shied away from any contact with me at the games. Then one day, I walked over and sat next to him and started making small talk. The conversation eventually began to lightly touch on the subject of the railroad. Finally, I asked him why he left.

"For a number of reasons," he said, the question obviously evoking dreadful memories of the circumstances that finally led to his decision to resign.

"I hope you understand that case in Chicago was nothing personal against you," I said, adding, "I understood that you only knew what you had been told."

"Actually," he confessed, "I believed all of the things you said and documented at the hearing, but I was just doing my job."

"You know," he said, turning to look at me, "you're Walter Rich's worst nightmare."

I chuckled to myself, relishing that thought.

After that, Sittler and I remained on speaking terms, but he was reluctant to discuss the railroad. I also knew that he was close friends with George Crippen, so I was always careful with what I said to him.

As time passed, I reflected on all the doors that had slammed shut in my face as I pursued my case against Walter and the railroad. Surely, it seemed to me, enough had happened over the years to warrant some type of investigation.

"It wasn't just me," I would tell myself. "There were at least eight other former employees who could have provided valid information that would shed light on how the railroad operates."

One evening, I climbed the stairs to my office above the garage; it had become my refuge. I could brood there without troubling Mary. Often, I would roll a sheet of paper into the typewriter and transfer my thoughts and memories there, adding yet more pages to my growing journal. Sometimes late at night, I would sit in my office as if it were a war room, strategizing my next move, my next plan, to find justice; or, to simply try to reconcile what seemed to make no sense.

That night, sitting alone in my office, I began to leaf through all of the files and news clippings I had accumulated over years of battling a system that seemed always to work against me.

"What am I missing?" I wondered.

Chapter Fourteen

"I cannot accept...that we are to judge [holders of power] unlike other men, with a favourable presumption that they did no wrong. If there is any presumption it is the other way, against the holders of power, increasing as the power increases. Historic responsibility has to make up for the want of legal responsibility. Power tends to corrupt, and absolute power corrupts absolutely. Great men are almost always bad men, even when they exercise influence and not authority, still more when you superadd the tendency or the certainty of corruption by authority. There is no worse heresy than that the office sanctifies the holder of it. That is the point at which the negation of [principle] and the negation of [tolerance] meet and keep high festival, and the end learns to justify the means."

— Lord Acton (1834-1902)
English historian, statesman

I read page after page, news clipping after news clipping, looking for what I had heretofore missed – the common thread, woven in the fabric of each document and each clipping, responsible for frustrating all of my attempts to find justice.

As I read, that common thread became apparent. It had to be corruption.

I looked over at the collection of news clippings on my desk and started reading them again:

"The Delaware Otsego Short-Line buys $5 million in rails after New York State Commissioner of Transportation, William Hennessy, pledged financial assistance for the line's operation and rehabilitation." "Delaware Otsego has hired William Hennessy, Former State Transportation Commissioner, at $2,500 a month to lobby the governor and the Transportation Department for a $3 million grant and other aid to Delaware Otsego for a "much needed" heavy locomotive repair facility. The Delaware Otsego says this facility would probably not be built with the $3 million grant, but would be constructed with future government grants. The company is also paying an Albany law firm $30,000 for lobbying."

"Of course Hennessy would have influence lobbying the State Transportation Department; I'm sure Walter Rich was counting on it!" I said aloud, stating the obvious.

"It's outrageous," I thought to myself in disgust, wondering why Transportation Commissioner Hennessy was never prosecuted for so blatantly using his government position to benefit the company that subsequently employed him to lobby the same government agency that he headed before the railroad hired him.

"If the company needed money so badly, how did they come up with $30,000 to pay yet another firm to lobby their interests?" I continued to wonder as I put the news clipping aside and picked up another.

"Boehlert re-election campaign in good shape; campaign fund-raisers held at the Washington Capitol Hill Club and the Delaware Otsego building in Cooperstown aided Boehlert's healthy bank balance."

"Another extravagant affair at Edgewater for one of Walter's political cronies," I noted.

"Boehlert raised 79% of his money through special interest Political Action Committees."

"One being the Delaware Otsego PAC," I acknowledged.

"Walter Rich and four other individuals donate $1,000 each to Boehlert."

Likely four of Walter's friends or members of the board of directors, I was fairly certain. The threshold individual political contribution was $1,000. There was no doubt in my mind that Walter quietly reimbursed each of the four $1,000 donations and made sure Boehlert knew it – I saw that happen with employees of the railroad when Walter asked them to contribute to the campaign of one of his political cronies.

Shortly after the articles about the campaign donations, Boehlert was re-elected. The subsequent news clippings reflected how Boehlert's campaign benefactor, the Delaware Otsego Corporation, benefited from his re-election.

"Congressman Boehlert proposes Federal Government set aside funds to be in a trust for the development of private railroads." "Congressman Boehlert, as liaison between the Delaware Otsego and the Federal Railroad Administration, instrumental in earmarking funds for a $4.1 million low interest FRA. loan to Delaware Otsego rail line." "$2.3 million given to Delaware Otsego for preservation and repair of short-lines in Richfield Springs and the company-owned railroad in Gloversville, both in New York. A portion of the money to be used on the small line running through the village of Cooperstown. Walter Rich said it was important that "we break this money loose this summer, so we can put a whole lot of college kids to work. If we can get the money free to work with, we can do quite a bit for the economy of the area."

Not very long after the Delaware Otsego Corporation received this money, those lines were permanently closed to rail service and the corporation began receiving revenue from leasing the real estate under the tracks and the associate rights-of-way.

"It's not just the Delaware Otsego Corporation," I said to myself as I sat there staring at the evidence that had been there all along. "It's much more insidious than that – it's corruption that has infected the entire system. No wonder whereever I turned, the door slammed shut on my case."

I knew from my experience at the railroad that Walter Rich, individually, through the Delaware Otsego PAC and through a variety of other creative means, made substantial political contributions to politicians whom Walter believed could benefit him and the railroad. The politician was always made aware that Walter was responsible for the contribution, no matter who actually wrote the check.

I also knew that state and federal government routinely made low-interest loans and awarded grants to railroads, purportedly "in the interest of preserving rail service." The distribution of such public funds to a railroad was always widely publicized, claiming the funds would boost the local economy and provide new jobs. The idea was that the public money used to fund grants and loans to railroads would spark economic growth in the community that the railroad served. However, that's not what happened – at least not in Cooperstown. The only economy in Cooperstown I ever saw grow from public funds channeled to the Delaware Otsego Corporation was Walter's.

I knew that the Delaware Otsego Corporation received state and federal funds to upgrade and keep in service several small short-lines the company owned. However, most, if not all, of those short-lines were closed down long ago and not in service – there was nothing left to upgrade. The only activity on those defunct short-lines involved not the line, but the real estate under the tracks. Cable, telephone, and utility companies paid the Delaware Otsego Corporation handsomely to rent that real estate and the associated rights-of-way. So, those defunct short-lines were valuable to Walter and the corporation because they didn't have to spend a penny operating trains on those rails to generate significant revenue. They simply pocketed the state and federal money and collected the rent. Observing the opulent lifestyle that Walter enjoyed as president of the Delaware Otsego Corporation, it didn't take much imagination to guess who was paying for it.

The incredible salaries, luxury company cars, extravagant food and beverage service, the mansion called Edgewater, and so many other perks the railroad provided to Walter, the board of directors and Walter's political cronies were excessive by any standard.

"Any business could do just as well," I supposed, "with friends in high political places to guarantee a million or two whenever needed."

I was amazed at how obvious the thread of corruption appeared to me when the documents and news clippings were read together, one after another.

"Doesn't anyone else see it? Why isn't anyone interested in investigating what's going on?" I asked myself incredulously, wondering if anyone would ever attempt to reconcile all of the public money this company had received with how it was actually spent.

I had to admit, the railroad business is complex, and its inner workings are essentially a mystery to the average person, a phenomenon that I'm sure got Walter's attention. By using carefully crafted catchphrases like "new jobs" and "economic boost" in their press releases and comments to the media, Walter and his political henchmen could mollify the unsuspecting public and blind the indolent media from recognizing the bigger story behind the cunning media speak it was spoon-fed.

Why hadn't the press read its own articles, put two and two together, and blown the whistle themselves? Other than the publicity when the railroad fired me and the later story in the *Times*, newspapers, it seemed, refused to print anything adverse to the railroad.

A number of years after the Poolville accident, I joined the twenty-first century, equipping myself with a computer and access to the internet. The information I found on the Internet was impressive, as it related to not only the local railroad but the industry as a whole.

In looking into Federal Railroad Administration issues, I was shocked at one of the first things I found – after I was fired, *someone* at the railroad created and filed an accident report with the FRA for the Poolville accident. Filing the accident report would have been my job, but, since they fired me, someone else had to file it. On the FRA website, I found copies of the report that was filed and although it was unsigned, the report was part of the official record of that accident. It appeared that instead of investigating the accident itself, the FRA simply relied on whatever information about the accident the NYS&W submitted, and the NYS&W had every reason to cover up the real facts. (It's my understanding that, for the most part, the FRA continues that practice today.) In any event, the report submitted to the FRA by the NYS&W was false and because there are no checks and balances at the federal level, the bogus accident report remains the official record to this day.

The report stated, among other things, that in addition to the "crossbuck" signs, there were "highway traffic signals and other" crossing warnings for the driver of the truck. That is an outright lie – there was no other protection at that crossing. The report also said there was a minimum twenty-second warning for the truck. But, the truth is there was no warning. The report further states that the "estimated" speed of the train was 15 mph. That's another outright lie. How anyone could *estimate* the train's speed at 15 mph without being present at the scene of the accident, as was I, is simply incomprehensible. During my investigation immediately following the accident, I reconstructed the accident several times at the scene, and each reconstruction revealed that the train's speed had to be far in excess of the required speed limit. Following those reconstructions, Charette and Walter Rich realized how obvious it was that the train's speed was excessive and Charette changed his official statement to the state police. Finally, notwithstanding evidence at the scene of the Poolville accident, the report indicated that the "train" was only a single engine and was not pulling any cars.

So, there it is. Can anyone *really* doubt that there was a cover-up and obstruction of justice in the Poolville case?

Chapter Fifteen

"Man, proud man, dressed in a little brief authority, plays such fantastic tricks before high Heaven as make the angels weep."

— William Shakespeare (1564 - 1616)
English poet & dramatist

The Woodsmen Builders continued to grow far beyond what I had expected in the beginning. For the first time in our lives, Mary and I and the boys were able to take a vacation, have things we never before could afford, and furnish our home the way we wanted.

I had always dreamed of purchasing a motor home, perhaps later in life; but we could afford to purchase one now, so we did and we traveled every time we had a chance – usually for just a weekend to nearby Lake George, but one time we splurged and took the boys to Florida for a week at Disney World.

Though the economy (especially in Cooperstown) remained uncertain, I felt more and more confident that we'd be okay. Even in a bad economy, the best businesses survive; and my team and I worked very hard to make Woodsmen Builders among the best.

Our two older boys (we called them David and Don now) had finished high school, and then Don completed three years of college. They both worked summers for Woodsmen Builders. Don decided to become a police officer and applied to my alma mater in Portsmouth. I was surprised by Don's decision, and, knowing what it was like to be a police officer in the tough streets of Portsmouth, I worried. But Don was an adult, he was smart, and he was very capable; I supported his decision and encouraged him to do what he wanted to do.

Don scored a ninety-nine percent on the Portsmouth civil service examination and was accepted at the Police Academy after passing the oral review board. He did very well at the academy, and I was immensely proud of him. Mary and I traveled to Portsmouth for Don's graduation, where he was listed as "Officer D. K. Butler," the same as I had been years ago.

At Don's graduation, I saw old friends from the Portsmouth Police Department that started with me in the late 1960s, fresh from the academy. Some were now high-ranking officers. Looking around, I realized that all of these people were now nearing retirement. For me, retirement was still just a dream.

Don started work immediately, breaking into the routine under the watchful eye of the field training officers. In record time, he was sent out on his own with excellent recommendations. I had no doubts that he would do well, and I couldn't have been more proud.

David continued as part of the Woodsmen team, although he told me that he didn't want to do it forever. He considered becoming a police officer, too, but he wasn't ready to leave Cooperstown yet. I didn't push him. Besides, he was a great asset to the business, and he ran heavy equipment better than anyone I had ever seen. I enjoyed working with him every day.

After being sworn in as a member of the Town Board in January, 1990, I faithfully attended and participated in the Town Board meetings. Citizens would often bring their complaints before the Town Board at its meetings. Some of those complaints concerned the railroad.

At one meeting, someone complained about the railroad not being required to pay taxes on the Edgewater property. Apparently, when Delaware Otsego Corporation purchased Edgewater, Walter Rich, with the assistance of the Otsego County Industrial Development Agency, worked out a deal exempting Edgewater from property taxes under the ruse that Edgewater would bring new jobs to the community, enhancing its economy.

"Where have I heard that before?" I thought sarcastically as I sat at the dais with the other councilmen listening to the discussion. I saw George Crippen sitting in the audience.

In reality, Edgewater resulted in no new jobs for the community. Instead, it provided an opulent tax-free residence for Walter Rich and an elaborate venue where he could entertain friends and court politicians. For eleven years, the railroad avoided paying property taxes on Edgewater.

I wondered about how other businesses that legitimately created new jobs in the community – like Woodsmen Builders, for instance – might have prospered if they could have enjoyed the perks and the benefits that the railroad enjoyed at the expense of the taxpayers.

I suggested that the board look into the matter of Edgewater's property tax exemption. The board agreed and, thinking it best to not directly involve me, we assigned the task to one of the other councilmen.

At another meeting, someone complained about the state of disrepair of the crossing protection at the railroad's two crossings in Cooperstown. Each crossing was equipped with rubber matting at the tracks and automatic gates with flashing lights, however the railroad hadn't run a train on those tracks for several years and the crossings were not being maintained.

I knew from my railroad employment that crossings like those in Cooperstown were a huge profit center for the railroad. It was my understanding that the state of New York paid the railroad around $200,000 for each crossing project, when the actual cost to the railroad was substantially less. The difference was profit to the railroad. The railroad also profited if a grade-crossing accident caused damage to the crossing protection mechanisms. In that case, it was the railroad's practice to convince the insurance company to bear the cost of completely replacing the crossing protection, rather than the cost of repairing the damage, by demanding either payment for the cost of a full replacement or a written statement from the insurance company assuming responsibility for future damages if the crossing protection mechanisms failed after being repaired. That seemed reasonable, except that when the insurance company paid the railroad for a full crossing protection replacement, the railroad repaired the damaged gates using surplus parts and pocketed the insurance payment as profit.

After some discussion, the town board explained that there was little it could do about the railroad crossings. Neither the town of Otsego nor the village of Cooperstown had the authority to make the railroad keep the crossings in good repair.

In the course of the Woodsmen Builders' remodeling work, I was contracted to renovate a house in Cooperstown. As with many of Cooperstown's homes, the house was used as a summer home by the out of town owner. When the project was nearly completed, I learned that the owner of the home, Dennis Lynch, was a lawyer and partner in a litigation firm in Nyack, New York.

Dennis and I had become friends over the course of the renovation project. After learning that he was a litigation attorney, I explained my situation with the railroad to him and asked his opinion. He listened with interest, but because so much time had passed by then, there was little that could be done. However, Dennis agreed that if my case had been handled differently from the start, it likely would have been a successful lawsuit against the railroad. After speaking with Dennis, I knew that if anything new developed, I'd call him. He was an aggressive attorney with a confident presence and local politics didn't intimidate him. I liked him and we remained friends.

In early 1992, Malcolm Hughes announced that he was retiring as Delaware County district attorney to run for the office of county judge. After my experience with Hughes, I was horrified by the thought that someone like him could even have a chance to fill a position requiring such integrity and trust.

Much to my relief, and I suppose Walter's disappointment, Hughes lost the election and went into private practice.

Right after the November 1992 election, I got a call from Sheila Ross, a fellow town council member.

"David, you were railroad police chief," she began. "I have a question about the jurisdiction of railroad police."

"Are you talking railroad jurisdiction, on railroad property?" I asked, thinking of crossing incidents or vandalism in the rail yards.

"No; I want to know if George Crippen has authority to make traffic arrests. He arrested a young man I know who was driving an injured friend to the hospital!"

"No, Sheila, I don't believe Crippen has that kind of authority, but, I'd like to talk to the man involved and learn a little more about what happened before I can say for sure."

"Why don't you come have lunch with him at our place?" she asked, and we set a date to meet at her small bar and grill in Fly Creek, The B&S.

Sheila went on to tell me about how George Crippen, who lived across the street from The B&S, had been harassing her.

"Crippen's always calling the police late at night, complaining of noise from The B&S," she said. "Then the police come, and because there's been no disturbance and they find nothing, they leave."

"So, what do the police say about Crippen?" I asked.

"That's the thing, David; the calls are always anonymous, though I know Crippen's responsible."

"How do you know that?"

"Once, he signed a complaint against me for being a disorderly person. The charge was tried and dismissed. Later, the local building codes official showed up armed with a bunch of complaints filed by Crippen stating that my building didn't meet fire codes. I had a certificate of occupancy from the town and everything. The B&S has occupied that building for a number of years. Do you know what Crippen's reasons were?"

"No," I answered, intrigued, but thinking this was beginning to sound slightly crazy.

"He said that my building, if it burned, would threaten his house, across the street!"

Oddly enough, on the site where Sheila and her husband had built *The B&S*, a business was destroyed by fire years before, but the fire was no threat to the buildings on either side, nor was it a threat to Crippen's house across the street.

"Meanwhile," Sheila continued, "he stalks up and down the street in front of my place, taking pictures. There'd never been a single complaint against me, for any reason, in the past, but I ended up having to go to Albany to defend myself!"

I didn't know what to say, but before I could reply, Sheila continued.

"George Chandler, the Fly Creek fire chief, went with me to Albany to testify for me."

"Sounds like George," I thought.

"Anyway, afterward, Crippen parked the railroad police car on the road by Chandler's property, roaming around taking pictures of his place."

Crippen also complained to the state Alcohol Beverage Control Agency that Sheila ran "disorderly premises," a ludicrous claim considering many executives from the railroad ate lunch every day at The B&S. Sheila's business was anything but "disorderly," but I guessed it galled Crippen to see people enjoying themselves without him. In my opinion, Crippen just didn't want a bar and grill across the street from his house, and he was apparently using whatever means he could to drive Sheila out.

"Unbelievable," I thought.

Charles Crist, the young man Crippen had arrested, and I met for lunch. He was twenty-two years old, somewhat muscular, but clean-cut with a boyish face and blonde hair. Crist had never been in trouble before, and he was upset as he recounted to me what had happened. Having been a victim of Crippen's mischief myself, I listened to Crist with empathy.

Crist's trouble that night began in a nightclub in Richfield Springs, a village north end of Cooperstown. In the midst of a fight, Crist's friend was knocked unconscious and Crist and another man loaded him into a car and headed to Bassett Hospital in Cooperstown, fifteen miles away. Crist was driving. While en route to Cooperstown, Crist passed Crippen, who was in his own car headed toward Cooperstown after having dinner and wine at a nearby restaurant.

Crippen pursued Crist, following him to Bassett Hospital, where he pulled Crist from the car and demanded his identification. According to Crist, Crippen was in plain clothes, in his own car, and showed Crist no badge or identification when he pulled him from his vehicle.

Ignoring Crippen, Crist and the man with him took their injured friend into the hospital's emergency room, where their friend's injury was deemed serious enough for him to be admitted.

In the meantime, Crippen had called his brother Mike, Cooperstown's chief of police, for assistance and the Cooperstown Police responded. They forced Crist to take a field sobriety test, which he passed. Not liking that result, Crippen complained that the test "must be wrong" and demanded another one. Crist was taken to police headquarters and given another sobriety test, which he also passed. Finally, because there was no reason to hold him, Crist was released. But, before he was released, Crippen ticketed him for speeding in the village and running two stop signs.

It sounded to me like classic Crippen intimidation and abuse.

Crist returned home with a court date in Cooperstown to answer to the traffic charges. Then, a week later, a state trooper appeared at Crist's door and arrested him on a reckless driving charge. The trooper explained that the arrest warrant was secured by Crippen, who had complained that Crist was speeding in the town of Exeter on his way to the hospital the week before. Crippen also charged Crist with speeding in the town of Otsego.

With no money to hire an attorney, and not wanting to post bail or go to jail until trial, Crist pled guilty to the charge in the Town of Exeter and paid the fine.

Subsequently, based on Crippen's lack of authority, Crist was allowed to withdraw his guilty plea in the town of Exeter and the charges were dismissed.

The town of Otsego also dismissed its charges against Crist on the same basis. Crippen was furious.

Cooperstown wouldn't dismiss the charges against Crist, and he was eventually convicted of the traffic charges. It was no surprise, since Crippen and the judge in Cooperstown were friends. However, Dennis Lynch appealed the conviction on Crist's behalf, and it was overturned by the County Judge who found that Crippen acted outside of his authority.

The case made headlines in the local newspaper. Crippen wrote a guest editorial attempting to justify himself. Letters to the editor criticized Crippen, and he looked like a fool. The railroad subsequently issued a public statement, which read, "Although we believe our policeman to have been justified in the Crist case, he has been instructed not to issue any more traffic tickets." I got a kick out of that.

A short time later, Crist called me one day and told me he had received a package in the mail that contained a lot of documents concerning me. Crist described the package as a brown envelope mailed to him at his street address, which he said was unusual since he used a post office box address for his mail.

"Is your street address listed anywhere?" I asked.

"Just on my driver's license," Crist responded.

The only person who recently had Crist's driver's license was George Crippen.

I arranged to get the package from Crist that afternoon. Inside were copies of the same documents that had been mailed to Margaret McGarrity of *The New York Times* in 1987. I had no doubts about who had mailed the package to Crist.

I wrote to the superintendent of state police again, and I received a letter back saying that there was no criminal activity and, therefore, no action would be taken. The superintendent stated that he had conferred with the Otsego County district attorney, Michael Coccoma, and Coccoma agreed that there was no indication of criminal conduct by Mr. Crippen.

I went to see Coccoma and I explained to him what had happened in the *Times* case, and now the Crist case. Coccoma seemed indifferent, so I explained to him that the documents that were mailed anonymously to McGarrity and Crist were not public information and the railroad was the only place in Cooperstown that had copies. After I signed a release, Coccoma wrote a letter to the railroad and asked them to furnish his office with all records they had concerning my employment there.

The railroad replied that they had no records concerning me.

"Maybe now Coccoma will listen," I speculated, and went to see him.

"They're obviously lying," I said, handing Coccoma a copy of the letter I had written on railroad stationary, requesting copies of my records from Portsmouth, when I applied for the railroad job and they were investigating my background.

"I'll investigate and get back to you," Coccoma assured me.

"Talk to the postal clerk, Thomas Redding," I suggested. "He can positively identify Crippen as the person who sent the first package to McGarrity."

I didn't think an investigation involving one witness was too much to ask of a district attorney, but I never heard from Coccoma and he never spoke to Redding.

Chapter Sixteen

"If one advances confidently in the direction of his dreams, and endeavors to live the life which he has imagined, he will meet with a success unexpected in common hours."

— Henry David Thoreau (1817 - 1862)

The railroad was soon in the news again, This time seeking money to "rehabilitate" the line near Richfield Springs, and justifying its need for the money on a statement by a company known as Sentinel that it was going to build a plant that, within a year, would employ one hundred fifty people in Richfield Springs.

The only announcement of government funding for that project came in the form of a small legal notice I happened to see in the newspaper one day. The notice said that the New York State Department of Transportation had applied to the Federal Railroad Administration for $966,945 to "rehab" the Richfield short-line under the Federal Local Rail Freight Assistance Program.

"Sounds familiar," I thought as I walked up to my office over the garage to look back through my files.

After a few minutes of leafing through a box of documents, I pulled out a news clipping. In 1975, the exact same line was given $865,000 for the exact same purpose!

I called a local reporter I knew and talked to him about what I had found. A few days later, a newspaper article announced the funding and state and local politicians were patting themselves on the back for arranging it. They touted their usual catchphrases about new jobs and a boost to the local economy. The article said nothing about the fact that the state had already funded this once before, and the line, like several others that had been funded for similar projects, was closed and the crossings paved over.

After the railroad received the funds, there was no further news about the project or that any new jobs were ever created to boost the local economy in and around Richfield Springs.

Then, the issue of the Edgewater property taxes resurfaced. The local newspaper reported that the Delaware Otsego Corporation had failed to make any payment on the property taxes due on Edgewater.

The Oneonta *Daily Star* ran an editorial critical of the tax-exempt status of Edgewater, stating, "There are serious questions about what the government's role should be in helping a company like the D.O. set its president up in a nifty mansion overlooking a lovely lake," and opining that Walter Rich and Delaware Otsego should be paying local governments just like other companies and "regular folk." "Most people," the editorial continued, "don't get the government to help them pay for a new home, except Walter Rich."

I couldn't have agreed more, and I would have paid anything to see Walter's face when it read it.

Apparently, he didn't like it much and the proverbial shit hit the fan the next day at the *Star*. A reporter friend of mine there told me the person who wrote the editorial was chewed out vigorously and almost fired.

It was apparent to me that the purpose of the author of the editorial was to objectively write the truth, and I thought, "Isn't that what newspapers are supposed to do?"

The next day, apparently in an attempt to prove that he simply occupied a room or two in the mansion, and Edgewater really was offices, Walter invited employees of the *Star,* including its publisher and my friend the reporter, to a luncheon at Edgewater. When they all arrived, Walter apparently had his employees running around various parts of the mansion with their sleeves rolled up, fretting over layers of complicated diagrams spread out on tables and discussing railroad matters.

Walter fooled no one. "It was all very transparent and disingenuous – clearly contrived for our benefit," my friend the reporter told me, laughing at its absurdity. Anyone who walks into Edgewater knows the building exists for one purpose – Walter's home. It's where he lives and entertains his guests.

The publicity resulted in the railroad being required to pay thousands of dollars in property taxes to the Town of Otsego, the Village of Cooperstown, and the Cooperstown School District.

"Proof to me," I thought as I read the article, "that even a small investigation can produce results."

The railroad knew that I had engineered the investigation into the Edgewater property tax issue, and I was glad they knew. I must have been right, or the railroad wouldn't have ultimately paid the thousands of dollars in delinquent property taxes. I just considered my involvement as part of my public duty as a town councilman.

In my view, Walter always did strange things to try to protect or improve his public image. However, what I heard next seemed very strange, given what I knew about Walter from the past.

With great fanfare, Walter got married, and it was announced that he now lived at Edgewater with his wife and two children. Apparently, his new bride came with two children from a previous marriage.

"An interesting new image for Walter," I mused, wondering how Bonfardice and Charette reacted to the news.

After that, the flurry of publicity about Edgewater and Walter Rich quieted down, and Crippen stopped coming to the Town Board meetings.

But Crippen continued his campaign against Sheila Ross and reportedly still had a lot to say about Charles Crist. I spoke with Crist's attorney, my friend Dennis Lynch, who told me that on behalf of Crist, he was going to file an action against the railroad and Walter Rich for damages resulting from Crist's illegal arrest. I told Dennis that I would provide any information I had and help in any way I could.

At the time, The Woodsmen Builders was involved in the biggest project we'd ever had. I received a telephone call one day from a businessman who lived on Long Island. He told me that he was going to build a Corvette museum in the Cooperstown area and, based upon references and reputation, he selected The Woodsmen Builders as the contractor. It seemed almost too good to be true, but it wasn't. A few weeks later, he came to Cooperstown to meet with me and talk about his plans. Less than six months later, I signed a contract in excess of one million dollars to build a 27,000 square foot building I immediately engaged the services of David Bassler, a contractor who had a lot of concrete experience and a sizeable assortment of heavy equipment, to work with Woodsmen Builders on the project.

Construction started in the fall of 1991. From the beginning, the project was a success.

We purchased pre-fabricated package for the steel outer shell of the building, which allowed us to get the building's shell up before winter so during the severe cold weather, we could work inside.

At the same time Bassler and I were building the Corvette museum, we worked out a plan with commissioners in the Fly Creek Fire District to build a new firehouse. Since I was a member of the Fly Creek Volunteer Fire Department, the project was especially meaningful for me. Bassler and I donated all of the manpower, equipment, and supervision for the entire project. It was a labor of love. The firemen volunteered most of the labor, working weekends and holidays. Since both the firehouse and the museum we were building were steel, we were able to coordinate a lot of the work between the two projects. Through all of our efforts, the fire district got a new firehouse for about a third of what it would have otherwise cost.

One day while I was working on the firehouse, Crippen drove up and parked in the triangle in the road opposite the corner where we were building the firehouse. He sat in his car staring at me for about fifteen minutes. Then, with a smirk, he drove away.

"Get a life, Crippen," I thought, although the incident troubled me.

In late summer of 1992, we finished the Corvette Museum, followed a few months later by the firehouse. The two successful projects significantly enhanced our professional reputation and standing in the community. We were being recognized as one of the area's leading contractors.

At the dedication of the firehouse, the Fly Creek Fire District installed a nice brass plaque recognizing those who had contributed to its construction. WOODSMEN BUILDERS, Inc. was first on the list. It was a nice gesture, and I appreciated it. That year, I was selected as Fireman of the Year for the department. I received the same recognition again in 1993. I worked hard for the fire department, both as a fireman and as a builder. To be honored in such a positive way was truly gratifying.

Chapter Seventeen

A man calumniated is doubly injured – first by him who utters the calumny, and then by him who believes it.

— Herodotus (c. 484-c. 425 B.C.) Greek historian,
Artabanus, in *Histories*, bk. 7 (c. 430 B.C.)

Crist's lawsuit against the railroad, Crippen, and Walter was served on the defendants. They weren't pleased. I guess Walter, particularly, was irate about being named a defendant. But, he was president of the railroad, had directed the railroad police in the past to commit illegal acts (meaning me, of course), and as for actions of the railroad police (Crippen), the buck stopped with Walter.

I knew for sure Crippen would be gunning for me now so that he could prove himself to Walter. After all, it was Crippen's actions this time that had resulted in Walter defending himself in another lawsuit. My guard was up and I was cautious every day, wondering when Crippen would strike.

Then, one afternoon in early 1993, it started.

I received a call from Norm Johannsen, another local builder. Although he and I were competitors, we shared a mutual respect.

There was urgency in Johannsen's voice. "I'd like to see you right away."

The following morning, I left the house to meet Johannsen. As I drove past the Bruce Hall Corporation, I saw Crippen standing outside. He looked at me with a big smile on his face as I passed by. When I arrived to meet Johannsen, he handed me a brown envelope he'd received in the mail. With no return address. The envelope contained the same photocopied documents about me that Crist and McGarrity had received.

"I'm giving this package to you because I don't want it and I think you should know about it; I don't believe in this sort of thing," he said.

I thanked Johannsen, took the envelope from him, and walked back to my car, laying the envelope in the passenger seat. As I drove home, I remembered the smile on Crippen's face earlier that morning. At the time, I had wondered what that was about. Now I knew.

At that moment, I absolutely filled with rage, and it took all of the focus I could muster to control myself and drive home. As I drove, I remembered Coccoma's words, "no criminal conduct involved."

"Like hell!" I thought. "Why wouldn't this qualify as aggravated harassment under New York law?" I asked myself, making a mental note to look up that law when I returned home. I couldn't believe it. If Coccoma had done something the first two times this happened, it might have stopped.

Albert, our St. Bernard, was at the door when I got home. Usually a source of comfort, he had no effect on my mood just now and I ignored him. I went into the kitchen where Mary was preparing a pot roast, my favorite cold-weather supper. She turned to me, and then recognized the storm raging within.

"What happened?" she asked, the smile disappearing from her face.

I told her, and she looked at me, wide-eyed and stunned.

"Oh, my God!" she cried, her eyes filling with tears. "What are you going to do?"

"At the very least, I'm calling Dennis Lynch," I said.

It wasn't that I had anything to hide. I had never even had a parking ticket in my whole life. I was not ashamed of the indictments, either, but Crippen took them out of context and didn't relate the whole story, so in his packages, they appeared very sinister.

Then, there was the added twist with the Johannsen package. In it was inserted a "cover sheet" on which The Woodsmen Builders' logo was copied and enlarged on a letter-sized sheet of paper. Below the enlarged logo, someone had typed a very vicious message, cautioning voters to inform themselves about the "echoes" of my past. *It said, I had been a patient in a local psychiatric ward; I had been fired from my position as a police officer with the railroad;And, it questioned: Why my wrongful discharge lawsuit against the railroad had been dismissed; If I had "made a deal" with the courts in Virginia; My credibility and integrity as a public official*

It said a lot of sleazy things designed to denigrate and malign me, and call into question my character and integrity, with the obvious intent to ruin my reputation, ruin my construction business, and embarrass me publicly. It was unadulterated malice at the lowest level. In my mind, it was defamatory and it was libelous.

Less than two days later, I became aware of eight more packages, all the same. The contents were identical to those received by Crist and McGarrity, with the added sordid cover sheet that came in Johannsen's package. All were mailed in brown envelopes with typed mailing labels. None had a return address. Each had postage stamps affixed and obviously dropped in a mailbox. Each was sent with the intent to destroy me.

I started receiving telephone calls from each recipient. All of them wanted me to know, which I appreciated. Some of them were embarrassed to speak with me about it. Each of them was upset.

"What kind of a low-life would do something like this?" many of them commented. Others expressed their hope that whoever it was would get caught.

Although the reactions from those who received packages were sympathetic, it was very difficult to try to provide an explanation and thank them for letting me know.

By the time I was able to sit down with Dennis Lynch, I was trembling with rage.

"There's little doubt in my mind that Crippen is behind this," I declared indignantly. "If we have to, I know we can prove it, especially since Redding, the postal clerk, identified Crippen as mailing the first package to McGarrity."

Dennis talked to me for a long time and then said he would immediately file a lawsuit against Crippen and the railroad.

"Good; maybe that will stop it," I thought.

But, by the next day, I was aware of yet another package. This time it was left on the table of the coffee shop at Taylor's Tower, for anyone to see. A friend of mine saw it and picked it up and brought it to me.

It had become a nightmare. Instead of focusing on work, I was wondering when and where the next package would appear. I also wondered how many people had received them who had not called me. That night, Mary answered the business phone and listened to a mechanical laugh. I knew Crippen owned one of these contraptions when he worked part-time for the village years ago. It was a little plastic box, and at the push of a button, it laughed for several seconds. Over the next few days, we received several more "mechanical laugh" telephone calls. By the time I was able to get the telephone company to install a "trap" on our phone lines, it stopped. Whoever was doing this knew I would attempt to trace the line.

Two days after my friend picked up one of the packages in the coffee shop, five more new packages surfaced. They were apparently now being mailed to my suppliers, my business associates, my friends, my car dealer, the Town Codes officer, the Highway Department and the town clerk. I was livid and Mary was distraught. Even Danny had heard about it in his sixth grade class at school.

Somebody would pay for this someday.

The railroad's smear campaign was spinning out of control. In February, 1992, I wrote a letter to Coccoma alerting him of the situation and suggesting that Walter was "a powerful and dangerous man" who should not be underestimated. I remembered my experience with Walter wanting to plant drugs on a railroad employee, a memory I didn't take lightly. Frankly, I was worried about what Walter might try to do to me.

The packages started showing up all over town. I called Coccoma's office and made an appointment to see him. Something needed to be done. A day or so later, I got a call from Coccoma's secretary telling me the appointment had been cancelled and there was no need to reschedule. No explanation, nothing. Coccoma, the district attorney, was simply ignoring the matter.

The packages kept coming at a rate of two or three a week. The same thing would happen over and over. I would get a call from someone I knew in the community. They would tell me that they had received the package in the mail. Each package was identical, and the sender was now highlighting certain portions of the documents. Each package was sent in cowardly anonymity, the mailing labels all the same. Each package contained eleven pages, and the sender had put obvious effort into the preparation and mailing of each of them.

With virtually no cooperation from the district attorney's office, I contacted the Otsego County Sheriff's office and spoke to Undersheriff Don Mundy. Mundy agreed that something should be done, but said that the sheriff's department couldn't do much without the support of the district attorney, who decided who to prosecute and who not to prosecute.

On May 12, 1993, I hand delivered a letter to Coccoma's office, once again stating my concerns that the smear campaign against me was continuing. I even included one of the packages that someone had received so that he could see for himself that the material was obviously being prepared and sent with malicious intent.

On May 24, 1993, I fired off another letter to Coccoma, complaining that I had not even had the courtesy of a reply from my May 12th letter. I stated that I had provided more than enough information for him to conduct an investigation, and I suggested to him that perhaps the reason I was being ignored was because Mr. Crippen enjoyed special privileges because of his status as a railroad policeman. I further advised Coccoma of the potential damage being done to my business reputation, and I asked him to inform me of his intentions in the matter.

No response.

"If Coccoma doesn't do something pretty quick, I'm going to settle the matter with Crippen in my own way," I finally said to a friend I was talking to one day when I was mad.

I guess my friend took me seriously and went to see Coccoma.

"You'd better do something before the situation escalates any further," my friend told Coccoma. "David's ready to settle this with Crippen himself."

Surprisingly, Coccoma told my friend that he would take action. In the first week of June, Coccoma called me.

"I want your assurance that you will not take the law into your own hands," he said, explaining that he would ask the state police to conduct an investigation.

"That's all I've ever asked for," I said, thanking him and assuring him I'd restrain myself.

Coccoma told me to expect a call from an investigator in the State Bureau of Criminal Investigation.

That same evening, I received a call from Investigator Art Daniels, Bureau of Criminal Investigation, State Police. We made an appointment to meet at state police headquarters for Troop C in Sidney, New York.

I met with Investigator Daniels for an hour or so and explained to him what was going on. Daniels promised me that he would conduct a thorough investigation. He also told me that he would be back in touch with me later that week.

That week ended, as did the following week, with no word from Daniels. Almost two weeks after our initial conversation, Daniels called and asked me to meet him again in Sidney.

When I arrived at Daniels office, Investigator Jim Aloi was present. They told me that Aloi would be taking over the investigation because Daniels was being transferred.

I went through the whole thing again with Aloi. He asked me for copies of documentation that I showed him, and I assured him I would send him copies of everything as soon as I got back to my office.

The following day, I sent Aloi the copies he requested.

I knew Crippen's fingerprints were on file with the Otsego County Sheriff's Office because of his pistol permit, and I was pretty sure that the state police had them too, because of his railroad police commission.

I crossed my fingers, hoping they would now be able to come up with something.

Through June and July, the packages kept coming on a regular basis. We had now recovered over thirty of them, and I continued to wonder how many were out there that I didn't know about.

In August, tourists began to stream in to Cooperstown for the Baseball Hall of Fame weekend and the annual baseball fever was transforming the quaint village. Lawns were becoming parking lots with small-town kids waving hand-scrawled signs hawking day-long parking for an outrageous fee.

The parking lot at Doubleday Field was full of refreshment booths attended by Cooperstown high school kids hoping to sell enough to finance their annual senior school trip. Main Street merchants set out sidewalk tables filled with baseball memorabilia.

The Otesaga Hotel hosted the baseball greats, who relaxed on the adjoining golf course, fans lining its fence along Lake Street and scanning the greens, hoping to catch glimpses of their heroes and get an autograph or two.

Guests at the Otesaga strolled in well-dressed groups down Fair Street and across Main Street to the Hall of Fame. Others, invited to Edgewater, strode over to Walter's hedged enclave, where the big white party tent catered to privileged fans and those whose power or influence could benefit Walter. A large red, white and blue vinyl banner was spread across the hedge by the gate to Edgewater's entrance saying, "Sherwood Boehlert again!" This all-American weekend was the perfect lure for wealthy fans who wanted to rub elbows with VIPs and donate money to Walter's political friend.

At home in Fly Creek, I watched the traffic going up and over the hill toward the Village.

There was no question that the packages were being read, believed and even embellished. The rumors had spread all over town, and not a single day went by that I didn't hear of them. Someone told me they had actually heard that I had killed someone in Virginia and that the federal authorities were after me.

Our business slowed considerably. Some projects we'd expected to do were suddenly cancelled without any reason. When I tried to find out why, no one would call back.

I couldn't defend myself against the rumors or challenge them because most came to me second-hand.

Mary and I were devastated. Everything we had worked so hard for was beginning to crumble.

My oldest son, David, decided to move to Reno, Nevada, to attend the police academy there. We had friends who lived there and could look after him. As much as I hated to see him leave, I encouraged it because I didn't want him here to see all that was happening to us. I was very worried about our future.

I wrote to Coccoma again and told him that I was not aware of any developments from the state police, and that the packages were still being received. I enclosed sections of law that I had researched and outlined in great detail. I specifically noted the section concerning aggravated harassment, a misdemeanor under New York law. Once again, I received no response.

I couldn't understand why Coccoma continued to ignore us and refused to discuss the case with us. I thought perhaps he had formed a negative opinion about me because of the Portsmouth indictments, and that bothered me. So I put together a lot of material, including all of my letters of recommendation from the police and fire departments in Portsmouth, the Cooperstown Police Department, and my military service accomplishments, and sent it to him in hope that he would look at it and see that I had been a victim of circumstances in Portsmouth and had done everything humanly possible to clear my name. Again, I received no response.

Then I wrote a letter to State Police Major Joseph Loszynski at Troop C Headquarters in Sidney, outlining the case and what had happened so far and expressing my concern that the trail Crippen was leaving might go cold. I also described the catastrophic damage from all of this to my business, my reputation, and now my family. I felt I had "turned the other cheek" for the last time.

The frustration was building inside me to a dangerous level. Mary was scared, and I think she had good reason to be. I was scared too, because I did not think I was going to be able to retain control much longer. Our business was at a dead-slow, and, for the first time, we had nothing to do and I had to send men home. Crippen continued to smirk when he saw me, and I reasoned that he was playing with fire. I couldn't take much more.

The next insult was a call from Investigator Aloi, asking me for a list of persons who had received the package to date. I reminded him that I had sent that information to him the day after our meeting, along with the other material that he wanted. I asked him if he had read what I sent, and he replied that he had "been busy, and hadn't had time to look it over."

"Good God," I thought. "Nothing has been done at all; they haven't even looked at all the information I've sent them."

Aloi asked that I send him another list of names, which I took to mean that he had lost the first one. I was furious, but told him I would send it, and I did that very afternoon.

I told Mary that I was concerned about what I might do about all of this. I was just human, and we all have limits. I was far beyond mine, and I knew it. We decided that I would take the motorhome and go away for a few days. It would give me time to think and get away from all that was happening.

Late the next morning, I was on my way to upper New York state, near the Canadian border. I stayed there five days, and did very little other than some sightseeing and riding my bike. I called Mary while I was gone, but there was nothing new to report from home. I felt a little better, but as I headed home again, I could feel my body tighten with stress.

Our business was now just hanging on by a thread and the phone had stopped ringing for the first time since 1985. We heard more and more rumors, and everywhere I went, I saw someone who had seen the package or heard of it. I heard that at a cocktail party hosted by a local doctor, the package of information concerning me was the hot topic of discussion. I believed that, because we often worked for doctors, and had, at least in the past, a good reputation in the medical community.

It had even infiltrated the fire department. Everyone there knew about it, and it became unbearable for me. The stories were now so far-fetched that I had no way of knowing what anyone thought of me.

Finally, I gave up and resigned from the fire department. It was a hard thing to do, because I had invested a lot there, and I received much satisfaction from helping people. I remembered a time when I had saved the life of a choking victim. I felt good for a week after that, but what was happening now overwhelmed me and I could no longer stay.

My term as a member of the town council was ending and I was being pushed to make a decision as to whether to run again in the upcoming November election. With all that I heard about me, there was no way I could face the politics of a campaign and subject myself to more public ridicule, so I decided not to run.

More of what I had worked so hard to attain was slipping away.

A noteworthy incident had occurred at the railroad while all of this was going on. Ron Bonfardice, who had in the past been a victim of Walter Rich's homosexual advances, was now himself accused of sexual harassment at the railroad for some of his actions towards female employees. I heard that he was suspended, and later that he was "gone." I think that would have been an interesting news story – "Bonfardice is accused of sexual harassment, and not long ago, he was the VICTIM of such harassment." Such a news story would be even more interesting if it revealed who it was that had victimized him. As it was, though, he quietly went away. I wonder how much that cost the company.

One day right after I left the fire department, I heard that Coccoma was now saying that Crippen couldn't be prosecuted for aggravated harassment because the packages were not mailed to me, who was supposed to be the aggrieved party. Coccoma apparently interpreted the code to mean that the one receiving such a package would have standing as a complainant, but anyone who did not receive one of the packages would have no such standing.

If that were the case, I felt that I had a solution. I contacted twelve of the people who had received the packages. There were now forty-two that we were aware of, and I picked prominent, well-known businessmen. I asked each one if they would write to Coccoma and indicate that they were "annoyed or alarmed," if, in fact, they were, because this is what the code required of the complainant. In just a few days, the district attorney's office received several letters.

"...I was disgusted with its contents. I have known Mr. Butler for many years and he has always been honest and straightforward with me. If this was done to either annoy me or alarm me, then they succeeded, because it alarms me that there is a person or persons out there that would stoop so low as to do this and it annoys me that they would stick it in my door in the middle of the night."

- Don Olin, Don Olin Realty,
Cooperstown, NY

"The papers in the envelope dealt mostly with Mr. Butler's police career many years ago. My first reaction was to wonder why anyone would think this would interest me. However, the further I read, the more evident it became that this was simply an attempt to discredit him and to especially destroy his character in the eyes of the voters in the Town of Otsego. I find such tactics very distasteful and question the character of whoever put it in the mail."

- David Willsey, Councilman,
Town of Otsego

"Whoever put this package of information together is out to destroy this man, his business, and his family."

- Raymond Bennett,
Oaksville, NY

"I hope that your department can put a stop to this sort of malicious vengeance as I'm sure I would not like this to happen to either of us."

- E.C. Smith, Smith Ford.
Cooperstown, NY

"I was shocked and annoyed to receive such material and I am angry about the manner in which it was delivered. I would hope that prosecution of the person responsible is possible."

- Jim Tongue, Owner, The Cupboard,
Cooperstown, NY

"I was disturbed, upset, and insulted that anyone would mail me this garbage. I received this material this spring in a large plain envelope with no return address and addressed to me as Fly Creek Fire Chief. I would hope that something could be done to stop this aggravation."

- Jim Pernat, Fire Chief
Fly Creek, NY

"To those of us who know Dave, the information in the package did little to cast any doubt as to his integrity. But to those who do not know Dave, I can see how such garbage could be damaging. There is talk of this throughout the area and I would hope that something is being done to find those who are responsible."

- Steve Barringer, Electrician,
Mohawk, NY

"Now that base is covered," I thought, humbled by the enthusiastic response to my request.

Week after week passed, and each time I called Coccoma, my call was ignored; each time I called the state police I would be told that they were under instructions not to discuss the case with me and that any information would have to come from the district attorney. I finally wrote again to Coccoma and told him I had reached the end of my patience and could not predict how I might react under any given situation. Ideas were beginning to enter my mind on how to permanently settle the score with Crippen, and perhaps with Coccoma, too.

"It's no wonder," I thought, "that people go off the deep end out of sheer frustration with a system that clearly doesn't seem to work." The sad part is that it might work, if those responsible did what they were in office to do.

Coccoma finally did call one day, and simply told me that the investigation was secret and he could not talk about it.

"Apparently as victims," I told him, "we're not entitled to any rights at all."

I had an overwhelming urge to go to his office and demand to see him, but I knew, of course, he would refuse, which would, at this point, incite me to conduct for which I'd ultimately be sorry. But maybe it would be a clue to him that I was serious, and I had little more to lose. Besides, as Mary reminded me, I would be providing the railroad something to use against me and, after all this time, I could not let that happen.

The only work The Woodsmen Builders had left was to finish a house we had started a few months earlier. I stayed on the job every day in order to keep busy and exhaust my energy as much as possible so that I could sleep at night. The frustration of an investigation that didn't appear to be happening together with Coccoma's conduct kept me awake most nights. I fought to keep control of myself – on an hour-to-hour basis.

On top of everything else that had happened, the owners of the house The Woodsmen Builders was renovating told me one day that they could not obtain the rest of the financing they had hoped for and, therefore, the construction would have to stop.

There was no sense fighting it any longer; it was over. That was the only work we had, and it had now vanished. With no income to pay the substantial overhead, I had no choice but to close The Woodsmen Builders. With the business gone, Mary and I would have no income. The week of October 11, 1993, was probably the worst week in my life, including my Vietnam tour of duty.

"At least in Vietnam," I thought, "I could fight back."

The constant frustration of the past few months, coupled with having to close the business, was more than I could handle emotionally. As I went through the necessary motions each day, tears often streamed down my face when I was alone. On Monday morning, when the men reported to work, I gave them the news.

"The Woodsmen Builders is closing effective today," I announced. I think they expected it; they had all heard the rumors too, and witnessed the steady decline in work. I felt as though I had let them down, even though I had done everything I could to survive. Until now, I had always been able to generate enough work to keep everyone working, summer and winter. I had provided them with paid holidays, vacation, sick time, and hospitalization benefits – not because I had to, but because I wanted to and because I cared about the people that worked for me. We had been like a family. Now they were unemployed and winter wasn't far away.

I made an inventory of all of my equipment and tools and typed a list to circulate among the employees and other contractors. I assigned a price to each item, usually a fraction of what it might cost new. There was no sense in pricing things too high; it was absolutely necessary that they sell. Mary and I needed the money to survive.

The following day, people were in and out of the shop all day, looking at and buying tools. They were all nice about it, but it was humiliating for me. After the tools were gone, I spent the rest of that day and the next cleaning up our shop building and the adjacent grounds to make it as presentable as possible for a potential buyer. People I knew dropped in from time to time while I was there, and I told the story of why we were closing over and over. I didn't want to talk about it, but some of these people were really concerned. That's the way it is in a small town.

Next, I sold one of our trucks – an expensive piece of equipment to own and maintain. That left one more truck, which I listed in the paper. I was also fortunate to find a buyer for our boat, which I hadn't expected, winter being so close. We took Mary's car to the local dealer, and left it there on consignment. I sold my gun collection, and an all-terrain vehicle that I had used to go woodchuck hunting with Danny.

Our house was on the market, too. This was the second time I was forced to sell my house because of Walter Rich and his railroad. This time, I also lost my business and just about everything I had worked so hard to build.

Dennis Lynch filed a lawsuit against the railroad and George Crippen. I knew that any benefit from that, if at all, would be a long time coming. But I was concerned now and determined to fight.

Finally, one day when I called the state police investigator, he told me that, although he still could not discuss details, he could tell me that they had completed their investigation and would be turning over a final report to the district attorney.

"I think you'll be pleased with the results," he added.

I took that to mean that they had probably been successful finding fingerprints, because that is primarily what they were looking for. I doubted that they would have ever attempted to arrest Crippen on circumstantial evidence, no matter how strong it was. That's politics, especially where the railroad and Walter Rich are concerned.

With fingerprints, I couldn't see any defense for Crippen – especially since the packages were turned over to the state police from different people and at different times. If Crippen's fingerprints were there, then he had been there too; it was as simple as that. And, if Crippen's fingerprints were inside the packages, his fate was sealed. At least that's the way I saw it.

A few days later, I got a call from Marty Ralph, the Otsego County sheriff. Marty told me that the state police had met at his office, and then had gone to Edgewater to question Crippen. They reported back that Crippen had actually turned white with fear, and didn't want to talk beyond simply denying any knowledge of the packages and saying that he wanted his lawyer.

Marty and others in the sheriff's department who had spoken with the state police investigators told me that they had raised many of Crippen's fingerprints from the packages. They said his prints were "plastered" on the various packages. I was elated because I felt there was now no excuse not to arrest him. The sheriff said they should have arrested him right there on the spot, adding that in a routine case involving an average person, they wouldn't have hesitated because all that's needed to make an arrest is probable cause, and there was plenty of probable cause in this instance.

I couldn't acknowledge what I knew, but called Coccoma again to find out where things stood. He wasn't available and he never called me back. Finally, Mary called his office and announced that if Coccoma didn't call her back, she would come to his office and sit there until he spoke with her. That apparently prompted him to call late that afternoon and again tell us that he couldn't talk about the case. He said only that the investigation was complete, and that we could "be assured" that he would do his duty.

"Bullshit," I thought.

As the days passed, word filtered to me through law enforcement friends that the fingerprint evidence was "overwhelming," and the investigators who had handled the case apparently were now confused, too, as to why nothing had happened. That week, a grand jury was sitting in Cooperstown, and a friend who works for the county told me that Crippen's name was on the grand jury's docket. That seemed to explain all of the secrecy. I was now looking forward to hearing of an indictment. But, after three days, the grand jury was canceled, apparently because someone was sick.

I was furious. I knew there was more than enough evidence to indict Crippen, if it was just presented correctly. Grand juries give a lot of weight to the district attorney's aggressiveness and his competence. Unfortunately, I believed, both of those criteria were questionable in this case.

Friends knew of my frustration with the process, and two of them actually called Coccoma to voice their concerns. One was Jim Dow, the County Coroner, and Helen Chetner, an older lady for whom The Woodsmen Builders did some work. Helen told me that she attended the same church as Coccoma. Jim and Helen both called Coccoma to question him about what was being done on the case, and both got the same answer. Coccoma told them that there was "a lack of evidence" to prosecute Crippen. Coccoma wouldn't talk to me, the victim, because the investigation was "secret," but he apparently felt free enough to tell others that he wouldn't prosecute.

"Now, I don't fancy myself a lawyer, nor do I have a formal legal education," I thought, "but I would bet my own life and everything I own (which, unfortunately isn't much right now), that there is more than enough evidence to not just to make an arrest, but to convict as well."

I had studied the case law, too, just in case Crippen was convicted and appealed; and, in my mind, he didn't have a prayer. The evidence appeared to clearly establish that Crippen had violated the code of Aggravated Harassment in the second degree, a misdemeanor crime according to New York State Penal law, with each element of the crime met. It seemed clear to me that Crippen definitely acted "with intent to annoy or alarm," the essential element. His motive seemed very clear and evidence seemed overwhelming. According to my read of the case law, in a case like this involving the distribution of derogatory and damaging communication, a conviction will be affirmed "if the communication served no legitimate purpose."

Now, the matter was no longer on the grand jury docket, and I was outraged. It seemed apparent to me that someone had intimidated Coccoma. The sheriff was angry, too. Crippen should have been arrested weeks ago, and now I wondered if he would be arrested at all. I also wondered if there was one, just one public official anywhere, that was capable of doing his job without allowing himself to be subject to outside influence, and in particular the influence of Walter Rich. I wanted nothing more than that to which I was entitled.

I called Coccoma's office the next day and requested an immediate appointment. I also dropped off a letter to him complaining that his focus seemed to be on finding ways to avoid prosecuting Crippen instead of doing what should be done. I informed him that I knew the elements of the case and I knew about the fingerprints, although I didn't divulge from whom I acquired the fingerprint information. I concluded my letter by telling him that anything less than Mr. Crippen's immediate arrest was, as far as I was concerned, unacceptable. It seemed to me that Coccoma believed his prosecutorial discretion as district attorney allowed him to do whatever he wanted with this case and remain insulated from criticism for failing to do his job. Whatever and whomever had convinced him to close his eyes to the evidence in this case must have held out a pretty plump carrot.

In any event, I made it clear that I wasn't walking away from this. "If you won't do your job, I'll find somebody that will," my letter concluded.

That same afternoon, Coccoma called me and said he would meet with me the next day. I asked him if it we could meet in the morning as I had afternoon plans. He responded that he would call and set up a time. When he called back, he announced that the meeting was set for four o'clock the next afternoon.

"So much for any consideration to us," I thought, disgusted by his lack of courtesy. Of course, he had never shown the slightest concern for us as victims, so I guess I really shouldn't have expected that he would do so now.

Mary and I arrived at the office of the district attorney at four o'clock the following afternoon. When we walked in, I was surprised to see one of Coccoma's deputies and a captain from the state police present for the meeting.

"Looks like a gang-bang to me," I thought as I stood there feeling ambushed.

Coccoma assured us that he had taken an oath, as had his assistant and the state police captain. "I'm going to uphold that oath," he said righteously.

I brought a tape recorder with me to record my conversation with Coccoma, explaining that my purpose was to have an accurate record of our conversation. But Coccoma wouldn't allow it.

I reminded Coccoma that Crippen had also taken an oath, and violated it, quoting the public officers law Crippen offended.

"Look," he said, "no matter what I do in this case, I'm going to get heat from someone."

"Well, then, why don't you simply do the right thing and not worry about outside influence?" I suggested.

Coccoma didn't respond to that, but the captain piped in and told me he thought that the investigators had done an excellent job.

"I can't really make a judgment on that because I have not been able to see the report, or even hear its contents," I responded.

"There is some administrative action that the state police can take," the Captain continued, "after the matter is resolved at other levels."

I asked him if he was referring to Section 88 of the Railroad Law, where it states that "railroad police commissions are issued at the pleasure of the superintendent of state police," reminding him that there was no need to delay revoking Crippen's commission if the evidence was there as I suspected it was. I also reminded him that when I was fired, my railroad police commission was revoked the very next day, notwithstanding that I had never been charged with a crime or afforded any type of hearing at all.

"Do you understand what I'm saying?" I asked.

The captain moved his head a little, indicating that he was listening.

"What a lie," I thought, knowing they were trying to throw me a bone in hopes that I would leave quietly.

"You have a good civil case," Coccoma commented.

"Does he think I'm stupid?" I wondered. "Of course I have a good civil case, but, that has nothing to do with the criminal case," I thought.

"I'm going to have a special prosecutor handle the Crippen case from now on, because a police officer is involved," Coccoma announced.

"Why," I asked. "Where is there a conflict of interest that prevents you from investigating Crippen, policeman or not?"

Coccoma didn't answer.

"Does that mean we will have to wait for another investigation?" I asked.

"No," he responded; "I'm turning the reports over to Richard McVinney, an Oneonta attorney who has been appointed the special prosecutor."

And, that was the end of the meeting. If there were political consequences to Coccoma doing his job in this case, he had most certainly avoided them.

Later, when Mary and I returned home, I learned that the local judge was retiring for health reasons.

"Of course," I reasoned. Knowing that the two seated judges had both been district attorneys before becoming judges, I knew that Coccoma was likely the obvious candidate to succeed the retiring judge – assuming he didn't upset the political apple cart.

Although there was now a new prosecutor, I would not forget Coccoma's performance over the past few months. I made a commitment to myself that some day I would expose him, too.

The following morning, I got a call from Tom Grace, a local reporter for the Oneonta *Daily Star*. I acknowledged that a special prosecutor had been assigned, but was unable, at least for now, to comment. Tom had told me a few days before that a public relations firm hired by the railroad had contacted him to discuss how the story would be printed in the event that Crippen was arrested.

"So much for the big, secret investigation," I thought. Here they were making plans for something that hadn't even happened and was supposed to be a secret.

The following day, I wrote a letter to Richard McVinney, the newly appointed special prosecutor. I introduced myself and outlined some of my concerns about the case and told him that I hoped that the case would be considered in the very near future. We had waited for what now seemed like an eternity and I wanted things to get going. According to the district attorney, everything was complete and all that McVinney had to do was look things over and make his own decision. It all seemed so clear that I couldn't see how he could possibly reach any conclusion other than to prosecute the case.

I sent the letter on a Friday and called McVinney the following Monday morning to see if he had received it. McVinney seemed nice enough on the phone during that first call, but made no commitment other than to say he would be "looking into the matter." I told him again of the extent to which I had been damaged, as had my family and my business, and expressed my concerns about further delays.

That was the last I heard from McVinney until twelve days later when I called his office again. He was busy, so I left a message and asked that he call me back. Late that afternoon, he did return my call and spoke with Mary, telling her that he hadn't had time to look at the Crippen case yet, and that he had just received some case law on the subject from Dennis Lynch, our attorney.

I was puzzled why our attorney had to provide legal research to McVinney, but I was grateful that he did. The case he looked up involved a person who had been charged with aggravated harassment and it had been overturned. The defendant in that case had made a "freedom of speech" claim with regard to his distribution of slanderous material concerning another person. The facts in the case were quite different from those in my case, which Dennis pointed out, and it appeared that case law was on our side.

After McVinney spoke with Mary for a few minutes, he said that he would be in his office the following morning and that I could call him around eight thirty in the morning. At precisely eight thirty the next morning, I called and asked for McVinney. His secretary told me he was on the phone, so I asked that he call me back. I waited at home for his call. Three hours passed, and no call from McVinney. The longer I waited, the angrier I became. I had other things I could have been doing, and I was offended that McVinney apparently lacked the courtesy to call me back. At noon, I typed a letter to McVinney and faxed it to his office. I asked that since he apparently was not interested in talking to me, would he please consider the information in my letter in making whatever decision he might make. I told him that I was aware that Crippen, when questioned by the state police, had denied any knowledge of packages of documents concerning me that had been mailed; yet it now appeared that he was going to make some free speech claim if he was arrested. I asked McVinney how someone could have standing to claim freedom of speech and at the same time deny they ever said anything. I also asked McVinney to call me after he had a chance to read my letter, and I assured him that I would come to his office and meet with him if he wanted. I was hoping he would do that, because I wanted to point out to him that the freedom of speech claim was apparently brought up to the district attorney by the railroad's public relations firm, who had provided a copy of the case law to the newspaper.

At four thirty that afternoon, I finally called McVinney again. His answering machine informed me that his office was closed for the weekend. I cannot even describe the rage that rose within me.

The election was just a few days away. Orrin Higgins was running against Marty Ralph, the incumbent, for the office of sheriff. I learned that the railroad's public relations people had suggested to the newspaper reporter that the possible arrest of Crippen was somehow a political move connected to the sheriff's race. Orrin Higgins was Crippen's deputy at the railroad. The incredible story being concocted was that if Crippen were arrested, it was a ploy by Marty Ralph's campaign to make Higgins look bad.

I had heard a lot of stupid reasoning in my life, but, honestly, this had to take first place for the "bullshit of the year award." How anyone could connect Crippen's actions over the past year to the election and Higgins' candidacy was beyond me.

Chapter Eighteen

Normally a grand jury will indict a ham sandwich if a prosecutor asks it to.

— Anonymous

Mary and I filed for unemployment.

Obviously, with the business closed, we had no income at all and it was going to take some time to get reorganized and find work to support us. Mary worked on reactivating her nursing license, and I was preparing a new resume and writing lots of letters. We thought that the unemployment check would take up the slack in the meantime.

We went together to Oneonta and filled out the applications. No one there was able to give us any information; we were simply told that our application "would be considered." After completing all of the documents, we were told to return in a few days for an interview. Later that week, when we arrived for the interview, we were herded into a room with about fifteen other people. There, as a group, we were instructed on the proper procedures for filling out even more forms and the correct way to call in each week to verify employment status and receive the check. We were told that we would have yet another interview the following day, by telephone, and were instructed to be at home between eleven o'clock in the morning and noon to receive the call. The next day, we got a call from someone who identified himself as our "counselor."

I advised our counselor that we had closed our business and dismissed all of our employees. I also told him that the business had no bank accounts, no insurance, no construction tools or equipment, and no customers – we were no longer "in business." He asked if we had dissolved the corporation, and I replied that I had not, as that in itself was an expensive procedure, requiring further services of our accountant and attorney, and, under the circumstances, we had no money to retain those services. Our counselor then informed me that in order for us, as owners of a corporation, to receive unemployment, we would first have to show three years of continued loss in the business, followed by an official dissolution of our corporation filed with the state."Then you can be considered," he said.

Of course, I couldn't show that The Woodsmen Builders sustained a continued loss for three years because, until my business was recently devastated by Crippen's smear campaign, The Woodsmen Builders was a very successful business.

I wondered why our counselor didn't seem to understand that small businesses like ours could not sustain a three-year loss in revenue and stay in business. "So, how would it be possible to show that?" I asked.

Our counselor had no answer.

Then I explained to our "counselor" that I was forty-eight years old, and, although I had never in my life taken a penny of unemployment, as a businessman, I had paid into the system for each one of my corporation's employees, including Mary and I, as evidenced on each employee's paycheck. I asked the man where that money went, and he said "into the system," adding that we had no claim to it.

None of what I said mattered to him in the least.

"So much for the system; no wonder the last interview is conducted by telephone," I thought. I was, again, frustrated beyond belief. "It's no wonder that we constantly hear that New York is not the place to own a business."

A few days later, we got our "official notice" that our request for unemployment benefits was denied. I was becoming more bitter by the moment.

In November's election, Higgins lost by almost a three-to-two ratio. I was glad that Marty was re-elected, and glad that Higgins' defeat could not be blamed on me.

Late in the afternoon, on the day following the election, we had still not heard a word from Special Prosecutor McVinney, so I called his office again. He came on the line and said, "Yes?" as if he had no idea why I was calling. I asked if we would have the opportunity to meet this week, and he replied "probably not; maybe next week." I told him that I had to go out of town and that I had re-scheduled my trip twice in order to be available to meet with him.

"Hang on," he said and then and put me on hold. A minute later, his secretary came on the line and asked if the following afternoon at one thirty was okay.

"Yes," I replied, and asked her if McVinney was coming back on the line.

"No," she answered. "He'll see you tomorrow." Then she hung up.

"How rude," I thought, believing that McVinney should have at least had the common courtesy to come back on the line to finish our conversation after his secretary scheduled the appointment. But, then, we hadn't been shown a display of courtesy from anyone yet, so I guess my expectations of McVinney were too high. I had no idea what to expect with regard to our meeting with him in Oneonta the following day.

Mary and I drove to Oneonta early so we could have lunch before meeting with McVinney. At a little after one, we located McVinney's office and went in. We waited a few minutes and then he came out, introduced himself, and escorted us to his office. He was about thirty to thirty-five years old and seemed friendly. McVinney explained to us that he planned to take the case to the grand jury on December 8th. December 8th was my birthday, and I thought, "What a great birthday present!"

McVinney explained to us the four options that would be available to the grand jury after they heard all of the evidence.

"They can either indict; order a 'Prosecutor's Information,' leading to an arraignment; not indict; or initiate a further investigation of their own," he said, and added, "Crippen will be subpoenaed and will have to testify with no immunity from prosecution. The DuPont case, may well have an effect, because if Crippen admits that he sent all of those packages, he'll likely be protected by First Amendment free speech rights."

I didn't like that, and said, "His rights? What about mine?"

McVinney answered that the courts have dismissed similar cases on those grounds when the information published to others involves a public official. "Public officials are inherently less immune to the distribution of derogatory information about them than are private citizens," McVinney explained.

I was considered a public official because of my position as an elected member of the town board.

"Remember, I wasn't a public official when the first package was sent to McGarrity at the *Times* in 1987," I reminded McVinney.

"Yes, but the statute of limitations on that mailing would now be expired," he responded.

I was dumbfounded.

The whole system just continued to work against me.

"What about his intent?" I asked, protesting vigorously that Crippen never intended to be exercising political free speech when he engaged in his smear campaign against me. "His intent was simply to ruin me, and it worked."

"By the way," I added, "how can he claim he was exercising political free speech when he denies having sent the packages?"

McVinney said that if he denied it to the grand jury, he would probably be indicted for aggravated harassment and perjury, for lying to a grand jury.

That was somewhat encouraging, but McVinney then added, "Crippen's lawyer would be crazy to advise him to continue to deny it."

I reminded McVinney that Crippen had denied any involvement and said knew nothing of any mailing when the state police questioned him. "Wouldn't he effectively be admitting that he lied to the state police?" I asked.

"If nothing else, at least if Crippen contradicts his statements to the state police by now admitting he sent the packages and claiming 'free speech,' his contradictory assertions can perhaps be used to impeach his veracity in future civil proceedings related to my lawsuit," I thought, deciding not to argue with McVinney. "On the other hand," I continued my thought process, "if we're lucky, Crippen will continue to deny any knowledge of who mailed the packages and the grand jury will indict him."

The state police report, I learned, indicated that of eleven packages submitted for analysis, six had Crippen's fingerprints all over them. That was very good news, and I could not imagine how he could defend himself against that. I also found out that Crippen now knew about the fingerprints, and I enjoyed the thought that the son-of-a-bitch would have some sleepless nights worrying about it.

McVinney told us that another Oneonta attorney had joined Crippen's legal team. Otto Rothermel was a lawyer in the same building McVinney was in. Rothermel had told McVinney that Crippen said, "I didn't do it, but I know who did." I knew that was just another of Crippen's lies and a clear indication that he was beginning to sweat. After all, who else could have done it? How was it that his fingerprints were all over most the packages? Who else would have known to mail it to Crist? What about the information from Tom Redding at the post office? What explains the fact that since the day Crippen was questioned by the state police, not a single new package appeared?

I suspect he may have had some help, but I was convinced that he was the principal in this thing, the one who obtained the information and went through the trouble of putting it all together.

We were with McVinney for about two hours. All in all, I had rather a good impression of him and came away with the feeling that he might give us a fair shake, but I wanted to wait and see what developed in the next month, keeping my fingers crossed with regard to the grand jury. I was all too aware of how much depends on how the prosecutor presents a case to a grand jury. Grand juries generally accommodate prosecutors. But, that works both ways. If the prosecutor doesn't want a defendant indicted, it's a good bet that he won't be.

My final questions to Special Prosecutor McVinney concerned Crippen's railroad police commission. I explained to McVinney that Crippen's commission was issued by, and could be revoked at the pleasure of, the superintendent of state police. McVinney said that he didn't have jurisdiction in that area and didn't know who did. I told him I would write a letter to the superintendent and give McVinney a copy, which seemed okay with him.

When we concluded our meeting, McVinney told me to call him "anytime," and even gave me his home phone number, a gesture that made me feel much better about the whole thing.

If the case law did prevent criminal prosecution – as stupid and unfair as that sounded to me – I could understand. But, it seemed to me that by admitting he did it, Crippen would be subjecting himself and the railroad to serious civil liability.

"I don't care how we win, I said to Mary," "as long as we win."

The next morning I wrote a letter to the state police superintendent and asked that "appropriate action" be taken with regard to Crippen's police commission. I outlined the whole case, including the information in the state police report, pointing out that Crippen had committed the act, regardless of the free speech issue. "In mailing out confidential records," I stated, "Crippen violated his oath and sections of the Public Officers Law that pertained to the appointment of Railroad policemen." I enclosed copies of the pertinent law. Believing that I had made a good case for Crippen's commission to be revoked, I sent the letter.

That afternoon, I saw Sheriff Marty Ralph. He asked me to write him a letter expressing my concerns about Crippen, as he was going to write a letter to the Superintendent, too, requesting that Crippen's commission be revoked. I wrote a letter to Sheriff Ralph similar to my letter to the state police superintendent, but added that I was concerned for my safety and the safety of my family. I knew Crippen to be a very vindictive individual and he now knew about the fingerprints, explaining that Crippen was caught and he knew it.

Crippen really did worry me, and I carried my own pistol with me when I was around home. At this point, I had done all I could do, so I returned my attention to the lawsuit Dennis Lynch filed against Crippen and the railroad when the big flurry of mailings had begun around the first of the year.

The lawsuit didn't stop the mailings. In fact, after the lawsuit was filed, the mailings intensified.

Rather than file an answer to the complaint, the railroad filed a motion to dismiss the case, stating that we had "failed to state a proper cause of action," and we suffered another setback.

A state judge in Norwich heard the motion and, ruling in favor of the railroad, dismissed the case. I was shocked. Once again, not one piece of evidence or one word of testimony had been presented.

Several members of the railroad's board of directors were Norwich businessmen and friends of Walter Rich. I was very suspicious. It seemed clear to me that Walter was using all of his big guns to fight me. And he had the resources to do it. Litigation is expensive – for both sides – and, unlike me, Walter had unlimited funds at his disposal. His apparent strategy was to fight us with technicalities, staying away from evidence and the actual facts of the case. I didn't blame him; if I were he, I wouldn't want a fair hearing of the facts either.

Dennis appealed the dismissal to the higher court in Albany, and the appeal was scheduled to be heard in February, 1994. Dennis felt that there was no logic to the dismissal and believed it was contrary to the law.

"I'm confident the decision will be overturned," he told us.

"I hope he's right so that the case can eventually be decided on its merits," I thought. Mary and I knew it would be a long fight, and we took every day one at a time. We vowed to not give up, no matter what happened.

In the meantime, I sorted through the facts of our case and found two that were interesting: The railroad claimed that, "they had received a package, too." The date they "received" their package was right after the lawsuit against them was filed.

Crippen must have thought that mailing one of the packages to the railroad would shift suspicion to someone else, apparently not counting on the state police finding his fingerprints all over the packages.

With nothing more to do but wait for the Grand Jury to convene in January and our appeal to be heard in February, I made plans to join my friend, Jim Dow, on a trip to Florida. Jim had to take care of some business in Florida and asked me if I wanted to go along. He knew I was close to the burnout point, and I think he was trying to help me.

A few days later, Jim and I left for Ormond Beach, Florida, just north of Daytona, where Jim had a lovely house with a pool, a spa, and tranquility. I needed the peace and quiet. We stayed for about ten days, puttering around the house fixing a few things; but, for the most part, we just relaxed.

While in Florida, I spent some time looking for employment, at least on a temporary basis for the winter. There was obviously nothing left for me in Cooperstown, and Mary and I had decided that when we were able to sell the house, we would leave the area. Housing in Florida, at least in the Ormond Beach area, was cheaper than in Cooperstown, and the winter climate was much more hospitable. I tried to approach it as an adventure for us and focus on the bright side, but the reason we had to leave our home in Cooperstown disturbed me.

After my little respite, I returned home somewhat encouraged that a move to Florida was the right thing to do. Mary and I talked about it and decided to explore the idea. We sent for newspapers from the area and wrote letters to potential employers and real estate companies.

David and Don were coming home for Christmas and the holidays, and I wanted us to enjoy them together in Cooperstown's winter wonderland. So we temporarily abandoned our search and enjoyed a lovely family Christmas season.

But, by January, we had decided that I would leave Cooperstown for the balance of the winter to find work and a new home in Florida so that when our house sold, we'd have a plan in place. We tried to protect Danny from the harsh reality, knowing that our talk of moving upset him. He was a kid and looked at things from a kid's perspective. He was happy at Cooperstown Central School and doing quite well. He loved to play baseball and enjoyed being on the Little League and All-Star teams. He had a lot of friends in Cooperstown.

I remembered how painful it was for me as a child to be taken from my beloved Cooperstown and transplanted to Florida, and although I could accept the ultimate consequences of the victimization I had experienced, it broke my heart to see my son suffer because of it. It made me hate Walter Rich and his corrupt system even more.

Each day I prayed for something favorable to happen for us.

Chapter Nineteen

"It warms the very sickness in my heart,
That I shall live and tell him to his teeth,
"Thus diddest thou."

— Shakespeare
Hamlet, IV, 7 (1600-1601)

When I returned home from the Florida trip, a letter from the Superintendent of State Police was waiting for me. I ripped it open, hoping for good news; but the letter was short and not so sweet.

"Your letter regarding Mr. Crippen's police commission as been received. Please be advised that this office will take no action on the matter while it is pending before the grand jury."

"What?" I shouted in disbelief. "What the grand jury is looking at has nothing to do with the conditions of Crippen's railroad police commission!"

"I hope he doesn't just think that his letter is going to be the end of it," I thought. Annoyed, I threw the letter on my desk.

December 8th was just a week away, so I settled in to wait and see what the grand jury would do. Sitting in my living room one evening, I picked up a newspaper article that I had clipped and read it again in disgust. "Walter Rich has been named to the State Transportation Safety Board...Senator James Seward said the appointment was fitting because transportation safety and Walter Rich are synonymous."

I felt like throwing up.

As I sat there, I reflected on my perspective of the events that significantly altered my life over the last several years. *I had worked for the railroad for a little over four years as a police officer. To feed his insatiable greed, Walter Rich, the president of the railroad, had made affirmative decisions that jeopardized railroad safety and put innocent lives at risk. As a result of one of those decisions by Walter Rich, two innocent people were killed by the railroad, and I was fired for refusing to lie to protect Walter Rich. I had nothing to gain and everything to lose by acting with integrity. Challenging Walter was tantamount to economic and professional suicide, but I had believed that the system I had sworn to uphold as a police officer would protect me. For the almost ten years since then, I had worked within the system to pursue justice. For the almost ten years since then, Walter, his henchmen, and his political cronies have worked zealously to destroy me. The system had not only failed me, it had succumbed to the insidious corruption that allowed Walter Rich and his unscrupulous henchmen to succeed.*

On December 8th, the day the grand jury was to convene, I would be forty-nine years old. I wondered what I was going to do. I had started over once, after I was fired, and successfully rebuilt my life. Now I had lost everything. There was nothing left for me in Cooperstown, but how was I to just pick up and start over someplace else? Everything I needed to start over was gone, including the spirit to survive.

I had lost faith in the lawsuit, the legal system, and the judicial system. I was bitter, and I believed I had a right to be.

On December 6th, two days before the grand jury was scheduled to convene, I received a telephone call from Special Prosecutor McVinney that extinguished the last small ray of hope.

"The grand jury date has been rescheduled to December 16th," McVinney said unconcerned, and then added, "Do you mind?"

"It doesn't appear to matter whether I mind or not," I responded. "I suppose I can live with it if the delay is for a positive reason."

"After all," I thought, "what's one more week?"

McVinney told me that he needed the additional time to contact some of the people who had received the packages.

Apparently, McVinney had done little, if anything, to prepare for the grand jury even though the case had been turned over to him about eight weeks ago on October 14th. Coccoma had told us that the investigation was complete. Any questions would probably have been answered in the state police report, which McVinney now had. If there was other information that he needed, he had eight weeks to gather it. There was little I could say about the delay, but I did ask to keep a previously scheduled December 7th meeting with McVinney.

On the morning of December 7th, Mary and I arrived on time at McVinney's office for our ten o'clock meeting. His secretary informed us that he was not there, but would return in about twenty minutes. Mary and I left and returned at eleven o'clock. We were ushered in to McVinney's office.

McVinney talked with us again about Crippen's political free speech rights and showed us a letter that he had received from Otto Rothermel, Crippen's lawyer. The letter stated that Crippen "had a right" to say these things about me and threatened legal action against McVinney if charges were brought against Crippen. The letter stated, "Any criminal action taken against George Crippen would be grounds for a civil rights action for malicious and frivolous prosecution in violation of Mr. Crippen's rights under the constitution." That last statement went through me like a knife.

"His rights? What about mine?"

The last paragraph of the letter said, "In the name of justice, we request that you not bring any charges against George Crippen before the grand jury."

"In the name of justice?" It was the most outrageous thing I had seen so far.

It appeared that McVinney was beginning to agree with all of this, and I was starting to feel like he was setting us up for the fall.

I don't believe that retaining Rothermel to represent Crippen was a mere coincidence. The strategy behind that was pretty obvious to me. Rothermel wasn't a renowned civil rights attorney or even an esteemed criminal defense attorney. He was just an average lawyer who also served as the local public defender. But he was cozy with McVinney, the special prosecutor. In fact, his office was right next door to McVinney's.

Mary and I left the meeting with McVinney feeling spiritless. Before we left, McVinney told me to be at the grand jury room at the county courthouse at nine o'clock in the morning on the 16th of December.

I clung to the hope that something positive might happen on the 16th. At least it was still going to the grand jury, and Crippen continued to deny sending anything to anyone.

It was beyond me how someone could claim free speech protection while denying he ever did anything that amounted to "speech."

The night of December 8, 1993, was my last meeting as a councilman on the Town of Otsego Board. When the meeting ended, I came away with a feeling of emptiness, although I believed that during my four years as a councilman, I had made a contribution to my community. I had intended to run again, and I think I might have been re-elected if all that had happened had not happened. It didn't seem fair.

The following morning, a friend of mine in the local court system called and told me that the grand jury had been dismissed and that a new grand jury would be called on January 3, 1994.

"That can't be true," I said, "because I'm scheduled to appear on December 16th." Nonetheless, it was confirmed; the grand jury had been dismissed. I couldn't believe what I was hearing. "There must be a mistake," I thought. I was numb.

"What now?" I wondered. I called McVinney's office and spoke with him. He said he didn't know anything about it, and suggested that it might be a communication problem between him and Coccoma.

"I'll check and get back to you later today," he said. The day ended, and I heard nothing from McVinney.

On Friday, December 10th, I called McVinney's office again and told his secretary that I wanted to confirm the day that I was to appear before the grand jury.

"I need to know today," I said, not wanting to go into the weekend without that confirmation.

She said she would check with McVinney and call me back. I waited all day and heard nothing from McVinney's office. At four thirty in the afternoon, I called again and asked to speak with McVinney. He came on the line and told me that he hadn't been able to confirm anything yet, but commented, "It just might be in January, after all."

"What now?" I asked, feeling the rage well inside me. "How long do we have to wait? It's been one delay after another." If I had not been living through this, I wouldn't have believed it. It was a simple enough case with some pretty convincing evidence. For several months, just about nothing had been done. After my case started, the World Trade Center had been bombed, the crime investigated, arrests made, and criminal trials begun. But, my case remained in limbo. Something was really wrong here.

McVinney now said that he wanted to talk with someone from the court in Portsmouth, Virginia, to see who, if anyone had access to the records about me that had been mailed in the packages. He told us that he had checked with the police department there and had been told that no one has access to those records except the person involved (me) and then only with a notarized letter of request, which is exactly how I requested my records from Portsmouth when I applied for the railroad job. I knew that the court had the same policy. Those records were not public information.

What now really infuriated me was that I had signed a release many months ago for the state police to check on this very same information. Again, it was plain that nothing had been done. I wondered what difference it made anyway. Even if the information was accessible, it was Crippen's fingerprints that were all over it. We know that he had access to the information, regardless of who else might have seen it. Not only that; Crippen also had motive and he was identified by the postal clerk in Cooperstown as the person who mailed the first package to McGarrity at *The New York Times*.

McVinney sounded peculiar and a little evasive.

"Someone's getting to him," I thought, wondering who that might be. It was the same feeling I had with Coccoma. McVinney's focus seemed to be changing and it appeared that he was now looking to find ways to not prosecute this case.

My stress level was approaching the danger point again.

McVinney ended our conversation telling me that he would get back to me "next week, after I see where we're going with this thing."

"Another weekend wondering if there would ever be any justice," I thought, seething with anger towards the whole frustrating mess.

Monday, December 13th, came and went without word from McVinney. Officially, the last instruction I had from him was to be at the grand jury room on

December 16th at nine o'clock in the morning. I decided not to call him and just wait to see what he did.

Late that evening, Tom Grace, the local reporter for the Oneonta *Daily Star*, called me.

"I checked on the status of the Grand Jury," he said. "I was told that it had been dismissed and would not be called back; a new Grand Jury will be convened on January 3rd."

That was the same information that I had heard.

Tom agreed with me that something was wrong here, and I was being shown very little consideration, which was nothing new.

"They all do whatever they please with no consideration for how all of this has affected my life and that of my family," I groused. "They're apparently answerable to no one."

I promised myself that sooner or later, I would change that. "Everyone is accountable, at some point," I said.

At the end of each day, I found some peace detailing the latest events and my feelings in the journal I kept as an ongoing record of this nightmare, believing that some day my journal would be instrumental in exposing the cesspool of corruption that foiled the justice to which I was certainly entitled.

I wrote another letter to the superintendent of state police and sent it certified mail. I told him that I had exhausted my patience with receiving what I felt was a brush-off from the state police administration. I enclosed copies of my recent letters to state police officials and the responses (if any) that I received. I made it clear that the case might or might not go before the grand jury, but in any event, that had nothing to do with the fact that Crippen had violated his oath and the Public Officer's Law. I requested once again to meet with him or his representative, and informed him that if I did not receive this courtesy, I would take the whole matter to the media, and he could justify his actions to them. The media was one of the few options I had left, and I had every intention of acting on that option.

During the second week of December, David and Don came home for the Christmas holidays. Don had time off from work, but would have to return to Portsmouth before Christmas, so we made plans to celebrate Christmas Day a week early. David was freshly graduated from the Reno, Nevada, Police Academy and was home for three weeks. It was wonderful for us all to be together again. I tried to put the uncertainty of the future out of my mind while they were home.

David and Don both asked me if things would settle down after the grand jury met on December 16th. Even Danny was aware that something was going to happen on that date because he heard about it in school. I had no answer for my sons; I had no way of knowing from day to day what was going to happen, and I had no way of assuring them that things would work out okay.

David and Don were both beginning careers in law enforcement and had to rely on the system in just about everything they would do. I was worried about the miserable example they were witnessing of how the system works. In light of what was happening to me, I wondered what they were learning about the values I had always tried to instill in them. It seemed pretty clear that power, money and influence could corrupt the system.

I heard from Tom Grace again on Tuesday, December 14th. He told me that he had received a couple of phone calls; one from the railroad's public relations firm, and one from Otto Rothermel, Crippen's new lawyer. They both told Tom that my case was "frivolous bullshit."

It was interesting to me that before the November election, the railroad's public relations firm had told Tom that the case was about politics in the sheriff's race; and now that the sheriff's race was over, they were advancing a different theory. Obviously, Rothermel would say whatever he believed might work to prevent a prosecution.

At nine o'clock on the morning of December 16, 1993, Mary and I went to the grand jury room in the county courthouse. When we arrived, the building was virtually empty. We asked the court clerk if the grand jury was to meet that day.

"No," she said, "they've been dismissed; a new grand jury will be convened on January 3rd."

I stood there for a minute and stared at her, trying to suppress what I wanted to say. It wasn't her fault. My body was trembling with rage as we left the building and it worried me. Each time something like this added insult to injury, the rage grew. I wondered what my limits were, and what I would do when I had reached them.

When I got home, I called McVinney and told him that I had just been to the grand jury room and that no one was there.

"I know," he said; "they won't reconvene until January."

"No one told me," I said.

"I thought you knew," he responded.

"The last I heard from you was that 'it might go in January,' but you said you'd let us know; I never heard from you."

"January's better anyway," he said.

"For whom?" I asked.

"For me and the state police investigation," he answered, adding, "I still need to talk to them, and I haven't decided yet what direction to go on this."

I was so angry I could barely restrain myself. I asked him if I could have a copy of the state police report.

"I don't see why not," he said, "but I'll ask the state police."

"In the past, the state police have always referred me to the prosecutor when I've asked for anything," I reminded him.

"Yes, but I still feel that I should ask them first," he balked, and I knew then that we'd never get a copy.

McVinney said that the grand jury would meet "about the second week of January" to consider the case, but wouldn't confirm what his goal would be. Our conversation was over.

This was the third time that the grand jury had been cancelled, once by Coccoma and now twice by McVinney. One thing was abundantly clear to me – no one gave a damn about me and my family. As naive as it sounded, I told Mary that I still expected the pendulum to swing the other way, and that sooner or later, this whole thing would be exposed. I opened my journal and began writing.

Apparently, when District Attorney Coccomas first authorized the state police investigation, he did so simply as a gesture to pacify me and likely believed that determining who was responsible for mailing the anonymous packages would be a difficult at best, but more likely impossible. I think he was counting on being able to tell me that the investigation reached a dead end with no convincing evidence. But, then suddenly the state police discovered some very convincing evidence – the fingerprints – and I think Coccoma was taken aback. At that point, everyone, including the state police investigators, expected Crippen's arrest, but that never happened because, according to Coccoma, I had not personally received one of the packages, so he could not prosecute. That's when he received letters from those who had received packages. But still Coccoma resisted, saying there wasn't enough evidence. When he finally figured out that I had done my homework, he raised the "freedom of speech" issue and threw the case to a special prosecutor, insulating himself from me and the political heat he told us he was getting.

Then, when McVinney first got the case, he pretty much ignored me for the first few weeks, in spite of the fact that he knew the case had been dragging on for months. When we finally did meet, I thought at first that he was sincere, and might give me a fair shake. Then we learned about his cozy relationship with Rothermel and he started to suggest that the free speech issue would prevent prosecution without even discussing the issue of "malicious intent."

His next attempt to convince us that there might not be a case was the letter from Rothermel, threatening McVinney with federal civil action. Dennis had responded to the letter, and McVinney didn't bring it up again. Then he said he wanted to talk to the central files division of the Portsmouth Police Department to see who might have access to the documents regarding me. Again, he was stopped, because no one other than me had a right to have access to this material. He had stated that he would check the courts too, but I don't think he ever did, and I imagine he would have received the same answer. Now, he was wondering "which direction" he should take.

With each delay, the trail was getting colder. To my knowledge, none of the witnesses had ever been contacted by anyone.

"Some investigation," I thought.

The whole system was working against us, but we had a good case in spite of them. They knew it, and I would make sure that they knew that I knew it. I would also make sure they understood that I was a problem that was not going to go away.

Then it occurred to me that it wasn't long until the statute of limitations would expire on the first packages that were mailed and, if that happened, the matter would never go to a grand jury.

Maybe that was their plan.

Chapter Twenty

"The torment of human frustration, whatever its immediate cause, is the knowledge that the self is in prison, its vital force and "mangled mind" leaking away in lonely, wasteful self-conflict."

— Elizabeth Drew (1887-1965)
Anglo-American author, critic

By December 1993, I was living in a world of stress and anger. I tried to clear my head, to decide what to do next. Late on the afternoon of the 16th, I called the state police and spoke with Investigator Aloi. I asked him if he objected to my having the fingerprint report. As usual, he said it was up to the special prosecutor, and that he was not at liberty to discuss the case. He did say that he had no particular objection, as long as it was okay with McVinney. I called McVinney's office back and left a message that I had checked with Aloi, and I wanted to arrange to pick up the report the next day. No one returned my call, so I waited until the morning of the 17th and called again. This time, McVinney said I could pick it up at his office that afternoon at three o'clock.

My son, David, and I drove to Oneonta that afternoon, and arrived at McVinney's office promptly at three o'clock. When I told the secretary I was there to pick up some papers, she looked confused and said that Mr. McVinney was not there and had not left anything for me to pick up.

"Can you come back?" she asked.

"No, I can't. I made an appointment to pick this up, and it would be very inconvenient for me to come back."

Then she told me that she didn't know where to find the information.

"I do," I volunteered, and told her it was on a table in McVinney's office.

She started for the office, and I followed. On a table was a file with my name on it. She said, "I don't even know what that report looks like." And again, I was helpful and pointed it out to her. She hesitated, and I reminded her again that McVinney said that I could have the report, and even gave me a time to pick it up. Finally, she made a copy and gave it to me. At last, I had proof of Crippen's involvement. I was sure that would be a big plus for the civil case, regardless of his defense on the criminal charges.

When I returned home, I read every detail in the report, noting that it was completed and notarized on August 12, 1993.

"That's interesting," I thought; "When I met with Coccoma on October 14th, he told me that the report had "just been completed," giving no indication that it had been around for a couple of months.

According to the report, the state police made sixteen positive matches with Crippen's fingerprints. Several packages had been submitted to the state police for analysis, and it sure looked like they had Crippen locked down cold. The last package that was tested was one that one of my employees had received. He had been expecting it, and when it came, he gave it to me unopened. I had hand-carried it to the state police laboratory. Of the five fingerprints that the state police raised on that envelope that were suitable for identification, four were Crippen's.

Later, I wrote yet another letter to McVinney, and told him that I was concerned by the delay again in the case and the casual attitude with which it was being handled. I also informed him that I was concerned that politics seemed to be influencing Coccoma's decisions in the case. I didn't say anything negative about McVinney himself, but I wanted him to know that I was willing and able to speak out about this case, regardless of the politics. But, I doubted my concerns had any effect on McVinney.

"At least he gave me a copy of the fingerprint report," I conceded.

After a few days, I contemplated going to the press, thinking the many delays in this case were newsworthy and justifying them to the media would be difficult. However, as much as I wanted to expose all of this publicly, I decided to wait until after the grand jury so that I couldn't be accused of "trying the case in the papers." Besides, the grand jury indictment would make a much more interesting news story.

On the personal economic side, things were looking pretty bleak for Mary and me. The approaching Christmas holidays made that reality even more difficult. I was doing everything possible to pay our bills and survive, but I knew it was just a matter of time until our money and our credit ran out. If the shop building sold, things might be easier, but with winter now upon us, that prospect didn't look good. I was looking for any kind of work I could get, even on a temporary basis, but I was having no luck finding anything. Jobs are scarce around Cooperstown in the winter. Silently, I wondered how we would survive. So did Mary.

Dennis seemed frustrated with our civil case. We were fighting a company that essentially had access to unlimited funds to litigate. I didn't; and Dennis and I both knew the railroad and its attorneys would exploit that weakness.

"Don't put all of your eggs in one basket," Dennis would cautiously advise me, suggesting that I should pursue options other than just the lawsuit to get my life moving forward again. Dennis had always been a good friend, and I know he was concerned. The constant delays in the case were a strain on both of us, but they particularly frustrated me because I had so much at stake.

I'm sure Dennis tired of my frequent calls to his office and the less frequent calls to his home; after all, he had other cases and priorities, too. But the case was all I could think about. When I realized that the case was straining our friendship, I started to look for another attorney to handle the case. I didn't want to risk losing Dennis as a friend.

The case gripped my every conscious moment, and I was zealous in my efforts to find a way to move it forward. I called the American Civil Liberties Union, thinking they might take an interest in the case since a police officer was involved and evidence was being suppressed. They never called back. I contacted the producers of the television program "Case Closed." I never heard back from them.

At Thanksgiving, Mary's brother, who lived in Albany, recommended a friend of his who was a lawyer.

"Christopher Rutnik," he said, "went to school with me; and, he was assistant district attorney in the Albany area for several years."

Three days before Christmas, I called Rutnik.

"It appears that your legs have been kicked out from under you," he said after I explained the case to him. "Your case has potential," he said, "and it appears rife with political corruption. It's time to fight back."

It was the reaction I needed to hear. We agreed to meet at his office on December 30, 1993.

Our first impression of Rutnik when we met with him on the 30th was very favorable. Mary and I both liked him, and he seemed extremely knowledgeable. He was also expensive.

"I'll need a $5,000 retainer to take the case," he told us.

"I was hoping you'd consider taking the case on a contingency," I responded.

"I'd want a third of any recovery," he said, "but, I still need $5,000 up-front."

Obviously, I didn't have that kind of money.

"I can probably find $2,500 to get things started; then, when the shop sells, I can pay you the balance," I offered. It was about all the money we had left in the world.

"$2,500 will handle the pending appeal," he said. "I'll need the balance to proceed with the case after that."

Rutnik told us he would do some research and argue the appeal in February. "I think we have a pretty good chance of success," he offered as encouragement.

I gave him copies of everything Dennis had done so far, and authorized him to notify Dennis that he was taking over the case. I felt guilty doing that, but I also knew that, with so much at stake, I would be very demanding in the coming months, and I just didn't want to risk ruining our friendship over the case. I hoped I hadn't burned an important bridge.

That night, I wrote a personal letter to Dennis to explain my feelings about not wanting to risk jeopardizing our friendship and to advise him that we were changing lawyers. A few days later, I got a letter back from Dennis acknowledging the change and telling me that he understood. I hoped he did.

Before leaving Rutnik's office, we made an appointment to meet with him on January 6th to deliver the retainer check to him.

In the meantime, January 3rd arrived and a new grand jury was seated. I didn't hear a word from anyone. That didn't surprise me; I would just wait and see what happened.

On January 6th, I handed to Rutnik a check for the $2,500 I had scraped from the bottom of our financial barrel. I didn't have a clue how we were going to survive; I only knew I had to fight this battle.

"You need to understand that it's going to be a long and bitter fight," Rutnik warned.

Mary and I drove home that night in a snow storm, overcome with worry about our future. Neither of us said a word.

On January 7, 1994, I finally got a call from Special Prosecutor McVinney informing me the grand jury was now scheduled for January 26.

"Before then," he said, "I'll meet with and question each of the witnesses to pin them down on their stories so they can't come into the grand jury on the 26th and change their answers." I was cautiously optimistic. My experience with McVinney so far was that he said a lot of things but had done very little. As yet, no witness had been questioned. All I could do was wait and see what happened.

On January 12th, I got a letter from Lt. Col. Bennett at state police headquarters responding to my latest letter concerning Crippen. The letter advised me that it was the opinion of the state police legal counsel that Crippen was "not a public servant" because he was paid by a private corporation.

"He's dead wrong," I said, and rolled a sheet of paper into my typewriter. "Have your legal counsel look up the Criminal Procedure Law and he will then see that Mr. Crippen, as a police officer commissioned by the state, signed an oath that subjects him to the public servant's code of ethics," I typed in response to Bennett's letter and mailed it off.

In the very early hours of the morning of January 13, 1994, our phone rang, jolting us awake. Mary answered. It was our son, David, calling from Reno, Nevada. By the tone of Mary's voice, I knew something was very wrong.

"Oh my God, is he dead?" She cried. I jumped out of bed and grabbed the phone from Mary.

"What's happened?" I asked David.

"It's John; he killed himself."

I went numb. John Peevers and I were the best of friends. "What could have happened?" I thought in disbelief. The tragedy had happened earlier in the evening, and David had been up all night. I couldn't talk; I didn't know what to say. I told David to try and get some sleep and that I would call back around noon.

About mid-morning, John's wife, Nancy, called. She was distraught, and, other than her two daughters, she had no family in Reno. Mary and I knew that we had to be there for her and for our son, David, so we made plans to fly to Reno the next day, charging the expense to our American Express card, not knowing how we would pay it. But, we had to go. It was a very difficult trip.

At the end of a week, Nancy drove us to the airport and we flew home. Over and over, I tried to understand what had happened to John – why he elected to end his life. There was never a clue in any of our conversations. Whatever it was, he had reached his limit and snapped.

The incident made me stop and think about how the stress of my situation, which often pushed me to my limits, was impacting my own state of mind.

John's death would haunt me for a long time.

Chapter Twenty-one

"God, grant me the serenity
to accept the things I cannot change,
courage to change the things I can,
and the wisdom to know the difference.
But God, grant me the courage
not to give up on what I think is right,
even though I think it is hopeless."

— An adaptation of *The Serenity*
Prayer, written by Dr. Reinhold
Niebuhr, Theologian (1892-1971)

After returning from Reno, Mary and I each mounted an aggressive job search. We had no income. The money we had borrowed from family and the proceeds from what we could sell was just about gone, and we were receiving demand letters from creditors. We were doing all that we could do, but we were in financial chaos and the damage would get a lot worse before it got better.

Crippen's campaign to ruin my reputation essentially made anything in law enforcement out of the question for me. So I concentrated on everything else, sending my résumé to companies around the country hoping for work. I wrote nearly forty letters. Not one responded. It was disheartening. Nevertheless, I persisted. I was desperate for work, and I resolved that no job was beneath me.

Because of her nursing credentials and experience, Mary was more fortunate in her search. After reactivating her nursing license, Mary quickly found a job as the night charge nurse at Thanksgiving Home, Cooperstown's adult assisted care facility. Other than keeping the books and other work she did for The Woodsmen Builders, Mary had not worked outside of our home for over eight years. The adjustment would be difficult for all of us, especially with her working nights.

I looked forward to January 28th when the grand jury was scheduled to meet. McVinney called and wanted me to meet with him in the grand jury room the day before to go over the case and prepare me for my testimony. When we met, I asked if he had talked to any of the other witnesses and pinned them down on their answers. He said he hadn't. Right then I knew he had no interest in getting an indictment and was just going through the motions hoping to appease me.

"I'm going to give you a lot of leeway in your testimony," he said.

I took that as an invitation to tell the grand jury my story, and I intended to do that in vivid detail.

The following morning a severe ice storm hit the area, closing schools and many roads.

I grumbled as I heard the weatherman's predictions for the day, knowing what was going to happen. And, predictably, at eight thirty that morning the phone rang.

"It's McVinney; the grand jury has been cancelled because of the weather."

I was, of course, disappointed, but at least the delay was legitimate this time.

"I'll get back to you with a new date," McVinney said and hung up.

By the afternoon of February 1st, I had heard nothing from McVinney and called his office. He wasn't available, and didn't return my call, so I called again the next day.

"The grand jury is scheduled for Friday, February 11th, at nine thirty in the morning," he said abruptly. I thanked him and hung up.

The following Sunday, February 6th, I learned that my good friend, Sheriff Marty Ralph, had a heart attack and died at his home the night before after returning from his son's wedding. Over 200 uniformed law enforcement officers attended Marty's funeral, all of us mourning his death.

Just a couple of days later, McVinney called again.

"I have some more bad news for you," he said.

"Now what?" I wondered, assuming from the tone of his voice that it concerned the grand jury.

Sure enough. The grand jury was now postponed until March 3rd.

Angry and frustrated, I yelled, "When the hell is it my turn?" This was the fifth delay, and I felt like I was becoming the insignificant man to whom justice would never come.

"The jurors simply didn't want to come in just to hear one case," McVinney explained, adding, "and, if I insist on it, they'll all be pissed off during the proceeding."

"They'll be pissed off?" I snapped back sarcastically. "Why was this case the only one scheduled before them?" I asked rhetorically. I was furious. "Fine," I barked into the phone. "I'll see you March 3rd."

I couldn't believe it. Now I had the added burden of worrying about whether or not the members of the grand jury were having a good day and if they were "pissed off" about having to appear.

It seemed the whole case was swirling around in a vast pool of technical delays while I was going broke paying legal fees and my day in court nowhere in sight. Meanwhile, the railroad continued to prosper.

"Where's the justice in that?" I wondered.

As my quest for employment continued, I continued to function as "house-husband" while the days droned on.

Not soon enough, February 24th arrived and Rutnik argued the appeal in Albany. He called later to tell me that he thought everything went okay, but that there was no way to really tell. We'd just have to wait for the court's decision.

On the weekend before March 3rd, the date scheduled for the grand jury, I watched the news and weather report. Sure enough, another major snow storm was predicted to hit us March 3rd and, sure enough, on March 3rd, we got another twenty inches of snow in the fifteenth major storm of the season.

The grand jury was re-scheduled for March 8th. That morning, I arrived at the county courthouse shortly before nine o'clock and didn't have to wait very long before McVinney called me in to testify. After I was sworn in, I answered McVinney's questions about what had happened in 1973 in Portsmouth, about the first package mailed to McGarrity of the *The New York Times*, and about the package mailed to Charles Crist after he was arrested by Crippen and the charges were dismissed. Then, we got into the mass mailings of 1993, and its effect on me, my business, my reputation, and my family. McVinney's open-ended questions allowed me to tell the grand jury the whole story. It was difficult to maintain my composure as I recounted all that I had lost as a result of Crippen's smear campaign. As I testified, I watched the expressions on the juror's faces change from bewilderment to horror as they comprehended the profound malevolence behind Crippen's efforts to destroy me, my business, and my family. I sensed that the jurors would hold Crippen accountable if they could.

The question of whether Crippen would be held criminally accountable was finally in the hands of the grand jury.

That afternoon, McVinney called.

"Bad news," he said. "The grand jury found no criminal conduct."

I was devastated, and my faith in the system of justice evaporated.

I was sure that now Crippen, believing he was invincible, would be relentless.

I clung to the hope that my civil lawsuit might survive, although my confidence in everything judicial had reached a new low.

Sleep that night was impossible as I kept running the entire issue over and over in my mind. About the time the sky began to brighten into a new day, its tinges of pink reflecting off the still white and frozen landscape, a thought occurred to me.

I remembered that McVinney told me once that his role, and the role of the grand jury, was to investigate the violation of any law. "Yesterday," I thought, "the grand jury considered only one issue – whether Crippen's conduct in distributing the smear packets was criminal." They hadn't considered whether Crippen had violated his oath of office as a police officer or the statutes governing the conduct of public officers.

"Certainly," I thought, "the statute governing public officers in New York is a *law*, and, even though Crippen is employed by a private corporation, he is commissioned as a police officer by the state, and took exactly the same oath I had taken." As part of that oath, Crippen stated, "I hereby acknowledge receipt of a copy of Public Officers Law, Section 73 through 78, have read the same, and agree to conform to the provisions thereof." Those sections prohibited the disclosure of confidential information obtained in the course of his police duties.

"How clear did it have to be?" I wondered.

That morning, I made copies of everything I had obtained from the library and highlighted all of the appropriate sections. Then I wrote yet another letter to McVinney and asked if it was something he could take before the grand jury. Although it wouldn't result in criminal prosecution, it seemed to me that a grand jury report stating that Crippen had violated his oath of office would carry a lot of weight with the state police in the administrative matter of Crippen's police commission. I also thought it would also be beneficial to my civil lawsuit.

I put everything together and hand-delivered it to McVinney's office in Oneonta at nine o'clock that morning.

McVinney was in court, so I walked around the city for an hour or so and thought about what I would say, knowing that I risked annoying him but figuring I had nothing to lose at this point.

When I returned to McVinney's office, he was there, but said he had a busy schedule and had only a few minutes for me. After apologizing for dropping in without an appointment, I told him my thoughts and handed him the envelope of material I had put together. He listened to what I had to say and agreed that the grand jury could, indeed, look into the Public Officer's Law and the issue of the oath.

Relieved by McVinney's response, I drove back to Cooperstown.

By the end of the week, I had heard nothing from McVinney. I called his office. He had not had time to look into the matter. His secretary suggested I call back on Monday.

Meanwhile, Mary went to work at the Thanksgiving Home every night, usually with just a few hours of sleep. She found it difficult to sleep during the day, the domestic responsibilities she was accustomed to handling on her mind. She was tired when she left for work and exhausted when she came home. We saw less and less of each other. Our evenings together were a thing of the past. I woke up often during the night, ridden with guilt that I was home sleeping while Mary worked.

I thought about psychological counseling and even asked my doctor about it, needing a referral from him for my insurance policy to cover such a visit. Mary thought it was good idea, but I was unsure, believing that someone would surely use it against me while we were involved in litigation.

Beginning in mid-March, the assistant superintendent of state police, Wayne Bennett, and I exchanged a flurry of heated letters regarding Crippen's police commission and whether he was subject to the statutes governing public officers. The state police closed their file on the matter.

After not hearing back from McVinney, I called his office on Monday and left another message. No one called back, so I called again Tuesday and Wednesday and Thursday and Friday. He was never available. I wrote McVinney a heated letter suggesting he, too, had succumbed to political pressure and faxed it to him, Coccoma, and Judge Nydam, the judge who appointed McVinney at Coccoma's request. McVinney and I exchanged a couple more spirited letters, and he refused to initiate any further grand jury action regarding Crippen.

I then wrote a four-page letter to Judge Nydam outlining all that had happened and requesting that he require McVinney to provide him with a detailed summary of the investigation, including the names of all persons McVinney questioned, the date he spoke with them, and all information he obtained from them. I also suggested that Judge Nydam request from McVinney justification for almost five months of involvement with the case. Lastly, I requested that he assign a special prosecutor to the matter that would not be influenced by anything except the facts and the law relevant to the case.

Dennis Lynch called me to ask how things were going. We had remained friends and although he was no longer actively involved in my civil case against, he was still interested and was always a source of encouragement. It didn't seem that I had a lot of friends these days, but I was very grateful that Dennis was among those who remained.

With every day that passed, I worried more about the results of our appeal in the Albany court and wondered if my lawsuit would ever proceed to the next stage. All I had ever wanted was a chance to present to a jury the truth about everything that had happened. All I wanted was for a jury made up of regular, everyday people who had jobs, families, mortgages, a dog and a cat, and who lived their lives and raised their families according to ethical principles and values, to hear my case.

I tried to maintain my faith that things would turn out okay and that, sooner or later, justice would prevail. While not religious, I have my own relationship with God – a relationship that was forged in Vietnam. Each night, I prayed for the strength to continue fighting for what is right and just, and to ultimately have my day in court.

At the end of each evening, I would pick up the small card that I kept on my desk and, before retiring for the evening, I would read the message printed on it. It helped me garner strength when I thought I had no more, and it helped me find peace in the midst of all of this turmoil. It seemed to be written just for me:

"God, grant me the serenity
to accept the things I cannot change,
courage to change the things I can,
and the wisdom to know the difference.
But God, grant me the courage
not to give up on what I think is right,
even though I think it is hopeless."

Chapter Twenty-two

Anybody who has ever tried to rectify an injustice
or set a record straight comes to feel that he is going mad.

— Mary McCarthy, "My Confession,"
in *The Art of the Personal Essay* (1994)

The newspaper article was relatively short, but its headline caught my attention. Coccoma had announced his candidacy for surrogate court judge in the upcoming election.

"Just what I predicted," I thought. "Certainly answers the question why Coccoma didn't want to alienate the railroad by taking the Crippen matter before the grand jury himself."

The article quoted Coccoma as saying, "I am committed to public service and my reputation as a hard-working, ethical public official and private practitioner is a strong quality."

I'm always amazed at the ease with which politicians can pat themselves on the back and toot their own horn knowing that the public generally has no idea about what has gone on behind the scenes. I made a mental note to do all I could to expose Coccoma before the election. Surely, I, too, have a right to political free speech.

It appeared to me that, in the Crippen matter, Coccoma elevated his personal interests in a seat on the bench (with a ten-year term, a hefty annual salary, and virtually no accountability) above his public duty as district attorney, dishonoring his own oath of office. As far as I was concerned, he was a disgrace.

After waiting two full weeks, I had not received a reply to my letter to Judge Nydam so on April 2nd, I wrote to him again and sent it certified mail. In the letter, I suggested that he might not have received my first letter, "which is why," I noted, "I am sending this letter certified." I didn't want to sound accusatory or anger him; yet, I was suspicious that cronyism may again be at play.

When Nydam was still an attorney in private practice, his office was in the same building as McVinney's and Rothermel's. Then, before he became a judge, Nydam was the local district attorney and Coccoma was his assistant. Nydam-Coccoma-McVinney – it was quite a triangle.

Two and a half weeks later, I received Nydan's response. It was about what I had expected. He referred to the discretion a prosecutor enjoys in the decision making process and the judicial presumption that prosecutors "act impartially." "Based on that," he said, "your request cannot be honored."

"Absolutely no accountability," I fumed.

I wrote back and thanked Nydan for his response. I also challenged the "presumption" that the prosecutor in this case was impartial and suggested that I would take the question to the panel charged with regulating attorneys' conduct, the Committee on Professional Standards.

I started making notes of past events and researching the procedure for making a formal presentation to the Professional Standards Committee.

Meanwhile, my personal finances were in crises. Mary's nursing income helped, but not nearly enough; my efforts to find employment were fruitless. So, I started contacting previous customers to let them know I was available for small jobs. I still had an assortment of personal tools, and I could work by myself as a handyman. It paid off.

For a year or so, our next-door neighbors, Dr. Mike Ries and his wife Linda, had been planning to remodel their basement. Mike called me one day and asked if I was still interested in the job. I was, and told him I could do it myself, subcontracting the electrical. Mike was happy because the cost would be a lot less than if he had to hire a professional contracting company. I was happy just to have the opportunity to generate some income. Mike and I went over the plans, and I started the job a few days later. It was a relatively small job, just about right for one man, and I felt good about being productive again.

Mike's house was situated at the end of a long driveway approximately 1,000 feet from the main road. The house was barely visible from the street. The door to the basement was on the back of house, which was secluded from view by the trees and vegetation that surrounded the yard.

Just about a week after I started, Neal McManus, the local building and codes officer, showed up at Mike's house. Since the work that I was doing didn't require a building permit, we were all curious about why he was there.

"I'm responding to a complaint," he explained, looking somewhat perplexed himself.

"What complaint?" I asked.

"A written complaint from George Crippen," Neal responded.

I felt an instant wave of rage shake me to the core, and I held my breath, trying to control my response.

"How much of this am I suppose to take?" I silently fumed.

"What's the basis of the complaint?" I asked.

Neal handed me a copy of Crippen's letter.

It has recently been brought to my attention that David K. Butler, Sr. is allegedly remodeling the basement of a home owned by a Mr. Michael Ries. Mr. Ries' home is located just adjacent to Mr. Butler's home in Rambling Ridge Estates.

During the week of April 4th, it was evident that some type of construction was being done at the above residence as Mr. Butler's vehicle was present and what appeared to be tools, equipment and materials were being taken into the residence throughout the week. This leads me to believe that my sources of information are correct and that construction or remodeling of the basement may be currently underway.

Under the circumstances, I am respectfully requesting copies of the building permit application and building permit issued for construction of the aforementioned premises. If these documents do not exist, I am requesting an immediate inspection of the aforementioned premises for violations of the Uniform Code per my complaint. When this is complete, I would like to have copies of all inspection reports as well as any stop work orders, if applicable.

I do believe that all requests for copies of documents pertaining to this complaint are covered under the Freedom of Information Act. If there is a charge, please advise and I will forward the appropriate fee.

I would appreciate a timely response to this complaint.

Sincerely,
George Crippen.

I was furious. The work I was doing didn't require a building permit, and, anyway, there's no way Crippen could see from the road that "tools, equipment and materials were being taken into the residence" when the door to the basement was in the back of the house and impossible to see from the frontage road or any other public vantage point.

Linda Ries was also very upset. She told me that just a few days before, she had seen someone approaching their property line from the field behind the house.

"What does Crippen look like?" she asked.

After I described Crippen, Linda said she was sure it was him that she had seen in the field.

Crippen would have had to walk quite a distance through an adjoining field just to get close enough to see activity in the Ries' backyard.

Neal McManus wandered through the basement looking at the work I was doing.

"This doesn't require a permit, and there's no need for you to be concerned about this," he said walking back to his car. He said he would write a brief report and send a copy to Crippen.

Now that the project had been inspected and nothing was found to be improper, Crippen would look pretty stupid.

"Will Crippen ever stop his annoying harassment, his stalking, his menacing behavior?" I wondered, concerned about what he would pull next, but, believing that ultimately it could all be used against him and to my advantage.

That night, I wrote a letter to Coccoma, detailing Crippen's continued harassment of me. I didn't expect an answer and I didn't receive one.

I also wrote a letter to the new superintendent of state police, James McMahon, requesting a meeting with him.

Right now, my typewriter was the only weapon I had.

Dr. Ries called Walter Rich to complain about Crippen and his building code complaint.

"I've already seen the letter Crippen wrote and I've reprimanded him for it," Walter said to Dr. Ries, embarrassed by the incident.

Apparently, Crippen showed the letter to Walter after he wrote it, likely thinking he'd be praised for his creative strike against me. Unfortunately for Crippen, his strategy backfired when Walter learned that it was Dr. Ries who owned the house in question – the same Dr. Ries that had recently operated on Walter's mother.

When I was in town one day, I stopped off at the County Offices. It occurred to me that McVinney would have to submit a detailed bill for his services as special prosecutor to the county for payment. It would be a public record. I walked over the counter and asked the board clerk for a copy of Richard McVinney's bill for his services to the county as special prosecutor.

"He hasn't submitted his bill yet," the clerk explained, offering to send me a copy when McVinney submitted it.

I looked forward to receiving it. Maybe it would explain what witnesses McVinney interviewed and exactly what else he did to prepare for the grand jury.

Each night, I worked on the complaint against Coccoma and McVinney that I planned to send to the Committee on Professional Standards, striving for detailed perfection and a professional presentation. When I finished, the information was neatly compiled and organized under appropriate descriptive headings, and each detail was supported by attached exhibits. The twenty-page complaint was securely bound and placed in an addressed envelope, which I mailed to the professional standards committee on April 13th, not knowing how long I would have to wait for an answer.

Crippen continued to mock and malign me whenever he had the chance. I had endured his disdain and disrespect for almost sixteen months, and it was getting very old. I tried to avoid him, but he was always there leering and staring, his eyes reflecting the absolute evil in his soul as he continued to wear away at my sanity. I was only human, and I worried that sooner or later he would push me over my emotional threshold and I would react. Once it started, I knew I wouldn't be able to stop. I was very near the breaking point.

"It's time to do something about it," I conceded.

I called Bassett Hospital and made an appointment to see someone in the Psychiatric Department.

Once again I thought, "The railroad will probably find out that I'm going to see a psychiatrist and use it against me." But, that no longer mattered – the alternative was too severe to risk.

I took a few days off to clear my head and went fishing. Mary agreed it would be good for me to just get away from everything and give my mind a rest. Being alone gave me time to think of other things, and I felt a little better. I had hoped when I returned home, there might even be some good news for a change. But I was wrong.

The first thing I saw was a letter from the Commission on Professional Standards stating the matter regarding Coccoma and McVinney had been dismissed based on prosecutorial discretion. I was disappointed, but not at all surprised. I wrote back and told them that I didn't feel that the presentation I had made to them had even been reviewed and that I should have known better than to make a complaint about lawyers to a commission comprised of lawyers.

The next day, there was even more bad news. Rutnik's associate called and said the court decided against us on the appeal in Albany. The news was devastating, and I was just about emotionally drained. I had expected that the case might be decided in our favor, which would have allowed us to move forward towards my day in court. Now, fifteen months later, we were nowhere.

I received a very formal letter from Rutnik's office with a copy of the decision enclosed. "Please call with any questions," the letter ended. I heard that Rutnik never appeared in court to argue the appeal as he represented to me that he had. Instead, he sent an associate to argue the case – one I didn't even know existed until then.

I had been curious about what might be going on with Rutnik because every time I called his office I got an answering machine. The few times that someone actually answered the phone, it was this "associate." I finally spoke with the associate one day, and she informed me that she would "be looking into other options" regarding our case, but that it would be a while because she had other priorities. Then she told me that Rutnik had suffered a heart attack and would be away for several weeks.

So for $2,500 I had received nothing. Rutnik hadn't even prepared his own brief for the court; he simply used Dennis Lynch's work.

I decided right then to discharge Rutnik as our attorney. Although I thought I deserved a refund of some of the money I paid him, I knew that it would never happen. The best I could do was cut my losses and move on.

The continued disappointments were overwhelming and I wonder sometimes how I continued the will to keep up the fight, especially when there was no clear route to take and very little support.

When I was home one morning our garbage man, Russ Smith, stopped in to talk to me. He told me that a week or so before, on a Monday around ten in the morning, he had seen George Crippen in the railroad police car parked in a driveway adjacent to the state highway. The driveway overlooked my house and the Ries house. It was Russ's impression that Crippen had been watching my house and he thought I should know. It was April 4th, the same day that Mrs. Ries had seen Crippen walking in the field behind her house.

I asked Russ to write down everything he told me in case I needed him to testify about it in court some day. He said that he would.

I got another call from Dennis Lynch and I filled him in on the current status of our case. I believed that he really wanted to help us out, as a friend. He made some calls to lawyers he knew and then told me of an attorney in Syracuse named Allen Rosenthal, who had experience in cases like mine and might be interested in our case. Dennis had talked with him about the facts and was going to send him copies of some of the pleadings.

I called Rosenthal and spoke briefly with him. We agreed that I would call him back in a week, after he had time to look at the case and see what options we might have. I was a bit encouraged, but any optimism was tempered with caution; I'd been down this road before.

The day came for my appointment at the hospital's psychiatric clinic. At the last minute, I felt humiliated by the thought and almost cancelled the appointment. But Mary wanted me to go and insisted that I at least give it a try.

When I entered the waiting room I was nervous that I would see someone I knew and be embarrassed. But, there were very few people there, and I was almost immediately ushered into another room to speak with a counselor. I spent almost an hour telling him about myself and my situation. He sat there and listened, and when I had finished he asked me a question.

"What can we do for you here in the clinic?"

"I think the answer to that question is something you're supposed to tell me after hearing everything that has happened," I responded, somewhat annoyed by the question. "If you don't know, then we have both just wasted an hour."

"The question is therapeutic," he explained, smiling. "You're supposed to suggest a solution to the problem."

"The solution to my problem," I said, "is a day in court. My reason for being here is to deal with all of the emotions I am experiencing until I get that day in court."

At the end of the session, another appointment with the counselor was made for the following week and another appointment was made for me to speak with the resident psychiatrist.

Although I didn't feel any better or any worse after this first appointment, I decided to follow through and see what happened. At least I was trying, but I was still humiliated and embarrassed by it all.

The following morning, I looked through my files and notes to see what inquiries I had made that might still be pending. I picked up the letter I had written to the new superintendent of the state police a month ago. It had not been answered.

I made a note to write him another letter and send it by certified mail. "Perhaps if I'm a big enough pest, I'll finally get an answer," I thought.

In May, I finished the basement project for Dr. Ries and continued to look for other similar small jobs. I also followed up on leads for other employment and continued to send resumés everywhere I thought there might be an interest, but I seldom received a response.

I was discouraged and worried. The stress from trying to juggle our limited finances increased each day. Every morning I prayed that something positive would happen and every night I went to bed a little more disappointed.

I continued the appointments at the psychiatric clinic and had a session with the resident psychiatrist, who told me that I was suffering from stress, severe anxiety and depression. He prescribed some anti-anxiety medicine and told me to take it whenever my stress was "getting out of hand."

It seemed I was stressed out most of the time.

It was suggested that if my condition worsened, hospitalization might be needed. That scared me; I was careful after that to not say anything that might make me appear to be a danger to anyone. Having to hide my inner thoughts from these people seemed to defeat the whole purpose of being there. I wanted the help, but I sure didn't want to make things worse.

Our financial woes worsened. Following a tax issue related to The Woodsmen Builders, the State of New York filed a judgment against us. The judgment was apparently based on a State tax due from past years, but no one seemed to be able to identify exactly what the tax was, which I thought was absurd. They filed a judgment anyway. It was the first big blow to our credit rating. In past years, when the business was operating, we would have had the means to fight the judgment or at least pay it: but we didn't have the resources now to deal with it, so the judgment would just have to remain.

When I went to the County Offices to look at the judgment entry, I was shocked to see that there was a second judgment that had just been entered. It was for $250 and was filed against us by Crippen and the railroad for "court costs" awarded to them by the appeals court in Albany when our appeal was denied.

I was numb as I sat there staring at the judgment, anger and frustration again washing over me. That big corporation, with all of its money and resources, wasted no time in filing this little judgment against me, knowing the damage it would do.

To make matters worse, we had not heard a word from Rutnik since the case was dismissed, and we were certainly never informed that the court had awarded the railroad $250 in "court costs," an award that we would be responsible for paying.

I doubt if I could describe my feelings then. I left the County Offices and went home and took a couple of the pills from my new prescription.

At my next appointment with the counselor, I was asked to describe my frustrations.

"Well," I started, "it's like if someone stood outside your house and threw rocks at it day and night, -- you would be upset, especially if a lot of damage was being done; but, the real frustration would come if you were to constantly call the police or other authorities and nothing was done about it, or if you were simply ignored – over and over and over."

I think he got the message.

I wrote another letter to the new superintendent of state police asking again for a meeting with him. It had been a full month since my last try and I had not received any reply at all. I also wrote to the state attorney general asking for a review of Coccoma and McVinney's conduct. I didn't expect any results, but I felt I had to keep trying. My parents always taught me to "knock on every door."

David called from Nevada and told us he had been accepted in the reserve police force for the University of Nevada. This could well be the final step for appointment as a full-time police officer. It had been a long selection process and he had stayed with it until he reached his goal. We were very proud and happy.

David asked about our situation and, as usual, I didn't know where to start or what to tell him. There was no logic or fairness to any of it, and it was very difficult to explain. I simply told him that we had spoken to our attorney, Dennis, and suggested there might be a small ray of hope. I told him I would keep him posted.

God, I looked forward to the day when I might be able to give my sons some good news.

About the middle of May, Allen Rosenthal called. He said he was interested in the case, and we made an appointment to meet on May 20th at his office in Syracuse. He made no commitment, nor did he hint as to what he thought about the case, but he wanted to talk about it and asked me to bring whatever I could to support what had happened. After that, I assumed, he would decide where to go with it.

That seemed fair enough, but I was afraid to be too optimistic. I knew I had more than enough evidence to prove the case, but getting around all the technical roadblocks we'd encountered in the past and finding the money to keep up the fight were real problems.

I tried to keep believing that with such an outrageous case, justice had to be out there somewhere.

Chapter Twenty-three

"Hope arouses, as nothing else can arouse,
a passion for the possible."

— William Sloan Coffin, Jr.

On May 20th, I went to Syracuse to meet with Allen Rosenthal. We spoke for a few minutes about the reasons that the original case was dismissed. Then he told me that because the courts "don't like" this sort of case; it's very hard to get something like this into court, let alone get it to trial.

"What about some sort of action on behalf of my business, The Woodsmen Builders?" I suggested, explaining that in the packages Crippen mailed out, he included a cover sheet with my business logo.

"There might be some merit to that," Rosenthal responded. "It would be a claim against Crippen for the tort of purposely attempting to ruin your business," he said.

"Of course," I beamed. "There's no doubt that's exactly what Crippen intended to do, and he succeeded."

Rosenthal said he'd "look into that area," but wanted $300 in advance. "After I receive your check, we'll research it," he said.

That hardly seemed fair to me. It would be one thing to pay him to file a lawsuit and handle the case, but it didn't seem fair to pay him to see if it could be done. As a contractor, I couldn't charge a customer to study the feasibility of remodeling their kitchen or building a house. A contractor doesn't get a dime until he actually starts the project.

"But this isn't remodeling," I reminded myself, "and with a case like mine, I have to have a good lawyer."

At this point, $300 would even jeopardize our ability to buy food. It was just about all of one of Mary's paychecks. But Rosenthal wasn't interested in my financial problems. He didn't even want to see any of the papers I had prepared for him.

I thanked Rosenthal for his time and left. When I got home, I called Dennis to tell him what happened. I explained to Dennis that I wasn't at all comfortable with Rosenthal, but I had to find someone, so I'd keep looking.

"Have you thought of moving someplace where you can find work?"

"Dennis," I said, "There's no way I can focus on something like that right now; I have to get this case back on track first. The statute of limitations will soon expire on the mailings, and then I'll be out of luck altogether."

I also couldn't bear the thought of having Mary and Danny home here alone, with me in God knows where, trying to make enough to live. And, what would I do? No matter how I looked at it, things were dismal.

For the next month or so, I continued to pester the state police and the results were always about the same as before. Something or someone had convinced them not to take any action, and it didn't matter what I said or what information I provided.

I never again heard from Rutnik. He simply faded away with our money. I discussed it with Dennis, and Dennis wrote him a letter demanding a refund, but Rutnik refused. I let it go, but Mary and I sure could have used the money.

In July 1994, a friend gave me an embossed invitation to a "fund-raiser" for state Senator James Seward. Of course, I was not invited, but my friend thought I would get a kick out of the invitation – the event was being held at Edgewater. The price was $50 per person or $99 per couple. There was no doubt in my mind that Walter had invited enough people to make this a profitable evening for the good senator, setting the stage for the special political treatment he would expect from Senator Seward in the future – the *quid pro quo* of politics.

That same month, I wrote to the attorney general of New York requesting an inquiry into the actions of Mr. Coccoma and his special prosecutor, Mr. McVinney. The attorney general's office referred me to another agency, the New York State Commission of Investigation.

I wrote to the New York State Commission of Investigation, and provided copies of everything I thought would be important, along with a detailed statement of events thus far. I asked for an investigation of the facts. They wrote back in a few weeks advising me, without explanation, that they had determined that action by the commission was not warranted.

"How could they determine that no action was warranted without any investigation at all?" I wondered.

I wrote back and asked that they provide me with the reasoning for their decision not to look into the case, thinking I was at least entitled to know that.

Their next letter advised me that because their internal communications are confidential, they didn't have to tell me anything. They suggested that I consult with private legal counsel.

In the late summer of 1994, I sold the shop building. A young couple called and inquired into the feasibility of converting the building into a small house. I showed them how that could be accomplished at a reasonable cost, and they agreed to buy the property. Even better, they hired me to do the work. Between the income from the sale of the building and the payment I received for the work, Mary and I had enough money to make it through the coming winter.

Shortly after that project was completed, Jim Dow called and hired me for a major renovation in his apartment, and that kept me busy through most of the winter.

Being busy not only helped our financial situation, but it was good for me psychologically because I didn't have time to dwell on all of the reasons for our predicament.

A month or so after I had asked for it, I got a call from the clerk for the Board of Representatives at the County Building telling me that I could finally pick up a copy of McVinney's bill that he had presented for his services to the county in his investigation of Mr. Crippen's activities and the grand jury hearing. His bill totaled $3,605.46 for thiry-five and a half hours of his professional time. Judge Nydam approved payment. Most of the hours were from meeting with me, or talking to me on the telephone. There was no indication on the bill that McVinney had questioned any witnesses or brought any witnesses before the grand jury.

Towards the end of summer, Dennis Lynch called again to tell me he had located another attorney. John P. Kinney was with a fairly large firm in Syracuse and, apparently, was interested in hearing about our case. I called him immediately and made an appointment to go see him. A week later, I drove to Syracuse and spent an hour or so briefing him on all of the circumstances of the case. The case was actually getting to be somewhat complex with motion hearings, court decisions, and the appeal, but Mr. Kinney seemed to grasp the situation well. After we finished going over the case, he said he would call me in a week or so with a decision about whether he would take the case.

He called within a week and told me that his firm would take the case. The downside was that they required a $5,500 retainer before starting any work on the case. With our financial situation in crisis, the retainer was a problem because we just didn't have that much money, but my mother offered to pay the retainer for us in order to keep the case moving. I suspect she borrowed it. Nevertheless, I accepted her offer. We all felt there was really no choice. We had come this far and invested dearly in the hope of ultimately finding justice. Like the throwers of dice across the green felt-covered tables, we had to give it one more try.

After the retainer was paid, Mr. Kinney filed an entirely new lawsuit against the railroad and Crippen claiming they tortiously interfered with my business contracts and future business. The Woodsmen Builders, Inc., and David K. Butler were the plaintiffs.

Once again, I was charged with hope, believing this time the case would ultimately be decided on its merits.

Chapter Twenty-four

"Trust me, no tortures which the poets feign,
Can match the fierce, the unutterable pain,
He feels, who night and day, devoid of rest,
Carries his own accuser in his breast."

— Juvenal, Satires, c. 120

The local newspapers carried several stories about the new lawsuit. In a story in the Oneonta *Daily Star*, the railroad's new in-house attorney, Nathan Fenno, was quoted as saying that Crippen "told us he's not involved, and as it stands at the moment, we have no reason to believe otherwise." In the same story, Coccoma denied ever saying that he "would get some heat" in the case; and Bennett, from the state police, said simply that the accusations against Crippen "although entirely possible, could not be substantiated."

"Incredible," I thought.

Later, in a story in Cooperstown's weekly newspaper, *The Freeman's Journal*, Fenno was again quoted. This time he said, "Mr. Crippen told us that he is not involved. He looked me in the face and said so. Mr. Crippen was not doing it with our approval, if he was doing it. To the best of our knowledge, he was not doing it on company time, if he was doing it."

"What?" I thought, bewildered by how equivocally Fenno denied Crippen's culpability. I actually thought Fenno's statement sounded absolutely stupid.

Interestingly enough, the fingerprint report was mentioned in both stories.

Crippen's comment to the newspapers was that "Butler's accusations are outrageous and full of baloney," and he added, "It would appear that Mr. Butler likes to fill newspapers. Maybe he should get a paper route."

The railroad immediately attacked the lawsuit with a variety of motions in an attempt to get the case dismissed. However, that process ultimately resulted in nothing more than a lot of delay; all of their motions were eventually and essentially decided in my favor.

With all of those hurdles behind us, Walter, Crippen, Soule and I were all scheduled for depositions, and I couldn't wait. Mine would be first.

Then Kinney was diagnosed with cancer. His prognosis was dismal. Joe Shields, another attorney in Kinney's firm, took over our case.

In April, 1996, I walked into the grand jury room at the Otsego County Courthouse. For several hours, the railroad's lawyers and Crippen's lawyers hammered me with questions. At the end of the day, they scheduled one more session for May 13th at the Syracuse offices of the railroad's attorney. That session was much like the first. They continued to hammer me with questions, and I continued to truthfully answer each one.

Crippen was next. His deposition was set for late June at the office of his attorney in Delhi, New York. Joe Shields grilled Crippen for several hours about his background, his position with the railroad, his police car, the mailing of the packages and the packages' content, and more. After a very long day, a second session with Crippen was scheduled for September 3rd at the Otsego County Courthouse, and Richard Grossman, Shields' senior partner, grilled Walter with impressive intensity.

After years of vigorous resistance, we were next going to hear from Walter. His deposition was scheduled for October 30th in rented office space at the Inn at Cooperstown on Chestnut Street. Grossman grilled Walter with the same intensity that he had grilled Crippen at his deposition.

Then, in December, Soule was deposed in Syracuse.

With all of the depositions behind us, we waited for the court to set the trial date and I notified potential witnesses to be ready to go.

Our two essential witnesses were Robert Miller, who, after receiving one of Crippen's anonymous packages, chose not to hire The Woodsmen Builders as the contractor to build his house; and Margaret McGarrity, the *New York Times* reporter who received the first anonymous package from Crippen. Without them, we would have no witness testimony to prove tortious interference with my business contracts and future business.

Robert Miller had left the area, but I was able to locate him in Arizona. When I talked to him on the phone, I offered to pay his transportation and expenses back to Cooperstown for the trial.

In January, 1997, the court set a trial date for that November. It would be a long wait, but finally, I hoped, we would have our day in court. I was using credit cards and every cent I had for legal expenses and trying to find enough money to get Robert Miller back to Cooperstown to testify. During the following months, I worked seven days a week at whatever I could do to try and keep things afloat.

As the trial date approached, Robert Miller suddenly disappeared. He would no longer answer the phone or return messages. I heard that he owed a lot of money to a lot of people in Cooperstown, and I assumed that he wanted to avoid coming to Cooperstown and facing his creditors.

Then I learned that Margaret McGarrity was in Europe and was not expected to return by the trial date.

Without those two witnesses, our case was in jeopardy.

Neither the defendants nor their attorneys were aware of our witness situation. However, a week before the trial was to begin, the railroad presented a settlement offer, which I immediately rejected without further comment.

On the Friday before the Monday the trial was to begin, Mary and I went to Syracuse to meet with our attorneys. It was a high-tension meeting, with calls back and forth to the attorneys for Walter, Crippen, and the railroad, trying to settle the matter without a trial. I wanted more than anything to have my day in court, but our attorneys were adamant that we wouldn't get through the first day without Miller and McGarrity. Without them, I had no choice now but to settle.

The attorneys made offers and counter-offers, and finally the railroad's attorney made one last offer. If we didn't accept it, we'd walk away with nothing at all.

The offer required that in exchange for payment of the settlement amount, I would be required to sign a confidentiality agreement as to the terms of the settlement and a statement that the case had been settled for twenty-five thousand dollars. I asked Shields why, and he said, "It doesn't mean anything."

"Why then," I asked, "do I have to sign it? Especially since it's not true?"

"Because they want it," he responded, "and the case won't settle without it."

"No wonder they want this statement," I said. "Now they will use that to convince everyone that the case was settled for "nuisance value.""

I decided I had to sign both papers, with the feeling that if one "didn't mean anything," neither did the other. That whole issue left me with even a worse impression of our legal and judicial systems. I was reminded of the form I was required to sign after being fired, when I received some $3,600 in cash to pay my medical bills and get the railroad to fill out the verification of employment so I could go back in the Navy. And, back then, they wanted me to sign a statement that "everything I said about Walter Rich, I made up." Now, I was being required to sign a statement that the case was settled for twenty-five thousand dollars and everyone in the room, including attorneys on both sides, knew the statement was *false,* yet no one even slightly objected (except me). It was considered simply part of the process.

We talked about the confidentiality agreement. I was to simply say that the case was "settled to mutual satisfaction," which I have always done, and I have always been careful not to divulge the terms of the settlement. If people want to believe that I settled a four year lawsuit for twenty-five thousand dollars, then so be it. The important thing is that the agreement in no way prevents me from writing this book.

The settlement did little more for us than to pay legal fees and some debts. During the long struggle to survive, we had been forced to refinance our house under a high-interest "predator mortgage," which we still struggle to pay. I still work at whatever construction jobs come along, and Mary is still a nurse at the Thanksgiving Home.

I have no real hope of retirement in the near future and continue to live one day at a time. When I worked for the railroad, I had an excellent retirement plan with "Railroad Retirement" mandated by federal law. When I was fired, I lost that benefit. Later, when I built the Woodsmen Builders, I set up my own retirement plan. It would have provided me with a comfortable retirement income. However, when the railroad destroyed Woodsmen Builders, all of the money in my retirement fund went to pay legal fees and personal survival expenses. So, rather than now being able to retire from either the railroad or Woodsmen Builders, Mary and I are left to worry about how we will survive in the future.

We have our health and we have our pride. Some of the wounds have healed; some never will.

Chapter Twenty-five

My final thoughts.

Railroad safety, in my opinion, has become a disgrace on a national level. First, we have the Federal Rail Administration, that is operated and supervised by those who are politically appointed. These people are not going to offend those who appointed them or "make waves" for the friends of those who appoint them.

Secondly, what are the qualifications to run the FRA? From 1989 to the present, none of the administrators of this agency have any railroad experience. They are, as previously stated, appointed, and have backgrounds in everything from car dealership to public administration and experience as lobbyists.

The purpose of the FRA is to promulgate and enforce railroad safety regulations that affect the lives of not only railroad personnel and passengers, but also of people living near to, or those crossing, railroad tracks. Unqualified, insecure and weak FRA administrators are vulnerable to becoming captives of the very industry they are entrusted to regulate.

It is bad enough that the railroads and the FRA share the same data, serve on the same committees, attend many of the same meetings and partner the same projects. Having an overly impressionable administrator simply compounds the relationship.

That leads me back to the Poolville accident. With all of the glaring circumstances that were present in that incident, why was there no FRA response? Why did I frequently see FRA inspectors going to lunch with railroad executives, and why were they frequently guests at Edgewater? Why did the FRA tell the state police there was no way to confirm the train speed? What other conclusion could a reasonable person reach?

In the past few years, I began to pay more attention to what was going on around the country. I talked to many people, including experts in various areas of the railroad industry. I was able to separate good, honest people, who took their jobs seriously, from those with some kind of agenda (usually political).

I learned about "FAILSAFE" crossing protection. The words mean just that; fail-safe. On railroad crossings where there are gates and lights, *federal law* requires a failsafe system. Put in plain language, that means that if the lights and gates fail for any reason, the gates go to the "down" position, effectively blocking traffic from crossing the tracks. Although that might be inconvenient for a motorist, it protects the crossing until repairs can be made. So, for weather-related problems, electrical malfunctions or any such defects, the gates GO DOWN. Or at least that is what is *supposed* to happen. Bottom line? These regulations are violated every day or simply ignored. The railroads just say you should "stop, look, and listen" at railroad crossings. That, my friends, is a *slogan,* not a *law.* The LAW is the FAILSAFE requirement, but it apparently means little to the railroad industry.

Put yourself here: you are driving along a rural highway at 55 miles per hour. Ahead is a railroad crossing, equipped with flashing red lights, and gates designed to block the road in the event of a train approaching. The gates are up; the lights are off. There is traffic moving along at the same speed behind you. What do you do? Stop? Of course not, unless you want to trigger a series of rear-end collisions. (Do you stop for green lights at intersections?) So you continue on across the tracks, just as anyone would do, and WHAM...you are dead if a train was coming, and the "failsafe" system did not work. Simple as that; someone ignored the law, and you, your family or some innocent person is DEAD. Any reasonable person would not just assume, but *expect* to be able to go over railroad tracks if the signal-system displayed "all-clear." Bottom line? Signals tell people it is safe to cross when it's not. They are setting them up to be killed.

A couple of recent and very real examples: In February, 2003, in Henrietta, New York, an elderly couple was killed while crossing railroad tracks. The gates and lights had been malfunctioning and, instead of going to the failsafe mode to protect the crossing, they had been just turned off. A "stop and flag" order had been issued for train crews, but for reasons unknown, it was ignored. The railroad could have easily put a flag crew at the crossing while repairs were made, but they didn't. And they ignored the failsafe...in violation of federal law. They made their own rules to fit their own needs by issuing a "stop and flag," but it didn't work. Two people are dead, someone's family, someone's parents and grandparents, dead all because laws were ignored.

Another accident, in Fonda, New York in early 2005 was even more outrageous. A woman had stopped in a line of traffic that was waiting for a stopped train to clear a crossing. When the train cleared, the lights went off and the gates went up. Traffic began to move ahead of her and cross the tracks. When she entered the crossing *another* train, coming from the other direction, hit her car and killed her instantly. Someone from the railroad, it was later shown, had disabled the protection warning so the stopped train would not hold up traffic. Had the failsafe done its job, that would not have happened, and traffic would have been warned about the second train approaching. Put yourself someplace in this picture, either as the victim or a loved one of the victim. Someone is *dead,* gone forever, families and children suffer. Why? Rules were ignored or violated.

As time went on and I continued to research railroad safety, I came upon an organization known as *The Angels on Track Foundation.* It was formed in 1997 by Dennis and Vicky Moore, from Ohio. I was able to speak with Vicky Moore and learned that in 1995, they lost their youngest son Ryan, in a tragic railroad crash. Ryan had been in a car with five friends. They were on their way to look at some land the Moore family was considering for a new house. When they entered an unguarded railroad crossing, their car was hit broadside by a Conrail train traveling at an estimated 60 miles per hour. Three of the six kids in the car, including Ryan, were killed.

The investigation of that incident showed that trees and thick vegetation blocked a motorist's view of the tracks. The only warning was a crossbuck sign, like in Poolville. State law in Ohio requires vegetation to be cleared back 600 feet in both directions on railroad rights-of-way at public railroad crossings. That law, apparently, was simply ignored. No one was held personally accountable. Outrageous? You bet! At that same crossing, just two months earlier a young man was killed and, just a week before, a couple ran into the side of a train there. In all, this serial-killer crossing had claimed the lives of at least six others over the years.

The Moores filed a civil action against the railroad and reached a settlement agreement. Rather than benefit from their loss, they formed *The Angels on Track Foundation,* the purpose of which is to work with local authorities in selecting the most dangerous crossings and assist in funding the installation of gates at unprotected crossings. To date, the foundation has funded fourteen railroad crossing gate and safety improvement projects in Ohio. The Foundation also established an educational subsidiary, *Crossing To Safety,* to provide education on railroad safety issues.

The Moore's case was also highlighted on a *Discovery Channel* documentary entitled *Trouble on the Tracks.* I have seen the documentary a number of times and my reaction is always the same: Why is there not public and political outrage? Maybe not enough people have seen it...maybe no one cares...I just don't know.

The Moore family has suffered a loss most of us cannot comprehend. Politicians brand Vicky as a "grieving mother" and attribute what she says to that motive – just like they brand me a "disgruntled employee." Of course, we are both just what they say. Who wouldn't be? But that doesn't change any of the facts. I am honored to know Dennis and Vicky Moore. It is the efforts of everyday people like them that might someday force a change in a corrupt industry.

On the subject of crossing protection, I wonder if our attorney general or any other authority will ever take a close look at how *that* little scam works. The state of New York, for instance, maintains a list of *priority* crossings, in need of gates, lights, whatever. These projects are funded according to their position on that list and as funding becomes available. If there is enough money this year for three crossings, it is the top three on the list that receive it...or that is the way it is *supposed to be.* Here is the catch: the state gives the RAILROAD the money to install the protection and do the work. The railroad bills the state for the material and labor from its own forces. That does not pass the smell-test! The railroad is then free to bill whatever amount it pleases and, as I mentioned a few chapters ago, there is usually a tidy profit involved. So railroads *love* to do crossing projects.

Don't believe me? Take a look at little Cooperstown. When Walter Rich ran his train on the local track, it was never more than a boxcar a month, and seldom did it go over maybe 5 miles per hour through the village. One engine, one boxcar. However, in less than a half mile, there were *two* state-of-the-art, brand new crossings, complete with the rubber road mat, gates, lights, bells – the whole nine yards. Of course, Walter's company furnished and installed these crossings, and was *reimbursed* with our tax money. A little special treatment from his political friends got the Cooperstown crossings elevated on the state-wide "priority list." Could anyone *really* justify these crossings? Of course, they are now GONE. What do you suppose happened to all that new equipment they had been paid for, and then removed? Do you think it was returned to the state? In fact, they were sold to the taxpayer *again* and re-used at other crossings, for insurance repairs or "new" crossings. The exact same things were done on Walter Rich's Richfield Springs line, as well. Three NEW crossings, one rail-car maybe each month and, as in Cooperstown, they are now paved over and gone. And, the list goes on....

Which brings me to another question: *why* is no one ever held accountable? Look at Walter Rich and what he did to me. How can these things happen? What happened in Henrietta and Fonda happens every day around the country. Some 500 people die each year in railroad accidents. Some of them are the victim's own fault, but certainly many others could be prevented. What do you think would happen if YOU were the cause of a train accident? If a witness saw you go around the gates or ignore the warnings, you would with a doubt be criminally prosecuted, and if you caused a death, you might end up in prison.

In any railroad accident, the railroad police are directly or indirectly pressured to find the motorist at fault. That was apparent in my experience with every accident I ever investigated. To be sure, I always looked at the actions of the motorist to see if there was fault there, but there often was not. Being commissioned as a railroad policeman provides the authority to do the job from a legal standpoint, but being paid and supervised by the railroad you work for certainly presents a serious conflict of interest. I believe most railroad police officers are honest and sincere in their efforts to be impartial, but, again, they are subjected to enormous pressure to be "loyal" to the company that pays their salary. What happened to me was the extreme, but consider the events that followed and the efforts I made to find someone in authority that would at least take a serious look into the circumstances. Money, power and influence in the right places - the little guy has no chance.

In recent years, we read and hear in the news that corporate executives are *going to prison* because of the actions of subordinates. Mostly, it involves financial matters and investment schemes. CEO's were using the defense, "I didn't know," blah, blah, but juries were able to see through this and *convict* them for the crimes that happened on their watch. So why, in the railroad industry, when the violations are so clear, and people are *murdered*, does *nothing happen?* Railroad executives simply thumb their nose at these questions. They are secure in the knowledge that because of political connections and donations to the right places they are well insulated on a personal level.

A series of articles in *The New York Times,* by Pulitzer Prize winner Walt Bogdanich in the past year was explosive in what was exposed. The most recent article, published in December, 2005, quoted from a report issued by the Transportation Department inspector general, stating, *"The Federal Railroad Administration should stop accepting the word of railroads when they blame drivers for most collisions at grade crossings and should instead do more of its own research into the accidents' causes."* The report noted that deaths at rail crossings had increased by eleven percent last year, but collisions declined by thirty-four percent from 1995 to 2004, and by six percent so far this year.

I could not believe when I read in the report that railroads had "failed to promptly report twenty-one percent of the most serious collisions at grade-crossings, reducing chances of a proper federal investigation."

And, even more outrageous, the inspector general found that in 2004, out of 3,045 collisions, the FRA investigated NINE! The report was prepared at the request of Congress, which expressed concern about rail safety problems previously reported in *The New York Times*.

I recently read that CSX Railroad Corporation was fined $298,000 by the FRA for "multiple violations of highway grade crossing safety regulations." Of course, no PERSON was identified or held accountable. We also read that New York Attorney General Elliott Spitzer allowed CSX to pay $1.5 million to settle complaints of the same thing. Keep in mind that any monies paid as fines or penalties would be corporate funds and not have any particular impact on anyone personally.

Just in November 2005, as we work on our final chapter for this book, I read that the FRA, regarding the *Fonda* accident in which the woman was killed, confirmed "the violation of regulations governing operation of grade-crossing signal safety systems." Did I miss someone being held to blame for this? Did it really require the big FRA to confirm this, when an idiot would have seen what happened just by talking to the witnesses on the scene? And why, as usual, was there no mention of the possibility of any human accountability? My guess is that if railroad executives were held responsible for what goes on in their company, just like the captain of a ship, things *would* change, and in a hurry!

And a little more on that subject: In April, 2000, the *Richmond Times Dispatch* reported that John Snow, President of CSX, was "taking personal control" after three "top officers were out in a CSX shakeup." He was to bring "new fervor and intensity to safety issues." Snow was quoted as saying "I feel an obligation to take a hands-on leadership role at the railroad." From my point of view, that sure leads to an obvious question: Does that mean he assumes responsibility for what now happens on his watch? Don't hold your breath.

Of course, John Snow has now found an even better job. In January, 2003, he assumed duties as the United States secretary of the treasury. At the same time, CSX was under investigation for many improprieties. He was appointed by President George Bush...the same George Bush that was entertained at Walter Rich's mansion in Cooperstown. And I wonder why all of my efforts over the last twenty-some years have been ignored by those in powerful places.

To add a little proof to that statement, consider this: In July 2005, I received a phone call from a staff member for congressman Steven C. Latourette. The congressman was chairman of a Railroad Sub-Committee that was currently holding hearings in Washington D.C. I was asked if I could attend and testify about some of my experiences. I said of course I would and I was told to "stand-by" for further direction and to be prepared to appear in Washington two days later. I immediately made the needed arrangements as far as work was concerned and some other schedule changes. Because I'd been told that I would only have five minutes to speak, I worked to put together a concise statement with the most impact I could muster. The next day, I still hadn't heard back, so I called the congressman's staff member. He said to me, "All of the slots have been filled, so we don't need you after all."

So, there I was, all ready to go, and like so many times before, the door was shut in my face. I wasn't even surprised. With the amount of money involved with railroads and politicians, I hadn't realistically expected too much anyway. For whatever it was worth, I took the time to write the congressman a letter to outline what had happened, and to offer to appear at some future time. I never heard back from him or his staff.

As time passed, I became more determined to make my journal into a readable book, to publish it and finally tell the truth about what had happened to me. Even now, many years after I had to close The Woodsmen, I still hear things related to the packages having been mailed and opinions that were formed back then and forged in steel. The only way to correct any of that was to publish the *whole* story, and let the chips fall where they may. As important, was to tell what went on with not only Mr. Rich and his company, but the railroad industry as a whole.

I had kept the journal since the time I worked at the railroad. Over the years, I wrote a lot of it as it happened, and I am still doing that. I have had the help of friends, and even the assistance of a professional writer, in putting the words of my journal into a manuscript, with the hopes of seeing it in print someday.

I shared the manuscript with family and close friends, and with those I met through my work and who had become my friends. Most of them encouraged me to publish my story and some even offered me financial assistance to make that happen.

In March of 2004, I had traveled to my son Don's house in Virginia to build him a deck. Work in Cooperstown was non-existent at the time, and Don's in-laws were paying for the deck, so it was good for all of us. When I finished a few weeks later, I was alone, and driving back to Cooperstown, which is about a 600 mile trip. I noted that I was feeling a little uncomfortable and had an unpleasant tightness in my chest. When I finally arrived home at about 7:00 o'clock., Mary had supper ready and I went upstairs to wash up. I was feeling worse so I sat down on our bed. A few minutes later, Mary came upstairs and asked me if I was okay. "No," I said, "something is wrong; my chest hurts and my left arm aches." Right away, she wanted to call an ambulance. Knowing this was different than anything I had ever experienced before, I said, "Let's not do that; you can drive me to the hospital."

A few minutes later, we arrived at Bassett Hospital in the village of

Cooperstown. I was immediately placed on a stretcher, and before I knew it I was hooked up to a variety of machines and IV fluids. Mary was near tears and I was upset because she was. I was a little scared now, and didn't really understand what was going on until the doctor said "heart attack." I was concerned that my kids would find out and everybody would be upset. The doctor told me I was being admitted and would have to undergo an angioplasty to clear a clogged artery. As it ended up, I went through that procedure twice, having two stents put in place because of blockage of two coronary arteries. After a few days in the hospital, I was home and on light duty for a few weeks.

Not long after I was back at work, I teamed up with Chris Chandler. Chris had his first job with me several years ago, and now in his late twenties turned out to be a pretty good builder. When he worked for me in the past, I knew he had promise, and I now looked forward to having someone to work with that could not only do the work, but someone that I liked and enjoyed being around. Chris was also someone I could trust, and seemed to have the same everyday values that I have. Aware of the health challenges that I have faced, Chris is selfless and constant in his efforts to relieve me of some of the physical demands of working construction. So to this day, we remain working together.

In looking into who might re-write my journal into first-person, I reconnected with Nancy Lee Varnum, the former Nancy Peevers. After her husband's death in 1994, she changed her name back to her maiden name. Nancy lives in Reno, Nevada. She was the secretary at the railroad who took Bonfardice's statement in shorthand. Nancy and John and Mary and I were close friends back then and, after John's death, we had somewhat lost touch with Nancy over the years. It was wonderful to rekindle our friendship. After leaving Cooperstown, Nancy earned a Bachelors' Degree and then a law degree from Emory University in Atlanta. She is now an attorney, and she expressed her interest in writing, so we asked her to write a couple of chapters for this book. We liked her style, and she soon came on board as our official editor, charged with the daunting task of transforming my journal into a book.

Sometimes I have to wonder about what everyone must think as I have relentlessly pursued the completion of this book – in particular, my family. Mary seems to understand and has stood by my side through all of the good and bad. My sons, I think, sometimes wonder why I don't put it behind me and move on. They all grew up with the railroad controversy always seeming to be swirling around in our lives somewhere. Originally, I was going to title the book "What do I tell my sons?" because I really didn't know what to tell them about the injustices that had taken place. Now, it is just a mission to complete something I started a long time ago. I *have* moved on with my life as well as circumstances permit, and I am able to hold my head high. But this story, for everything it exposes, is important to me; and for whatever the reason might be, I will complete it.

As we neared the completion of the book, I should point out that we had given most of the people named in the story an invitation to be interviewed. I felt that in the interest of accuracy and fairness to all involved anyone who wanted to respond or tell their side of any issue should have the opportunity to do so. We sent registered letters to Walter Rich, David Soule, Malcolm Hughes, George Crippen, Deane Winsor and Michael Coccoma. The only response, I ever saw were letters from Rich and Crippen's attorney, suggesting legal caution on our part.

As 2005 nears an end and I will turn sixty-one years old, I know that if this story is ever to be told, now is the only chance I have. Everything I have written in this book is true. The facts are outrageous enough; they don't need to be exaggerated.

There is no malice or revenge on my part towards anyone, including Rich. I only wanted the facts presented, as they happened, so a *reasonable* person could make an *informed* decision as to what really happened, without the legal blockades and mumbo-jumbo that is associated so often with politicians and corporate executives who don't like what they read about themselves.

In January, 2006, as this book was going to press, an article by reporter James M. Odato showed up in the front section of the Albany Times Union, a major newspaper in Albany, NY. It was titled " RAIL MAGNATE COMES UNDER SCRUTINY".

The article stated that the State Lobbying commission was investigating annual fund -raising parties at Walter Rich's Edgewater home during Cooperstown's Hall of Fame baseball weekend. The commission was trying to determine if Rich or his company provided illegal gifts to public officials and politicians. The report mentioned, among others, Congressman Boehlert, Senator Seward, Governor George Pataki, and George W. Bush.

Nathan Fenno, the railroad's lawyer, was quoted too. He said "We certainly followed the law and that's always our intent. I don't think there's anything suspicious".

Like countless times in the past, I felt my hopes rise as I read the article. Maybe *this* would start the process that would finally expose these people and support some of the things I have been trying to say for over twenty years. I was encouraged some, and although not bursting with optimism, I would try and remain hopeful.

It has been suggested by some that this book might give Cooperstown a "black-eye."

Certainly, it is not Cooperstown that is at fault. This is a beautiful place, unique in many ways. But, it is not *my* fault either. This is *my* home too. I didn't cause any of this. The book simply tells the story. Let those responsible for what happened finally be held accountable to the public. They made their bed through their actions. It is time they slept in it.

This story is a wake-up call to American communities everywhere. It is our hope that by telling you this story, the truth, and maybe even some justice, will prevail.

Supplement
May 2006

After the first edition of Railroaded in Cooperstown was published, I received an overwhelming number of comments about the book. They were all extremely positive and supportive. Some came from folks I know, but I also received many telephone calls, letters, and e-mails from people I'd never met. I was overwhelmed. Some called me a "hero." But, I did nothing more than decency asks of all of us: live honest lives and act from strength of character and integrity.

Each message I received was a great blessing, but I was particularly moved with emotion by the e-mails I received from Tom Flummer's brother, Scott Lewis, and his mother, Jenny. As you will recall, Tom Flummer was a victim in the tragic Poolville grade crossing accident I investigated as the railroad's police chief. Scott and Jenny both gave me permission to publish their comments.

Here' verbatim what Tom's brother wrote to me on April 21, 2006:

I was only 10 at the time and I arrived home from a Boy Scout camping trip to Canada. I was so relieved to be home, it was the worst camping trip I had ever had. I remember walking through the door of the house and yelling "Mom, Dad I'm Home!" and nobody answered. It was kind of late around 8 or 9 PM, I know it was dark outside. I thought how strange that they weren't home. They knew I was coming home that day. Then Susie who was my brother Georges wife came around the corner and said "Hi Scott!" And I said "Oh HI......What's going on?" She replied "Oh nothing, your Mom and Dad had to go somewhere." I had this gut feeling that something wasn't right. Then the phone rang........and Susie answered it and walked out onto the side porch. I thought why did she do that....why so secretive? So I snuck over by the door, she had left it open and I listened. She said "Oh No!" and shortly after she hung up the phone and came inside. I said "Susie what's wrong?" She answered "Oh Scott it's awful, something bad has happened, Tom was killed in an accident......." That moment was the first tragic experience I had ever encountered in my life. I had just lost my best friend. He used to come by a couple times a week and he would take me down to the convenient store on Main Street in Sherburne and we would play Ms. Pacman. He wasn't very good at it but he sure loved to play it. And fishing, boy did he like to fish, we would go out and spend an entire day from dawn to dusk and walk down the Chenango River and fish all the spots we knew so well. I could go on and on about all the great memories I have of my brother. Anybody who knew Tom I can say without a doubt would say he was the nicest guy they had ever known.

I spoke with my Mom last night and she told me my aunt had called and told her about your book. She gave me the website address so I could see for myself. I was wondering what on earth someone would be able to write about Tom's accident. I knew the railroad was at fault, but I never had any idea that it went so much deeper than a train engineer who failed to blow his whistle and stop for an unmarked crossing. I found the excerpt link at the bottom of the page and of course had to click over to give it a read. I must tell you sir I never knew these emotions where still here inside me. I began reading about the accident and after a few sentences I had to get up and walk away for a moment. I came back and finished reading through it as shocking as it was for me to read the details. I knew he suffered but I didn't know it was as graphic as you described. I told my Mom she shouldn't read it (the excerpt), she still can't read the newspaper article. When I got off the phone with my Mom I lied on the couch with my wife and I cried.

I want to thank you for standing up for Tom, Calvin, and Rocky (We all knew Earl as Rocky). And after reading Rockys quote on your home page I hope he knows I never blamed him. I don't think anybody did.

My Mom plans on buying a copy of your book for herself, and us three brothers, and Toms son Brian. I can't wait to give it a read. I am sure your story is going to affect me in ways that your normal readers can't even imagine.

Thank You again, from a Brother who will forever mourn the loss of a Brother, a Friend, a Gentleman.

Scott Lewis

Scott sent me a second e-mail the following day, which read:

I must say that Dave's story was extremely moving to me. And I've only read the excerpt from the Website. It brought out feelings in me that I didn't even know were there. It is so surprising to me after all these years to learn that there was more to the saga of my brothers death. As young a child as I was at the time I don't think I ever was able to deal with the loss of Tom. My parents were engulfed in their own grief and I'm sure weren't able to recognize that I was hurting so bad inside. As I said in my letter to David the accident was the first real pain I had ever encountered. It is apparent to me now that I locked all my emotions inside and moved on. But looking back now I realize it was a strong turning point in my life. It wasn't long after that I started my rebellious stage. I began drinking alcohol when I was 14 and using Marijuana when I was 15. I can't help but think how differently my life would have turned out had this incident never happened. If not for Mr. Butlers story I don't think I ever would have opened the emotions that I'm being confronted with now. So now maybe I can start to heal those wounds. I believe my family is having a reunion this summer in Syracuse, New York and I would really like to be able to meet with David so I can shake his hand for the sacrifices he has made not only for my brother and his friends, but for everyone in our nation. It takes a strong person to give up everything they had to do the right thing and for that he should be honored. I need to find out when the reunion is and I will update you when I find out.

Thanks ever so much,
Scott Lewis

On April 23, 2006, I received the following e-mail from Tom's mother. Here's verbatim what she wrote:

Dear David Butler:

Hi I'm Tom's mother. That train wreck in Poolville that took my son from me has changed my life forever. I just want to let you know how much I appreciate you standing up for what's right the Truth. I can't tell you how much that means to me. God Bless You And Your Family.

Thanks, Tom's Mom Jenny

Then she added:

I just wanted you to know how much I appreciated your honesty it did my heart good and speak for my son Tom who couldn't talk for himself.

Late in May 2006 another note arrived:

I read the book it was very hard for me to read about my son, but it gave me closure. I'm very thankful to you for that and all you have done for us as a family.

Book Review by Pamela R. O'Dwyer, Esq.

Pamela O'Dwyer is a railroad safety advocate who co-founded Orion's Angels with the parents of Hilary Feaster, 17 year old daughter of Norman Feaster and Maryellen McCone. Their daughter suffered the preventable death at a faulty crossing in Dechard, Tennessee In October of 1997. Pamela also represented Dedra Shanklin before the United States Supreme Court in 2000. The knowledge she gained in preparation for that historic plea for safety has been put to good use in educating the public about the fiction of federal preemption. Her work in that effort helped to provide the facts for the Pulitzer Prize winning article by Walt Bogdanich in 2004.

Pamela is proud to be a safety advocate and a Trial Lawyer. She is even more proud of her mother, Selma C Paty who led the way for many young women in the practice of law. Of her four sons Pamela has raised two young lawyers and a rising tennis star. Her third son, Charlie O Rymer was killed August 2nd, 2004. He was the most supportive and nurturing son and his memory continues to inspire her to work on for crossing safety.

This and all her work is dedicated to Charlie.

I was packing for travel for depositions to be taken for the wrongful, preventable death of James Cobb who was killed at a passive crossing in Wisconsin by a Wisconsin Central locomotive pulling one log car.

I almost chose Ball on Damages for my flight time reading but having promised this review; my hand fell to Railroaded in Cooperstown.

I had read the proofs for David Butler and his editor and liked what I read but did not recall enough detail to do a full review. The Prologue snagged me like the hook in the fly:

> "The horror of that moment, the king went on,
> I shall never forget,
> You will though, the Queen said,
> if you don't make a memorandum of it."

A quote from Lewis Carroll's Alice in Wonderland that I often repeat was not only a great lead in, but it also reflects the feeling of fantasy that surrounds the entire railroad industry's safety history.

I was Alice in Wonderland when I began my first case against a railroad for a death at a passive crossing back in 1987. The railroad's shenanigans fascinated and mystified me all the way to the United States Supreme Court. Like the author, David Butler, I could not stop making memorandums of what I saw as I plunged into the black hole of the deceit that is emblematic of the workings of the railroad from the post accident cover ups all the way to the Federal Administrations pandering to the industry they are meant to police.

In my journey down the rabbit hole; I have met men and women like David who have seen the corruption and will not bend a knee to the corrupt railroads and the politicians they control.

Almost to the man; they have learned the hard way that, as David Butler said: "Justice, I've learned, is within the province of the Universe, not the judicial system."

David also recounts the heart-rending journey for that justice that would seem to a casual reader to have ruined his life all together. The power of the book is in David's frank telling of the human toll the search for justice for his wrongful termination for having blown the whistle on the corruption that involved illicit sex, fraud, abuse of poser and the general corruption that had infected the railroad owned by the aptly named, Walter Rich of Cooperstown.

I was moved to tears as the also aptly named David took on his Goliath and would not give up on his efforts, that like mine, began with the lies told to cover up a tragic railroad crossing death in which the train could easily have been shown to be speeding. His fervor rose when he realized that in spite of the proof — no one cared.

David explains this attitude all the way to the Executive office of the United States government. The horror he memorized at the risk of his sanity was that railroad safety had become a national disgrace. The Fox was paid handsomely in David's journal to mind the Henhouse.

The New York Times was there to expose the truth in David's case just as they did in more recent years when Walt Bogdanich won the Pulitzer Prize for his work that included the Tennessee case of *Feaster v. CSXT* in which the railroad's only excuse for not reporting a double fatality was that the conductor's superior must have been on vacation.

David's story is, as he hoped it would be, a wake-up call to American communities everywhere. It was his hope that by telling the truth that some justice that was never done in court could be still be done.

Readers, you will surely enjoy David's success in that final justice.

Pamela R. Dwyer, Esq.

Epilogue

So, where is everyone now?

DAVID K. BUTLER, SR. I will be sixty-one years old on December 8, 2005. I still live in Cooperstown and continue to do construction work with no hope for retirement in the foreseeable future.

MARY BUTLER is still a nurse at Thanksgiving Home in Cooperstown.

DAVID KIRK BUTLER, JR.; DONALD KEITH BUTLER; and DANIEL KIRCHER BUTLER, our three sons, are all police officers and live in three different states.

SHERWOOD BOEHLERT is still a United States congressman from New York.

MICHAEL COCCOMA is the Otsego County judge in Cooperstown.

THOMAS CHARETTE is still employed by the railroad.

GEORGE CRIPPEN quietly left the railroad and became head of security at a shopping mall. He's now a private investigator.

MALCOLM HUGHES is a private practice attorney in New York.

WILLIAM LLOYD retired from the railroad.

RICHARD MCVINNEY is a private practice attorney in New York.

NANCY PEEVERS (now Nancy Lee Varnum) is an attorney in Nevada. After her husband's suicide, Nancy changed her name back to her maiden name.

WALTER RICH is still the president of the railroad and still lives at Edgewater in Cooperstown.

JAMES SEWARD is still a New York state senator.

DAVID SOULE left the railroad and is self-employed as a consultant.

DEANE WINSOR retired from politics.